Philosophy for Children in Tra

The Journal of Philosophy of Education Book Series

The Journal of Philosophy of Education Book Series publishes titles that represent a wide variety of philosophical traditions. They vary from examination of fundamental philosophical issues in their connection with education, to detailed critical engagement with current educational practice or policy from a philosophical point of view. Books in this series promote rigorous thinking on educational matters and identify and criticise the ideological forces shaping education.

Titles in the series include:

Philosophy for Children in Transition: Problems and Prospects
Edited by Nancy Vansieleghem and David Kennedy

Reading R. S. Peters Today: Analysis, Ethics, and the Aims of Education
Edited by Stefaan E. Cuypers and Christopher Martin

The Good Life of Teaching: An Ethics of Professional Practice
Chris Higgins

The Formation of Reason
David Bakhurst

What do Philosophers of Education do? (And how do they do it?)
Edited by Claudia Ruitenberg

Evidence-Based Education Policy: What Evidence? What Basis? Whose Policy?
Edited by David Bridges, Paul Smeyers and Richard Smith

New Philosophies of Learning
Edited by Ruth Cigman and Andrew Davis

The Common School and the Comprehensive Ideal: A Defence by Richard Pring with Complementary Essays
Edited by Mark Halstead and Graham Haydon

Philosophy, Methodology and Educational Research
Edited by David Bridges and Richard D Smith

Philosophy of the Teacher
By Nigel Tubbs

Conformism and Critique in Liberal Society
Edited by Frieda Heyting and Christopher Winch

Retrieving Nature: Education for a Post-Humanist Age
By Michael Bonnett

Education and Practice: Upholding the Integrity of Teaching and Learning
Edited by Joseph Dunne and Pádraig Hogan

Educating Humanity: Bildung in Postmodernity
Edited by Lars Lovlie, Klaus Peter Mortensen and Sven Erik Nordenbo

The Ethics of Educational Research
Edited by Michael Mcnamee and David Bridges

In Defence of High Culture
Edited by John Gingell and Ed Brandon

Enquiries at the Interface: Philosophical Problems of On-Line Education
Edited by Paul Standish and Nigel Blake

The Limits of Educational Assessment
Edited by Andrew Davis

Illusory Freedoms: Liberalism, Education and the Market
Edited by Ruth Jonathan

Quality and Education
Edited by Christopher Winch

Philosophy for Children in Transition

Problems and Prospects

Edited by

**Nancy Vansieleghem and
David Kennedy**

⊛WILEY-BLACKWELL

A John Wiley & Sons, Ltd., Publication

This edition first published 2012
Originally published as Volume 45, Issue 2 of *The Journal of Philosophy of Education*
Chapters © 2012 The Authors
Editorial organization © 2012 Philosophy of Education Society of Great Britain

Blackwell Publishing was acquired by John Wiley & Sons in February 2007. Blackwell's
publishing program has been merged with Wiley's global Scientific, Technical, and Medical
business to form Wiley-Blackwell.

Registered Office
John Wiley & Sons Ltd, The Atrium, Southern Gate, Chichester, West Sussex, PO19 8SQ, United
Kingdom

Editorial Offices
350 Main Street, Malden, MA 02148-5020, USA
9600 Garsington Road, Oxford, OX4 2DQ, UK
The Atrium, Southern Gate, Chichester, West Sussex, PO19 8SQ, UK

For details of our global editorial offices, for customer services, and for information about how to
apply for permission to reuse the copyright material in this book please see our website at www
.wiley.com/wiley-blackwell.

The right of Nancy Vansieleghem and David Kennedy to be identified as the author of the editorial
material in this work has been asserted in accordance with the Copyright, Designs and Patents Act
1988.

Wiley also publishes its books in a variety of electronic formats. Some content that appears in
print may not be available in electronic books.

Designations used by companies to distinguish their products are often claimed as trademarks. All
brand names and product names used in this book are trade names, service marks, trademarks or
registered trademarks of their respective owners. The publisher is not associated with any product
or vendor mentioned in this book. This publication is designed to provide accurate and
authoritative information in regard to the subject matter covered. It is sold on the understanding
that the publisher is not engaged in rendering professional services. If professional advice or other
expert assistance is required, the services of a competent professional should be sought.

Library of Congress Cataloging-in-Publication Data

Philosophy for children in transition : problems and prospects / edited by Nancy
Vansieleghem and David Kennedy.
p. cm.
Includes bibliographical references and index.
ISBN 978-1-4443-5040-1 (pbk.)
1. Children and philosophy. 2. Early childhood education–Philosophy.
I. Vansieleghem, Nancy. II. Kennedy, David, 1943-
B105.C45P4555 2011
108.3–dc23

2011042651

A catalogue record for this book is available from the British Library.

Set in 11.25 on 12 pt Times-Roman by MPS Limited, a Macmillan Company, Chennai.
Printed in Singapore by Ho Printing Singapore Pte Ltd

01   2012

Contents

Notes on Contributors

Aurelia Armstrong School of History, Philosophy, Religion and Classics, The University of Queensland, St. Lucia, QLD 4072, Australia.

Barbara Weber 3581 West 1st Avenue, V6R 1G9 Vancouver, BC, Canada.

David Kennedy Department of Educational Foundations, Montclair State University, Montclair NJ 07042, USA.

Gert Biesta The Stirling Institute of Education, University of Stirling, Stirling FK9 4LA, Scotland, UK.

Joanna Haynes School of Secondary & Further Education Studies, University of Plymouth, Drake Circus, Plymouth PL4 8AA, UK.

Joris Vlieghe Laboratory for Education and Society, K. U. Leuven, Andreas Vesaliusstraat 2, Box 3761, 3000 Leuven, Belgium.

Juliana Merçon Calle Argentina 70, Depto. 4, Col. Benito Juarez, Xalapa, Veracruz, C.P. 91070, Mexico.

Karin Murris University of the Witwatersrand, Wits School of Education, P Bag 3, P O Wits 2050, Johannesburg, SouthAfrica.

Maughn Gregory Department of Educational Foundations, Montclair State University, Montclair, NJ 07042, USA.

Nadia Kennedy Department of Mathematics, SUNY Stony Brook, Stony Brook, NY 11794, USA.

Nancy Vansieleghem Department of The Foundations of Education, Ghent University, H. Dunantlaan 1 9000 Gent Belgium.

Richard Smith University of Durham, School of Education, Leazes Road Durham, DH1 1TA, UK.

Robert A. Davis University of Glasgow, School of Education, Eldon St, Glasgow, G3 6NH, UK.

Thomas Storme Laboratory for Education and Society, K. U. Leuven, Andreas Vesaliusstraat 2, Box 3761, 3000 Leuven, Belgium.

Viktor Johansson Department of Education, Stockholm University, Fack 710 400, 106 54 Stockholm, Sweden.

Walter Omar Kohan Universidade do Estado do Rio de Janeiro UERJ/PROPED, S. Francisco Xavier 524, Sala 12037 F, 20550-013 Maracana, Rio de Janeiro, Brasil.

Preface

Inventive geniuses, such as Pestalozzi, Bronson Alcott, Rabindranath Tagore and Socrates himself, have inspired practices of teaching and learning fit for democracy: it is through them that children can become active, creative and curious citizens, capable of resisting authority and peer pressure; and there is, to this end, a contemporary source of practical guidance for teachers in the work that has become known as philosophy for children. This at least is the view expressed by Martha Nussbaum in her recent Not for Profit: Why Education Needs the Humanities (2010, Princeton University Press), a work in which she connects philosophy for children with the progressive tradition, with critical thinking, with Socratic pedagogy and with what she cares about most in the idea of a liberal education. She praises the pioneering insights of Matthew Lipman and Gareth Matthews into the capacity children have for interesting philosophical thought, and she commends the innovative resources in Lipman's Harry Stottlemeier's Discovery and its sequels. Not everyone can be an inventive genius, but here we have the methodology and curriculum materials that ordinary teachers need.

It is sad to record that, during the time that this special issue has been in preparation, both Lipman and Matthews have died, respectively on 26 December 2010 and on 17 April 2011. The tributes to them have been legion. Matthews' ground-breaking work in thinking, writing and teaching about philosophy and children was disseminated in particular through three books—Philosophy and the Young Child (1980), Dialogues with Children (1984) and The Philosophy of Childhood (1994), all published by Harvard University Press—and his influence spread world-wide. Lipman's considerable output and dedication to the cause originated, according to Douglas Martin in the New York Times obituary (14 January 2011), in the contentious years of the Vietnam War: Lipman had found that many Americans were having trouble presenting their views about the conflict cogently. This distressed him deeply and led him to the view that if the ability to think critically was not established in childhood, it would be unlikely later to flourish. Hence, he hit upon the idea of teaching philosophy to children, and the course that he developed spread, in its original or derivative forms, to more than 4,000 schools in the United States and more than sixty foreign countries, its materials translated into forty languages.

The legacy of this work is surely plain enough to see, in the various pedagogical movements that have sought to address philosophical questions with children, and in the increasing extent to which policy-makers are

Philosophy for Children in Transition: Problems and Prospects, First Edition. Nancy Vansieleghem and David Kennedy. Chapters © 2012 The Authors. Editorial organization © 2012 Philosophy of Education Society of Great Britain. Published 2012 by Blackwell Publishing Ltd.

turning to this work to explore its potential enhancement of mainstream education. Part of the appeal is perhaps what Nussbaum finds in Lipman's writings and pedagogical style—its familiarity and gentle humour. Indeed the success of the movement in promoting its work has come in part from its understandable exploitation of this image, as is captured perhaps in its displacing of the cumbersome word 'philosophy' with the text-style, child-friendly 'P4C'.

But the legacy has not been without its ideological disputes, with leading proponents zealously defending their preferred methodology and practice, and it has not been without its critics. What is it, then, it is sometimes asked, that philosophy for children does that is different from what good teachers have always done? Does the movement depend upon contrasting itself with a picture of traditional, supposedly uncritical teaching and learning that is little more than caricature? Why does it tend to insist upon its particular procedural protocols? Thus, to what extent does it end up, in spite of itself as it were, being overly directive? And how far, in its preoccupation with the procedures of thinking, does it hide the importance of attention to the objects of study? Finally, a classic criticism of the progressive educator, does friendliness become sentimentality? These are the kinds of questions that are not really entertained in Nussbaum's somewhat bland, eulogistic remarks and in the connections she too quickly draws.

Paul Standish

Introduction: What is Philosophy *for* Children, What is Philosophy *with* Children—After Matthew Lipman?

NANCY VANSIELEGHEM AND DAVID KENNEDY

Philosophy for Children[1] arose in the 1970s in the US as an educational programme, initiated by Matthew Lipman (1922–2010), which was devoted to exploring the relationship between the notions 'philosophy' and 'childhood', with the implicit practical goal of establishing philosophy as a full-fledged 'content area' in US public schools—a goal that has, with time, become an increasingly distant one. This is not so much the case in the UK, Europe and Latin America, however, where the theory and practice of doing philosophy for or with school age children appears to be of growing both interest and concern in the field of education and, by implication, in society as a whole. Examples of this emergent interest can be found not only in the growing number of curriculum materials published in this area, but in the many workshops and teacher training courses devoted to practical philosophy that are organised for educational practitioners, managers and teacher trainers.

This volume focuses on the emergence of this 'philosophy/child' relation, and more precisely, on the horizon against which it has been born and has taken shape. We attempt to locate the arguments that make it reasonable to think through the relationship between philosophy and the child, and that clarify its significance for teaching and learning today. Our aim is twofold: first, to become familiar with an actual educational practice that is not at all well known in the field of academic philosophy itself; and second, to offer an invitation to rethink the relationship between philosophy and the child 'after Lipman'. In this article, and as a means of contextualising the different contributions to this issue, we provide an introduction to some of the main arguments and ideas that have given

Philosophy for Children in Transition: Problems and Prospects, First Edition. Nancy Vansieleghem and David Kennedy. Chapters © 2012 The Authors. Editorial organization © 2012 Philosophy of Education Society of Great Britain. Published 2012 by Blackwell Publishing Ltd.

shape to the idea of philosophy for children in recent decades. In doing so, we follow Ronald Reed and Tony Johnson (1999) in subdividing the history of the movement into a first and a second generation. Characteristic of the first generation was its emphasis on a strategic uniformity of approach, given its ambitions for a place in public schooling, while the second broke with this mode of thinking, and welcomed difference as a principle of growth. This in fact fits our own purposes, in that we are interested in envisaging philosophy for children not so much as a totality, but rather as an assemblage of moving elements that forms a particular horizon—and thus as 'some-thing' that is in movement and can turn toward thought (cf. Deleuze and Guattari, 1994, p. 38). Hence, in what follows we focus not on one particular author or on one ideological or methodological subgroup within the movement, but rather attempt, first, to map the epistemological and pedagogical discourses within which this set of discourses emerged.

ON PHILOSOPHY FOR CHILDREN: A FIRST GENERATION

In *Modelle und Perspektiven der Kinderphilosophie* (1997) Stephan Englhart refers to three different horizons through which philosophy for children became a matter of educational interest in the 1970s. We begin with Matthew Lipman, whose arguments for the need for such a programme were based on a notion of critical thinking that was strongly influenced by the pragmatic philosophy of John Dewey. Enabled by Lipman's initiative, but migrating into a different but related discourse, Gareth Matthews approached the issue more from a philosopher's than an educator's point of view, and introduced a notion of philosophical dialogue with children that was grounded in the adult appreciation of a child's inherent sense of wonder. Matthews (1980) emphasised the need to rethink the child, not as an ignorant being, but as a rational agent who already has the capacity to reason philosophically, and he thereby opened a space for the emergent field of what is now known as philosophy of childhood (Matthews, 1994; Kennedy, 1992). This moment of confluence was clearly marked by a symposium held at the Eastern Division Meeting of the American Philosophical Association in 1980, in which both Matthews and Lipman presented papers,[2] which were addressed by three respondents. These were published in 1981 in a double issue of Lipman's journal *Thinking: The Journal of Philosophy for Children* (2, 3 and 4), accompanied by a rich literary compendium of childhood memoir, poetry, and philosophical and psychoanalytic reflection. Finally, following on these two related approaches, another emerged that understood philosophy for children as a means for reconstructing relations of power and agency in the classroom, and for communicating and reflecting upon personal meanings, with a goal of facilitating the self-actualisation of conscious moral actors. In what follows we offer a brief overview of these different lines of argument.

P4C AS A MEANS OF DEVELOPING CRITICAL THINKING SKILLS IN AN EDUCATIONAL ENVIRONMENT

The growing interest in critical thinking that emerged at the end of the 1970s was based on the conviction that an emphasis on reasoning was a necessary element of any deep-structural educational reform, and that the introduction of philosophy into the content of schooling represented the one best curricular and pedagogical hope for bringing that element forth in the culture and practice of schooling. The most important representative of this approach at this time was Matthew Lipman, who developed the philosophical novel *Harry Stottlemeier's Discovery* (1974), which, whatever its literary merits, established a new genre—the philosophical novel for children—with a single stroke. *Harry* represents the attempt to construct a pedagogical tool that functions as a model for critical thinking by describing 'real life' children engaged in critical dialogue about philosophical issues, with the goal of stimulating the same sort of dialogue among groups of students. At the same moment, several approaches—a revival of Leonard Nelson's Socratic Method, in particular—emerged that shared Lipman's assumption that the stimulation of communal critical thinking led to an improvement of thinking in the individual. Beyond that similarity, however, Nelson (1882–1927) and Lipman differed in their epistemic assumptions.

While Nelson's 'philosophical truth' is located at the foundation of experience, Lipman adopted an evolutionary view of knowledge. Following Kant, Nelson believed that knowledge from observation presupposes the application of categories that are not to be found through empirical inquiry but are already present in the person and determine experience itself. Thinking, in other words, is not derived purely from our experience; rather, our experience is structured and made possible by thinking. Nelson followed Kant in holding to the categories of *a priori* thinking but differed in his claim that these *a priori* categories cannot be proven. It is substance and causality not just in the external world that are knowable by induction, but in the inner world as well. For Nelson, knowledge of the truth is internal, is traceable in and through the conceptual presuppositions of everyday experience, and is gained by regressive abstraction from those experiences. As such, truth can be brought to light by a 'psychological factum' (Nelson, [1975] 1994), which entails introspection and the painstaking dissection of one's own experience. The search for a common order of things is no longer undertaken on the level of human nature, but is based on the connections that materialise in the experience of the individual person. It is as if the truth is present in everyone but needs to be made transparent through the method of regressive abstraction. Here we are dealing with a specific methodology that shows step-by-step how a person can achieve objective knowledge concerning her own thinking.

In his interpretation of the Socratic method Lipman turned not to Kant but to pragmatism. Although the trunk and branches of Lipman's programme can be identified with G. H. Mead, Lev Vygotsky, C. S. Pierce and Justus Buchler, its roots are clearly in the philosophical writings of Dewey (Lipman, 1996, pp. xi–xv). Lipman began with Dewey's idea that there is no distinction between the mind and the external world and, as a consequence, between philosophical truth and scientific truth (cf. Daniel, 1992; McCall, 2009, p. 102). Influenced by Darwin, Dewey had developed an evolutionary view of knowledge, which implies an ongoing adaptive human response to a changing environment. As a consequence, and in line with Dewey, knowledge for Lipman is not static, but the emergent product of a ceaseless interaction with the environment. Dewey used the word 'experience' to explain this interaction, and understood thinking as reflection on the consequences of this interaction, and thereby on the possibilities of further experience. Dewey wrote: 'Reflection involves not simply a sequence of ideas, but a consequence—a consecutive ordering in such a way that each determines the next as its proper outcome, while each outcome in turn leans back on, or refers to, its predecessors' (Dewey, 1933, p. 4).

What this means is that thinking enables persons to become aware of the consequences of their actions and thereby to reconstruct those habits from which actions follow. This does not imply that success is guaranteed; but because we have nothing at our disposal that offers us more certainty than the outcome of reflection, it is incumbent upon us to strengthen the reflective quality of our feelings and our actions, however counterintuitive that may appear to 'common sense'. While Dewey connected this effort to the ongoing reconstruction of habit through experience, Lipman went further and emphasised the efficacy of formal logic in the formation of judgments and the growth of 'reasonableness' (see Daniel, 1992). This is not merely about mapping diverse possibilities that may be realised but about the search for possible incorrect presuppositions in the activity of thinking. Accordingly, for Lipman, critical thinking means being able to determine the facts or issues (including ideas, concepts and theories) that cause a problem in order to make hypotheses about how to solve it. Moreover, the logic of the development of knowledge in a given environment and the application of knowledge for the improvement of the quality of living became the horizon against which Lipman's Philosophy for Children programme took shape. Accordingly, the aim of P4C for Lipman 'is not to turn children into philosophers or decision makers, but to help them become more thoughtful, more reflective, more considerate, and more reasonable individuals. Children who have been helped to become more judicious not only have a better sense of when to act but also of when not to act' (Lipman *et al.*, 1980, p. 15). Against this background, philosophy is no longer regarded as a theoretical activity separated from the world, but rather as a potential that has to (and can) be developed in order to get a grip on one's interactions with one's environment, and to influence change.

PHILOSOPHY FOR CHILDREN AS A MEANS OF CLOSING THE GAP BETWEEN THE ADULT AND THE CHILD

A second line of argument that entered the discourse on philosophy for children at the end of the 1970s focuses on the emergent *topos* of the philosophy of childhood. In these approaches, which are often described as Romantic, the notion of childhood as merely a prelude to adulthood is problematised. These studies, amongst which the work of Gareth Matthews is particularly prominent, criticise traditional education for limiting its focus to the transfer of knowledge and, thus, underrating the voice of the child. 'Children can help us adults investigate and reflect on interesting and important questions and ... the children's contributions may be quite as valuable as any we adults have to offer' (Matthews, 1984, p. 3). Matthews explicitly strives for a symmetrical relation between the adult and the child, and approaches the child as an equal companion in thought. Therefore he does not speak about philosophy for or with children, but rather 'dialogues with children', and argues that children ask the same questions as philosophers do, although differently formulated.

In his book *Philosophy and the Young Child* (1984), Matthews launched a philosophical critique of Piaget's claim that young children are 'pre-logical' and incapable of what Piaget called 'formal operations'. In so doing, he was in effect questioning the foundational genetic epistemology of the American educational establishment, whose teachers were (and are) socialised from the start into a naive version of developmental, Piagetian discrete stage theory, which itself has been the object of criticism among cognitive scientists for decades (see Brainerd, 1978). Matthews argued that Piaget's theory displayed an 'evolutionary bias' in assuming that the goal of development is maturity, and that each stage of development represents an advance (Matthews, 1994, p. 17). This does not hold for the development of philosophical intelligence, Matthews suggests, and in fact the opposite may be the case: children are likely to ask more interesting questions than adults. 'The standard response', he writes, 'is, in general an unthinking and un-thought-out product of socialisation, whereas the nonconforming response is much more likely to be the fruit of honest reflection. Yet Piaget would have the nonconforming response discounted and eliminated on methodological grounds' (Matthews, 1980, p. 38).[3]

Correlatively, Matthews argues that the central mission of the school should be to create spaces in which children can articulate and explore their own interpretations of the world and bring these into dialogue with others. Critical thinking means not so much instrumental problem-solving as the capacity and the disposition to fantasise and to wonder, to entertain profound ideas about the world and to confront problems concerning individual well-being. Logical thinking skills are not emphasised in this approach, or even the discovery of inconsistencies or contradictions in ideas, but rather philosophy as a form of desire—of the opportunity for children to explore and articulate what they have not said or even thought before. As such, philosophy's boundaries shift under the influence of childhood, and it opens itself to the expression even of what can *not* be said, thus intersecting in its practice with art, psychotherapy and what Pierre Hadot called *askesis*, or 'spiritual exercise' (Hadot, 1995).[4] Thus, the experience of interacting philosophically with children results in a profound critique of the normative adult view of the child and of its expression in the 'science as usual' of developmental psychology, which becomes exposed as a sort of epistemic ideology immersed in a discourse that is unaware of its own philosophical assumptions (see Polakow, 1982). In fact this critique finds its justification in developmental psychology with the arrival in the West, contemporary with Lipman's pioneering innovation, of Vygotskian learning theory, which represents a challenge to Piagetian stage theory that has not yet been internalised by institutiona-lised education, not surprisingly perhaps, given its structural asymmetry with traditional educational assumptions and practices.

P4C AS A STRATEGY TO RECONSTRUCT MECHANISMS OF POWER AND TO COMMUNICATE AND REFLECT UPON PERSONAL MEANINGS

Although clearly related to the previous lines of reasoning, a third (Englhart, 1997, p. 138) is to be found in the attempt to strive for a more human world—that is, a world that is free from any preordained orientation to what constitutes human thinking and action. Here philosophy appears as a form of communal deliberation that stimulates critical reflection on existing power relations, these being envisaged as historical constructions that are or should be open to reconstruction. An exploration of these constructs is expected to bring into the light the invisible relationships of power that inform them, thereby neutralising their force. This project calls for a form of education whose fundamental discursive engine is dialogue, which privileges inquiry over instruction and the multilogical rather over the monological. Dialogue as a form of speech inherently resists the reification of ideas or practices and trades instead on clarifying essences, postponing judgements, working with ambiguities and interrogating assumptions, these being achieved through dyadic or group deliberation. Its discursive goal is the installation of a Habermasian 'ideal speech situation', a free space in which all persons involved in the inquiry have an equal chance to bring their arguments forward in the interest of a an emergent, rationally founded consensus. Ekkehard Martens (1999), one of the proponents of this approach, writes that children need to learn that there are different orientations possible, that no orientation can be claimed as the only one, and that the practice of philosophical inquiry is necessary in order to learn to think beyond totality, dualism and exclusionary categories.

Martens suggest that two dimensions need to be present in designing a philosophical curriculum and pedagogy for children: on the one hand, motivational content, or what he calls 'homeric themes as food for their souls to grow', and, on the other, a critical method of thinking modelled on the dialogical style of Socrates, identified as a 'philosophical spoilsport' or 'gadfly' (Martens, 1999, p. 138). This approach finds the value of philosophy in its capacity to encourage a historically sensitive, trans-cultural approach to knowledge, in the interest of refining students' powers of detailed analysis and their ability to reach judgements through communicative action based on collaborative interpretation. This also presumes an emphasis on the cultivation of the art of speaking (rhetoric), questioning (dialectic) and writing (grammar), and the strengthening of casuistic reasoning in service of ethical action. Here thinking for oneself implies that one takes responsibility for one's actions, and it assumes that the capacity for responsible action is an outcome of growth in philosophical knowledge and procedures. Philosophy is then understood as a means of increasing the potential power of children (who are defined as essentially vulnerable) in order to neutralise unequal power relations by strengthening processes of communication and cooperation.

A SECOND GENERATION OF PHILOSOPHY FOR CHILDREN: A 'METHOD' BECOMES 'A MOVEMENT'

Today a second generation of 'P4C-representatives' has emerged within the discourse of philosophy for children—including, among others, Ann Margaret Sharp, David Kennedy, Karin Murris, Walter Kohan, Michel Sasseville, Joanna Haynes, Jen Glaser, Oscar Brenifier, Michel Tozzi, Marina Santi, Barbara Weber and Philip Cam—in whose work received ideas have been called into question and new thinking has taken form. It is characteristic of this generation that these new ideas are not considered an attack on its predecessors but as a necessary step that takes into account the changing circumstances of the global and educational environment and, hence, are understood as a form of self-correction. Ronald Reed and Tony Johnson write, for example:

> Given the rise of post modernity, one simply does not do philosophy the way one did it forty years ago. The assumptions about truth, perspective,

nature and so on have, at least, been challenged, thereby forcing attempts at justification and explanation that were considered unnecessary in previous days. To the extent that philosophy has an impact on everyday experience, to that extent the debate has had practical consequences (Reed and Johnson, 1999, pp. 64–65).

The most obvious object of the second generation's critique is Lipman's strong emphasis on analytical reasoning as a guarantee for critical thinking. As Karel Van der Leeuw puts it, 'In the novels, but especially in the accompanying manuals, stress on analytical skills, reasoning, categorizing, ordering, and so on, is pervasive. It is not immediately apparent, however, how improvement of analytical skills is conductive to the discovery of meaning' (Van der Leeuw, 2009, p. 111). In addition, the regressive, instrumentalist structure and discourse of 21st century Western traditional schooling is understood as particularly antithetical to the goals and purposes of philosophy for children. 'Reflection and reasoning', van der Leeuw suggests, 'can't be realized when we only reserve separate hours a week for a collective exploration of philosophical questions' (p. 112). He argues that, in our changing information society,

> ... we expect people to be able to reflect rationally on human life, which includes a view of reality, of the place of the individual in society, of values and norms, of the meaning of life and so on. [And] ... we expect them to be able to communicate these views to others, because we live in a common reality, and this common reality must be the subject of common discourse, and can even be regarded as a common construct (Van der Leeuw, 2009, p. 113).

Accordingly, philosophy is not perceived primarily as a provider either of skills or 'answers'—whether in the realm of fact or value—but as a site in which students can determine what the important questions for our time are, and where they can seek their own answers through the practice of thinking for themselves and with others in communal deliberation. 'Every generation', Van der Leeuw claims, 'has to find answers, because the world is changing and widening' (ibid.). What is needed, on this account, is an integrated educational system with an infrastructure that offers opportunities for reflective thinking and communication and that will serve to prepare us for the inevitable transformation in our attitudes towards knowledge. As such, the central mission of the school is to teach children how to think and communicate: to train them how to reflect upon knowledge on their own.

Striving for unity and consistency, and subjugating our thinking to logical categories or to universal reason, are no longer, for this second generation, ends-in-themselves. In consequence, we find that speculations about methods and approaches tend to be contextualised to particular communities, and the only broad consensus that does exist is that philosophy for children is about promoting the exchange of rational argument and thoughtful opinion. There is, however, no longer understood to be one best way of reasoning, for collective reason, it is held, is shaped and articulated by the social community in which it operates. Now philosophy *for* children becomes philosophy *with* children. The change in the preposition is an important index of difference: it betokens a still greater emphasis on dialogue as fundamental and indispensable to the pedagogy of philosophy, which is no longer understood as the modelling and coaching of an ideal of analytical reason, but as what generates communal reflection, contemplation and communication. In this respect, the second generation will no longer speak about philosophy for or with children in terms of a method, but rather as a movement encompassing a medley of approaches, each with its own methods, techniques and strategies.

Now it may be suggested that the logic of 'what works' is bound to be marked by aspects of what has been called, following Michel Foucault, the 'biopolitical structure of society'. Understood as an adaptation—or capitulation—to biopower, whatever critical potential philosophy for children carries, and whatever notion of freedom it endorses, have come to be associated with a particular work upon the self—a work that is oriented to the fulfilment of human needs or desires in a community. On this account, a particular subject(ivity) comes to the fore in the discourses of philosophy with children themselves—a subject who looks at her life in terms of a process that can be managed and who experiences philosophy as an efficient tool for that purpose (see Vansieleghem and Masschelein, 2010). In this respect it could be said that philosophy for children, whatever its efforts to resist doing so, has not remained unaffected by the general cultural movement that has replaced critique with sales promotion, reinforcing our dependence on an exploitative apparatus that, in satisfying our needs, perpetuates our servitude (see Marcuse, 1964). Biopower seeks a totality, and philosophy for children may be both an instrument and an effect of a power that generates a totalising vision not only for a child but also for a people and humankind as a whole.

On the other hand, it could be argued, in the light of Foucault's (2005) final turn to the 'care of the self' as an ethical practice, that the practice of philosophy for children represents a *dispositif* in the service of an emergent form of subjectivity, a 'global class formation' (2004, p. xvii) that Michael Hardt and Antonio Negri (2004, 2009), following Spinoza, call 'multitude'. Here they reformulate the concept of biopolitics as the form of collectivity of 'altermodernity' (2009, pp. 101–118), a collectivity of singularities for which the articulation between the social and the political grows ever more intense: the innovative and creative capacities that capitalism demands for its expansion produce forms of resistance to capitalism, intensities that manage from within it to produce alternative expressions' (2004, p. 263), and through which 'the multitude can develop the power to organize itself through the conflictual and cooperative interactions of singularities in the common' (2009, p. 175). 'Communication', they argue, 'is productive, not only of economic values but also of subjectivity, and thus communication is central to biopolitical production' (p. 263). This is to suggest that the discursive form that characterises philosophy for children—communal dialogue in an ideal speech situation—is inherently subversive of the goals of biopower, and as such represents a sort of Trojan Horse wheeled into the ideological state apparatus of Western schooling.

RETHINKING PHILOSOPHY/CHILDHOOD—AFTER LIPMAN

Against the backdrop of these multiple views on the implications of philosophy for children as a discourse, a methodology, a philosophical enterprise, and a form of biopolitical production, this volume is the outcome of an invitation to think the project philosophy/childhood, childhood/philosophy again and anew. After all, what philosophy for children may become is by no means a given: it is, as Gilles Deleuze and Félix Guattari might put this, created rather than formed, as is made clear by the shifts that our brief genealogy has charted. Hence, philosophy for children does not just appear as a solution to a problem. It emerges within a given field of experience, where it combines with other coexisting theories and practices that gives it a history and a determination as well as constituting it as an opening to something new. Thus, this collection of articles takes note not only of the question of what philosophy for children is, but of what determines its moment of emergence, the particular conditions of that emergence, and of what remains unknown as well—and this not only at a theoretical level but also in the spaces of concrete educational practice. There are contributions here not only by friends of philosophy for children but also by its doubters and antagonists as well, thus opening a space for confrontation and challenge to received views. We would like to think of this volume as an intervention that creates the possibility of verifying and affirming philosophy for children as a *possible* theory and practice—as a theory and practice that has a history and that has linked up with other theories and practices, that corresponds to other concepts and presupposes other philosophies and other subjectivities. Moreover philosophy for children will not be presented as a well-defined occupation and more or less precisely circumscribed activity, but rather as a concept that is created and that remains subject to the constraints of renewal, replacement and mutation. As a result, the articles collected here are not simply analyses, interpretations or conceptual clarifications: what they offer is not a presentation of philosophy for children as an object of knowledge: it is the presentation of a subject that is subjective. Hence, this volume is an attempt to think philosophy for children beyond existing representations and to create thereby a hyper-representation, from which new meanings, new forms of social expression, new forms of empowerment, new forms of encounter and new forms of collective action may emerge.

NOTES

1. The use of the term 'philosophy for children'—now commonly 'P4C'—has been the subject of some contention, especially among European practitioners, for two reasons: (i) the term, it is claimed, rightly describes one particular curricular programme, developed and published by the Institute for the Advancement of Philosophy for Children, and therefore should not be used generically; (ii) the word 'for', it is alleged, has certain paternalistic connotations, implying that the activity is something that adults provide for children, or furnish them with, as opposed to something they practise with them. In consequence, many consider the term 'philosophy with children' more appropriate. Here and throughout this volume we have used three forms of the term, depending on the author and the context: 'Philosophy for Children' when referring to the IAPC programme in particular, and either 'philosophy for children', 'philosophy with children' or 'philosophy for/with children', depending on the author's preference.
2. Lipman's paper was entitled 'Developing Philosophies of Childhood', and Mathews', 'Childhood: The Recapitulation Model'.
3. Matthews and Lipman were, in turn, challenged directly by the philosophical establishment in the person of Richard Kitchener, who attended that same meeting of the APA in 1980, where he argued in Piagetian terms against children's capacity to do philosophy. He later published a paper summarising his arguments (Kitchener, 1990), which was followed by an even more exhaustive critique by John White (1992). The arguments of both papers were contested by Karin Murris (1999) in the *Journal of Philosophy of Education*.
4. In fact, Lipman offered a 'prototype' of philosophical community of inquiry that included five steps or stages (the 'offering of the text', the 'construction of the agenda', etc.) the last of which calls for the 'eliciting of further responses in the form of telling or writing stories, poetry, painting, drawing . . .' (Lipman, 2003, pp. 101–103).

REFERENCES

Brainerd, C. J. (1978) The Stage Question in Cognitive-Developmental Theory, *Behavioral and Brain Sciences*, 1, pp. 173–182.

Daniel, M. F. (1992) *La philosophie et les enfants. L'enfant philosophe. Le programme de Lipman et l'influence de Dewey* (Montréal, Les Editions Logiques).

Deleuze, G. and Guattari, F. (1994) *What is Philosophy?*, H. Tomlinson and G. Bruchell trans. (New York, Columbia University Press).

Dewey (1933) *How We Think: A Restatement of the Relation of Reflective Thinking to the Educative Process* (Boston, MA, Heath).

Englhart, S. (1997) *Modelle und Perspektiven der Kinderphilosophie* (Heinsberg, Agentur Dieck).

Foucault, M. (2005) *The Hermeneutics of the Subject: Lectures at the College de France, 1981–82*, G. Burchill, trans. (New York, Palgrave Macmillan)

Hadot, P. (1995) *Philosophy as a Way of Life: Spiritual Exercises from Socrates to Foucault*, M. Chase, trans. (Malden, MA, Blackwell Publishing)

Hardt, M. and Negri, A. (2004) *Multitude: War and Democracy in the Age of Empire* (New York, Penguin Books).

Hardt, M. and Negri, A. (2009) *Commonwealth* (Cambridge, MA, Harvard University Press).

Kennedy, D. (1992) The Hermeneutics of Childhood, *Philosophy Today*, 36.1, pp. 44–60.

Kitchener, R. (1990) Do Children Think Philosophically?, *Metaphilosophy*, 21.4, pp. 427, 428.

Lipman, M. (1974) *Harry Stottlemeier's Discovery* (Montclair, NJ, IAPC).

Lipman, M. (1996) *Natasha: Vygotskian Dialogues* (New York, Teachers College Press).
Lipman, M. (2003) *Thinking in Education*, 2nd edn. (Cambridge, Cambridge University Press).
Lipman, M., Sharp, A. M. and Oscanyan, F. S. (1980) *Philosophy in the Classroom* (Philadelphia, PA, Temple University Press).
McCall, C. (2009) *Transforming Thinking: Philosophical Inquiry in the Primary and Secondary School Classroom* (London, Routledge/David Fulton).
Marcuse, H. (1964) *One-Dimensional Man: Studies in the Ideology of Advanced Industrial Society* (Boston, MA, Beacon Press).
Martens, E. (1999) *Spelen met denken. Over filosoferen met kinderen*, I. van der Aart, trans. (Rotterdam, Lemniscaat).
Matthews, G. (1980) *Philosophy and the Young Child* (Cambridge, MA, Harvard University Press).
Matthews, G. (1984) *Dialogues with Children* (Cambridge, MA, Harvard University Press).
Matthews, G. (1994) *The Philosophy of Childhood* (Cambridge, MA, Harvard University Press).
Murris, K. (1999) Can Children Do Philosophy?, *Journal of Philosophy of Education*, 34.2, pp. 261–279.
Nelson, L. [1975] (1994) *De socratische method*, J. Kessels, intro. and trans. (Amsterdam, Boom).
Polakow, V. (1982) *The Erosion of Childhood* (Chicago, IL, University of Chicago Press).
Reed, R. F. and Johnson, T. W. (1999) *Friendship and Moral Education. Twin Pillars of Philosophy for Children* (New York, Peter Lang).
Van der Leeuw, K. (2009) Philosophy for Children as Educational Reform, in: E. Marsal, T. Dobashi and B. Weber (eds) *Children Philosophize Worldwide. Theoretical and Practical Concepts* (New York, Peter Lang), pp. 117–126.
Vansieleghem, N. and Masschelein, J. (2010) Creativity or Passion? What is at Stake in Philosophy with Children?, *Teoria de la educacion*, 22.2, pp. 131–149.
White, J. (1992) The Roots of Philosophy, in: A. P. Griffiths (ed.) *The Impulse to Philosophise* (Cambridge, Cambridge University Press), pp. 73–88.

1

The Experience of Childhood and the Learning Society: Allowing the Child to be Philosophical and Philosophy to be Childish

THOMAS STORME AND JORIS VLIEGHE

INTRODUCTION

It is noteworthy that even though the notion of the child has a ubiquitous presence in our everyday language, it is nevertheless rarely present within the field of philosophy of education.[1] If theories of learning are dependent upon a conceptualisation of the child or of childhood, one might wonder why the notion of the child is so seldom explicitly conceptualised, whether it is taken as an empirical or a conceptual reality. One line of reasoning that might explain this absence is obvious. We are no longer in need of the outdated reference to children and adults in today's dynamic and ever-changing information society, because 'to learn or not to learn' has become the number one creed. This is, at least, what the analysis of the current educational reality offered by Jan Masschelein, Maarten Simons, Ulrich Bröckling and Ludwig Pongratz shows. They argue that, today, a 'discourse of the learning society' is in effect and that this particular way of thinking and speaking leaves little choice in the way in which we relate to ourselves as actors in the educational sphere.[2] The 'discourse of the learning society' objectifies and problematises educational reality in terms of 'learning' and defines its members primarily as permanent learners. This discourse 'increasingly expresses the way in which we "read" our experiences, relationships and attitudes. It increasingly determines the way in which we understand and organize ourselves' (Masschelein, 2001, p. 2). More specifically, we are permanently asked to see ourselves as learners (and as nothing else), i.e. as subjects that are exclusively concerned with accumulating competences in order to safeguard and strengthen our position in life: what is 'learned' is only meaningful in

Philosophy for Children in Transition: Problems and Prospects, First Edition. Nancy Vansieleghem and David Kennedy. Chapters © 2012 The Authors. Editorial organization © 2012 Philosophy of Education Society of Great Britain. Published 2012 by Blackwell Publishing Ltd.

relation to this ongoing struggle to position and reposition ourselves. This demands that distinctions that traditionally shaped the educational reality, viz. between teacher and pupil or professor and student, between the already-initiated generation and the as-yet-to-be-initiated generation, become more and more meaningless. Thus, no longer bifurcating society in terms of newcomers that stand in need to be taught and the older generation that sees it as one of its most important tasks to lead these newcomers to adulthood, today we *all* relate to ourselves as 'learners' and we do so throughout our lives, from cradle to grave. Consequently, childhood, understood in its usual, diachronic sense, i.e. as the period of life spent in preparation for an adult life, appears as an anachronism. Similarly, Nancy Vansieleghem (2009, p. 103) remarks that, when reviewing literature on education and educational research, institutions such as the school and the family no longer help to frame 'what can be thought of as normal and abnormal behavior [or show] what circumstances require intervention' (p. 112). The familiar distinction between children and adults has become problematic and is being contested. Nevertheless, this distinction is still present in our language; we keep talking about young people, quarter-lifers, and so on. But these words seem to refer to nothing other than target groups, and survive due to the functionality they have vis-à-vis the discourse of lifelong learning. Therefore the 'traditional' distinction between child and adult no longer carries meaning and, therefore, the concept of the child seems to us to be primarily an issue to be questioned rather than a well-defined referent in current educational discourse. We believe that this situation offers possibilities for thinking of 'an experience of childhood' that stands for something entirely different. This would consist more precisely in conceiving childhood not in diachronic terms, or in terms of a quarantine or a preparation for a public adult life—that is what this term traditionally (before the learning society came into existence) stood for—but instead in terms of an antidote to the downsides of the learning society.[3] It will become clear then that this alternative way of thinking about the child makes it possible to fathom the intersection between the experience of childhood and a critical practice of philosophy. At the end of the article we will elaborate more precisely this experience of childhood as relating to criticism and claim that it is exactly this notion of criticism that is at stake today both in education and in philosophical practice. Before setting out these rather strong claims, however, we will first provide a further analysis of the discourse of the learning society and its downsides, and then elaborate extensively this 'experience of childhood'.

THE DISCOURSE OF THE LEARNING SOCIETY AND THE LOGIC OF BARE LIFE

Inspired by the distinction that Arendt (1951/1973; 1958) draws between *zoé* and *bios*, between 'bare life' and life as a human form, Masschelein has, in his early work on the discourse of the learning society,[4] shown *bios* to be both an effect and an instrument of the reign of the *animal laborans*. This refers to the labouring animal that in modern Western society has become the victorious figure in the struggle between the interest in survival and the longing for a significant life, which dates back as early as the ancient Greek world. *Zoé* refers to the simple fact of life (bare or naked life): it is therefore detached from all particular forms of life. A life that has a singular shape, meaning, and destiny, on the contrary, would for the Greeks have to be called *bios*. It is very important to stress here that both notions only have meaning in relation to one another. *Bios* should be defined as the true, meaningful life of those people (the free citizens) that have the opportunity to not be continuously preoccupied with survival, while *zoé* refers to the (deplorable) condition of those (women, foreigners, slaves) who are excluded from the possibility of a significant life. So, in contradistinction to the meaningful existence of singular individuals who have succeeded in lifting themselves out of the sphere of survival, *zoé* 'refers to the natural and "biological" processes of the organism, to the essential properties of organized beings that evolve from birth to death by fulfilling functions that are common to them' (Masschelein, 2001, p. 6). Now, the main characteristic of modern society is, according to Arendt, that it is a society whose most important and perhaps exclusive preoccupation is *labour*, i.e. the activity that is necessary to sustain life. To live is in this sense a continuous process of appropriating the necessary energy to satisfy our needs. The victory of the *animal laborans* therefore constitutes the one-dimensional implementation of a logic of productivity: *the logic of bare life*.

In order to understand better the distinction between 'bare life' (*zoe*) and 'human life as a form of life' (*bios*), it might be helpful to elaborate upon the difference between the concepts *environment* and *world*, which are the respective correlates of these two modes of living. In an environment (which is thus connected to 'bare life'), all that surrounds us (objects, persons, knowledge, technical skill, etc.) is considered either as a possible resource to benefit from and is seen as a functioning for survival, or it is assessed as something that stands in the way of benefit and survival. In contradistinction to an environment, a *world* is, according to Arendt, a space in which human action is understood to have *meaning*. It forms as such 'the public space between human beings who appear to each other as unique and who act and speak together' (p. 6). A world is thus supposed to hold in itself the possibility of the appearance of something other and of something new.

The logic of bare life presupposes a solely functional notion of existence, i.e. life as preoccupied with survival, fecundity, and fertility, and only allows for life to take place in an environment. This logic turns life into a cyclical event that has neither a beginning nor an end, and that is 'characterized by an eternal return insofar as the life of each member of a species essentially constitutes the repetition of that of all the other members' (ibid.). The actions people undertake are 'evaluated as a function of the promotion and preservation of the process of life' (ibid.).

The discourse of the leaning society operates, according to Masschelein, on the basis of the very same logic, in the sense that the process of learning mirrors this anonymously biological life process of continuous and cyclical appropriation. In this sense, the predominance of learning means that we are permanently encapsulated in learning environments. So, a first reason why the predominance of learning might be criticised is that this notion presupposes a conception of life that merely expresses a struggle for survival and, as such, 'does not create a common world existing between human beings, but only guarantees participation in a common process' (p. 15). Second, given that the educational sphere is to be understood as the space where 'the new' can arise, the learning society implies that 'newness itself has been made functional and productive for the given order' (p. 16) in the sense that what is 'new' or 'other' is immediately made operative as an asset to be used.[5] As such the willingness to allow newness does not have a chance of appearing as anything other than a competence to be acquired. Newness is no longer a challenge for thinking, or a nuisance vis-à-vis the identities and positions that we have acquired (but to which we care to stick to in spite of their contingent nature).

The overall presence of learning, and the regime of bare life that is supported by it, consequently installs 'a soft totalitarianism which constricts the imagination and inhibits our longing for something totally different than the given' (p. 3). This 'soft totalitarianism' is evident in the fact that it seems absurd to question our identity as learners or to question the benefits of lifelong learning. The logic of bare life therefore seems to be an almost inescapable aspect of the current educational reality.

THE EXPERIENCE OF THE LIFELONG LEARNER AS AN EXPERIENCE OF OMNIPOTENTIALITY

To clarify, living in the learning society can be described in terms of a specific experience that we believe to be typical for the inhabitants of this environment, and that we would like to call the experience of omnipotentiality. As life-long learners we are supposed to have a life-long capacity for gaining *assets*, and to be unceasingly interested in putting them to use.[6] We are thus all supposed to appropriate an endlessly diversified set of *competences*, which, once attained, is supposed to form a unique cluster specific to each individual. As a result we believe ourselves to be unique *because* we possess a host of competences that we specifically need and through which we realise ourselves (as truly our *selves* and distinct from any other). Nevertheless, this quest never reaches a definitive end. The interest in becoming (uniquely) competent implies a never-ending process of acquisition of better and new competences, and of mobilising these in order to strengthen one's position in relation to the position of others (who are also involved in a similar, continuous, and ruthless competitive battle to be more competent). It is this that gives rise to what we will call 'the experience of omnipotentiality'.[7] The experience of omnipotentiality is to be found in the desire to make the most of our possibilities by translating them into competences that are employable. Through this translation the experience of omnipotentiality holds within itself the desire to be maximally competent and as such the promise of success.

The experience of omnipotentiality is, however, precisely something that narrows down the possibility for education to take place. As we said, what the analysis of current society as a learning society has revealed, is that all of us are encapsulated in learning environments. In spite of the predominance of this regime, however, experiences are possible that are properly educational and that might allow something other than a mere turning back to the old idea of schooling and teaching (constituting a preparation for an adult life and thus being based on a teleological view of history). Since we are all permanently living in learning environments, education cannot be conceived exclusively as a preparation for the world. What is at stake in education, then, is perhaps not a notion of preparation (for the world), but rather those moments that suspend this traditional aim and render inoperative the existing learning regime. Educational moments, then, take place when newness and otherness is allowed to appear—and here of course the figure of 'the child' comes to the fore. We should recall here, however, that newness under present conditions is immediately made functional to the existing (learning) society (that owes its continuation to the translation of potential into competence). If we are encapsulated in learning environments, then, where could this 'world' be found? The question remains how to allow or to make space for real newness to appear. This is not a question of how this newness itself can appear, for this will always remain an unanswered question. The point is rather that we cannot anticipate the new, for then it would be known in advance, and thus it would not be 'new'. So, the two questions with which we will occupy ourselves in what follows are: First, how can we conceive of a 'world' where this newness can take place? And, second, how are we to allow for such a newness to come into being?

THE EXPERIENCE OF CHILDHOOD AS AN EXPERIENCE OF TOTIPOTENIALITY

The appearance of that which is new can be understood as the coming into being of that which is *other* to the logic of bare life and which can never be made subservient to an all-encompassing learning environment.

According to Masschelein, this newness concerns the possibility of imagining an 'appeal' to what is given, or to the current state of affairs; and 'to imagine the possibility of such an appeal requires us to recover our sense of the experience of childhood' (p. 1). Childhood, as Masschelein conceives it, should be defined as 'the appearance of the possibility of a radical questioning and thus also of a radical change of the given order' (p. 16). Therefore, the educational sphere is the place where such a radical change or radical questioning of the current discourse can occur. It is then exactly in this place that one should be able to ask whether we should subject ourselves to a logic of lifelong learning and continual strengthening of positions. Interestingly, when searching for an alternative and an antidote to the downsides of the learning society, the notion of childhood comes back to the fore. It seems then that the notion of the child bears a different meaning. To elaborate this notion of the experience of childhood, and thus the notion of newness, and their place in education, we will turn our attention to a short passage by the Italian philosopher Giorgio Agamben (1995, pp. 95–98).

A leitmotiv in Agamben's continuously growing oeuvre, is his elaboration of the Heideggerian thesis that what characterises (wo)man, is that we are creatures of possibility. Agamben's work can be read as several entrances to and ways of discussing the issue of human potentiality, namely that we are beings that are capable of saying of ourselves: 'I can speak, I can act' (Agamben, 1999, p. 177). Interestingly, Agamben does not link this to an experience of omnipotentiality (which would correlate with the subject that is an inhabitant of the learning society), but to an experience of impotence (pp. 181–184). He tries to show that the expression 'I can' when it is taken in its deepest sense—*as such*—is only to be understood as the experience of an absence of the concrete possibility (to speak). And here he brings in the notion of childhood, against the background that etymologically speaking the child, the in-fant, literally means the one who 'does not as yet possess the potential of speech'. So, instead of expelling the impossibility of speaking to the outskirts of the experience of being human, Agamben places it at its very centre—thus conceptualising our lack of speech, our silence, and even the empty space within letters and words as an experience that is highly significant and even the most characteristic of human action (Agamben, 1993, p. 4). It should be added that this emptiness, this lack of speech or of competence, is a dimension that has no place whatsoever in the discourse of the learning society: as far as it carries a meaning in this discourse, it appears solely as something negative, i.e. as a problem to be overcome. For the learning society this emptiness is a lack and a temporary condition to be worked upon, and a situation that calls for certain competences to be acquired. Nevertheless, Agamben sees exactly this impotence, this im-possibility, as a form of affirmation in the deepest sense of this word.

A short passage from Agamben's *The Idea of Prose,* in which he elaborates 'the idea of infancy', might be instructive here to explain why the experience of childhood may count as a genuinely 'potentialising' experience that is, paradoxically, connected to an affirmation of impotence. Here, Agamben reminds his readers of the discovery of a peculiar albino salamander, named the axolotl, which has until now perplexed biologists and zoologists. This is because the salamander maintains, throughout its entire life, characteristics typical of the larval stage of the amphibian. It spends its entire life in water, without ever losing its gills or going to live on shore, as other amphibians would do when they reach maturity. Yet, it has the capacity for reproduction. Biologists cannot but classify this strange creature as a larva, albeit a larva with the capacity of reproduction; premature, yet mature. It manifests thus a 'stubborn infantilism' (Agamben, 1995, p. 96). This peculiarity, which in biological jargon is also called 'neoteny',[8] is now considered by evolutionary theorists to be an important key to the understanding of human evolution and '[it] is now supposed that man did not evolve from individual adults but from the young of a primate which, like the axolotl, had prematurely acquired the capacity for reproduction' (ibid.).[9] Even though human evolution is supposed to be better understood by relating it to this peculiar manifestation of neoteny, it challenges the way in which biologists are used to categorising life and their understanding of reproduction on the basis of the distinction immature versus mature. It challenges even the very distinction immature versus mature itself.

Agamben is, however, not particularly interested in explaining or mapping human evolution. Rather, he takes neoteny as the starting point for a reflection on what is proper to (wo)man. Keeping in mind that '[c]haracteristics which in primates are transitory became final in man' (ibid.), Agamben develops the idea that this gave rise, in some way, 'to a kind of eternal child' (ibid.). This hypothesis (as he calls it) then makes it possible for him to undertake 'a new approach to language and to the entire sphere of the exosomatic tradition which, more than any genetic imprint, characterizes *homo sapiens*' (ibid.). Otherwise stated: the concept of neoteny allows us to conceive of human action as a kind of eternal immaturity, a stubborn infantilism. It is in the elaboration of this argument that Agamben offers interesting insights as to what the 'experience of childhood' might mean and how the appearance of newness forms an antidote to the logic of bare life that currently is operative. We would like to read Agamben's invitation to imagine such an infant as the educational challenge we are facing today in the light of the former critiques on the learning society.

More concretely, Agamben invites his readers to imagine an infant that 'rejects any specific destiny and any determined environment in order to hold onto its immaturity and helplessness' (ibid.). If one is stuck in a determined environment one only develops 'the infinitely repeatable possibilities fixed in the genetic code' and thus pays attention only 'to what is written' (ibid.). What Agamben refers to as the 'infinite repeatability that is fixed in the genetic code' is read as an instantiation of the logic of bare life (and its eternal return). The 'infinite repeatability' refers to the experience of omnipotentiality, i.e. the experience of a subject that can only pay attention to 'what is written' in the sense that it presupposes a continuous confirmation of the possibilities that are inherent in the 'genetic code'. The logic of bare life presupposes this 'infinite repeatability' in the sense that one's inherent self-understanding confirms a continuous obsession and need for investment as well as an orientation to the continuous acquisition of competences. The experience of omnipotentiality is therefore a form of self-affirmation, in the sense that we realise competences that satisfy our own (individual) needs—and this in turn results in a reinforcement of the inherent regime of thinking in terms of functionality. As omnipotential beings that inhabit the learning society we are continuously occupied with the realisation of 'what is written' through the endless appropriation of our own competences. Therefore the logic of bare life gets continuously promoted and preserved, and there is no room for helplessness. Indeed, everything is accounted for, except helplessness itself.

The neotenic infant, in contradistinction to the subject of the learning environment, 'would find himself [*sic*] in the condition of being able to pay attention precisely to what has not been written' (ibid.). This attention to what has not been written might also be called 'infantile totipotency' and the neotenic infant would, in its infantile totipotency, 'be ecstatically overwhelmed, cast out himself, not like other living beings into a specific adventure or environment, but for the first time into a world' (ibid.). We can thus oppose the *omnipotential* and functional relating to an environment, to a *totipotential* existence in a world. The use of this last phraseology is clearly provocative and might sound a bit misleading, as totipotency refers to an experience of utter impossibility: this is because the neotenic in-fant is no longer interested in realising what he or she potentially might become as a life-long learner, interested in gaining a strong(er) position in life. On the contrary, leaving this interest behind, a space of radical possibility is opened, i.e. the coming of a future that is not determined by what is actually possible, but that leaves room for the unforeseeable, i.e. what counts *now* as impossible. So, the neotenic infant, while 'paying attention to what has not been written', grants the possibility of the new, i.e. of the impossible, to become reality, because it does not appropriate it, because it does not turn it towards what is immediately functional for what is given, but allows it instead to become an experience of what is given. As totipotential beings, we do not know who we are and what we are supposed to do. We do not merely leave, or easily stroll out of the determination of the environment, but we are 'cast out into a world' (ibid.). This is only realised when we abandon any determination and any specific destiny, which is a state of holding onto 'immaturity and [a state] of helplessness' (ibid.). This abandonment and rejection then means that the neotenic child is 'entrusted to oblivion' and can as such 'truly listen' (ibid.). Indeed, in order to *truly* listen one must be silent, one must have *a lack of words*. The possibility of having an experience in which we see, hear something 'for the first time', is something the learning society immunises us against.

Elaborating the metaphor a bit further, it should be said that within the discourse of the learning society we can only hear a predefined set of sounds, i.e. that which has no place in the given register is simply unheard (of). As such, imagining other sounds is simply conceived as impossible. Assuming that the register of possible human action is already fixed, this discourse conveniently places every particular possibility within that register and is deaf to whatever falls outside of it. The only way of being able to hear what falls outside of it, and thus to 'truly listen' is to abandon the register that is given, and as such become helpless, without destination. Thus in rejecting the determination of what we as omnipotential beings might become (i.e. maximally competent learners), we might experience, negatively put, a kind of impotency, but that is simultaneously, put positively, the opening of a radical, unspecified, and open future. This concerns *not* the possibility of realising already fixed capabilities, but rather the possibility of living without determination or any destiny whatsoever (Agamben, 1999, pp. 232–238). 'Totipotency' thus relates to possibility taken *as such* (p. 249); not the superficial kind of possibility that is defined in terms of a position (of being a learner) we currently occupy, but rather 'pure' possibility (pp. 177–184). Not knowing what to do or who we are, we are exposed, 'thrown into a world' and have nothing else to do but pay attention and 'truly listen'.[10]

This world we are exposed to is, then, not to be understood as the sphere where human beings appear to each other as unique and that allows them to act and speak together, or the sphere where a more authentic experience of human action might occur (presupposing the possibility of a 'true human form of life' to arise). If this last were the case, the inhabitants of this world would be interested in a more genuine way of life. Instead we understand this being thrown into a world as a *de*subjectifying experience. We argue, with Agamben, for the significance and subsequently the allowing-to-be, of an experience that renders meaningless all desire to stick to a defined position or identity in life and which, for precisely that reason, opens a future in which the impossible might become possible. This is an experience in which the unforeseen is actually new, and not immediately recuperated as a part of the functional spectrum of the learning society. Through the openness that is created by this desubjectifying experience, an appeal to, and a radical change of, the given becomes possible. What is at stake in education today then is exactly the preservation of the neotenic infant, of the openness, of the allowing to be of an appeal to what is given.

What is at stake then is being helpless. This is clearly to be distinguished from and opposed to an existence that is lived from the perspective of omnipotentiality, which implies that the scope of life is made functional and that narrows life down to functional competences.

Childhood—taken in a critical sense, i.e. as an antidote to current societal developments—relates then to an experience that renders it impossible to remain who one is or is supposed to be. In that way, the future is set radically free, which is to say without destination. 'Childhood', as it is conceived by Agamben, is thus obviously not referring to the usual meaning of this word, i.e. the first part of a diachronic development that ends in adulthood. The experience of childhood is to be understood apart from this distinction. Childhood is not the negation of adulthood (i.e. not yet being grown up), nor is it to be conceived in relation to an adulthood that it lacks. It should rather be taken *as such*, i.e. as the indeterminate openness that characterises or correlates with a world. The 'soft totalitarianism' of the discourse of the learning society can then be interpreted precisely as a way of closing down the neotenic openness, by singling out omnipotency as the exclusive way to experience our 'dwelling in being', and as such not allowing for an experience of totipotency to take place. We could say, then, that taking the Agambenian experience of childhood seriously, the learning society and its logic of bare life should be criticised because they immunise us against the possibility of living through an experience of totipotency. The full experience of potentiality is undermined by the fact that within the learning society the very possibility of rejecting our destiny has become unintelligible. Rejecting one's destiny as a lifelong learner would mean that one desires to become incompetent, and thus become a totally useless individual that has decided to exclude itself from the struggle for survival and of gaining assets. Lacking these assets, this struggle would be resolved pretty fast. Otherwise stated, the discourse of the learning society, in turning all actions into useful learning activities, not only reflects the logic of bare life, but in doing so, moreover, denies 'indeterminate openness'. So, the discourse of the learning society walls in the neotenic openness, and shrouds the in-fant with its competence-orientated cloak. It is then only through oblivion, forgetfulness, and helplessness that an unforeseeable alternative to the encapsulating logic of bare life would become possible, and that another way of living remains principally possible.

NEOTENY FOR BEGINNERS?

'Somewhere inside of us, the neotenic child continues its royal game,' Agamben says (1995, p. 98). Beautiful and promising as these words are, we still have to consider how we are to allow this eternal child to emerge from beneath the rubble of the learning society. Should we remind ourselves to be silent or should we tell ourselves that we don't have to be competent? Or, should we *learn* in some way or other how to truly listen? Even though these suggestions might seem interesting, the answer to these questions cannot be positive: this is because the very asking of *these* questions seems contradictory to the idea of totipotentiality. Denying the destiny of the life-long learner, the experience of totipotentiality *grants* a moment of *suspension* of the logic of bare life.[11] It is as a result of thinking in accordance with the figure of the *animal laborans* that we are continuously inclined to ask how to translate the remarks of Agamben into concrete pedagogical practices and didactic instruments, and that we desire to possess a manual that would give concrete guidelines and make us competent, omnipotential beings. The very occurrence of suspension can never be the result of the application of a trick that can be taught or learned, and can thus never be the object of method. Offering a 'manual of suspension' would consist in explaining how we should begin anew, but the only manual for beginning anew is a perfectly empty book that offers potentiality itself, in its emptiness, in its lack of destiny.[12] Nevertheless going through these moments of suspension might be the most truthfully educational experience that remains in a time of an all-encompassing learning society. The moments that are the most educational for the authors of this text are not characterised by a reassuring confirmation of our roles as lifelong learners, or even as (anachronistic) teachers, nor by the heart-warming knowledge that we have been at the right place at the right time to account for a so-called educational problem. Rather, what is educational comes in those moments at which we have 'lost ourselves' and undergone a desubjectivation of some sort, became immature and helpless, and experienced as such a suspension of the logic that seemed to determine us so strongly, and which made it possible to be exposed to a world 'for the first time'. At these moments we were neotenic infants, entrusted to oblivion. To be 'useless', instead of feeling ourselves obliged to account for the thoughtlessness and indeterminate openness of the world by identifying ourselves on the basis of omnipotentiality, is thus the challenge that we—educators, philosophers, and neotenic children alike— are facing today. This challenge is to be taken on through an endless search, by adopting attitudes that do not allow the immunisation against experiences that is totipotency to take place.

WHEN PHILOSOPHY BECOMES CHILDISH (AGAIN)

We have so far left the notion of philosophy out of our discussion, yet its presence has been, up to now, a *silent* presence. Some remarks concerning philosophical practice will have to suffice here in order to expand upon the promised cross-section between philosophy and the child.

We must, of course, confront the question of defining philosophical practice. Dealing with the same question in their book, straightforwardly titled, *What is philosophy?* Deleuze and Guattari define philosophy as the art of creating concepts (Deleuze and Guattari, 1994, p. 2). Concepts of course form a part of our everyday lives, where they are used to simplify communication, to make decisions and to form opinions. Yet this is not, according to Deleuze and Guattari, what is so interesting about concepts. Each philosopher, and, we should add, each reader of philosophy, creates her own concepts and practices this art of creation. A concept is not the same as an idea, a notion, or a function. What is distinctive about a concept is that it has a consistency defined by its internal components and thus has no reference to any external determination or presupposition concerning its coherence, which is the case for scientific functions or logical propositions.[13] In this sense concepts have no referent at all, but are intensive and express the virtual existence of an event in thought (p. 21). A concept, then, has no necessary reference to truth, for this would make the creation of the concept subject to an external determination and as such put it at the service of a dogmatic image of thought, of how one should think. A concept is then not to be seen as true or false, but instead as affective and active and should therefore be understood as a form or a force (p. 144). Concepts, taken as forms or forces, are means by which we are able to experience something anew, and are able to think of new possibilities (Parr, 2005, p. 50). The creation of concepts originates in a denial of being at the service of existing images of thought, and in its expression of an event in thought, the active means by which we can 'think anew'. Admittedly, we don't need this kind of concept in order to be able to think, as we can very well think according to current ideas and notions, following existing thoughts. Yet in order to be able to think anew, we have to engage in the philosophical practice of creating concepts. Philosophy is exactly that practice that makes the experience of the new possible through the creation of concepts.

Considering concepts to be the *material* of the philosopher Deleuze and Guattari immediately encounter rivals that lay claim to the creation of concepts. Most notably, in recent times 'the most shameful moment came when computer science, marketing, design and advertising, all the disciplines of communication, seized hold of the word concept itself and said: "This is our concern, we are the creative ones, we are the ideas men!"' (1994, p. 10). Dealing with concepts in this way becomes thinking of new ways to make concepts marketable, therefore restricting the concept's powers and making it subservient to a regime of thought. When turning the creation of concepts into the *engineering* of concepts, concepts are no longer means by which we answer an event in thought and through which we can think anew, but become instead mere functional instruments.

So, it might be argued that the art of creating concepts has today become subject to what we have been calling the logic of bare life. The engineering and development of concepts is yet another competence to be acquired. Rendering the creation of concepts subservient to the logic of bare life, makes dealing with concepts a question of functionality (e.g. Is this concept efficiently developed? Is this concept useful for our purpose?). The transformative power of concepts is denied, as they are turned into instruments. Yet the problem is not only that the philosopher's material is being turned into instruments, but concerns above all the functionalisation of the art of creating concepts, by making it subservient to external determinations in the name of the logic of bare life—'an absolute disaster for thought, whatever its benefits may be' (p. 12).

Yet Deleuze and Guattari's criticism is not to be conflated with the cliché that philosophy should be without functionality or use. Saying that 'the greatness of philosophy' is to be found in its uselessness 'is a frivolous answer that not even young people find amusing any more' (p. 6). In earlier work, Deleuze had already confronted this question of philosophy's uselessness: 'When someone asks "what's the use of philosophy?" the reply must be aggressive, since the question tries to be ironic and caustic. Philosophy does not serve the State nor the Church, who have other concerns. It serves no established power. The use of philosophy is to sadden. A philosophy that saddens no one, that annoys no one, is not a philosophy ... . Philosophy is at its most positive as a critique, as an enterprise of demystification' (Deleuze, 1983, p. 106).

Philosophical practice, as the art of creating concepts and as a critical occupation, is not, of course, of no use whatsoever. Yet *this* use is not to be understood functionally: *its use is not to be found in its not having any use, but its uselessness is its relevance*. Its specific relevance today might be understood in the fact that it should be totally useless vis-à-vis the logic of bare life. Deleuze and Guattari write that '[t]he philosopher is the concept's friend; he is potentiality of the concept' (Deleuze and Guattari, 1994, p. 5). This quote resonates with what we have said about potentiality. The figure through which we try to understand philosophical practice should not only be *the friend*, but also and perhaps more importantly *the neotenic infant*.

In order to be able to create concepts as a philosophical activity, one needs to suspend any established order. It is precisely here that the cross-section between the child and the philosopher is to be found. Philosophical practice could be seen as a practice that cannot of itself be reconciled with the logic of bare life, precisely because it arises from the neotenic openness, i.e. helplessness and rejection of any destiny. It is here that philosophy becomes childish. The question of philosophy's use, however, is no longer an ironic one under the conditions we find ourselves in today. As a rule, philosophers now are increasingly asked to account for what they are doing:

they have continually to explain why a particular philosophical investigation is useful, whereby usefulness is to be understood in terms of an external justification that mirrors the logic of bare life, manifested in an endless appropriation of publications and methodological expertise. The currently hard-felt need to define philosophical activity as a useful activity—in its content, its methods, or its objectives—jeopardises the very *potentiality* that characterises philosophy. Shouldn't we, we might ask, just because we are philosophers and educators be sharing the problematisation of our usefulness? In this sense the experience of childhood is what is at stake today; and this, then, is first of all to be understood as allowing the experience of childhood to occur so that we can 'think anew'.

We will end by saying that it is the 'allowing' that is particularly relevant where philosophy enters the school curriculum. Of course it seems convenient, if not practically inevitable, to define philosophy (for/ with children) as a set of practices, competences, methods, and skills that have a specific content and deliver specific goals, as is clearly seen in the Philosophy for Children program.[14] Yet this definition of philosophical practice, as the cultivation of critical thinking skills, turns these skills into competences to acquire, and thereby seems to undermine neotenic openness and to make it subservient to a regime of thought that is not its own creation. Now, we believe that philosophical practice is revealed here in an all too straightforward way, and that the experience of childhood is also a potential *threat* to any established societal and pedagogical order. This might explain why it is convenient to rely on the (anachronistic) immature/mature distinction and to conceive (anachronistically) children in such a manner that we simply cannot leave them in this state of helplessness, since they are in need of the support of an adult generation. This is to say that philosophy for/with children is therefore rendered subservient to the existing regime, i.e. as an interesting addition to the set of competences provided by the existing curriculum. Yet, as we have argued, it is exactly this experience of childhood as a suspension of the logic of bare life that can be shared amongst the participants of philosophy for/with children, making of every participant a neotenic infant. We can only hope that philosophy for/with children as a practice gives birth to experiences of childhood, and that the contributions in this Special Issue that discuss more practical applications offer occasions to do so. If, however, the reader finds that these contributions render both the notions of philosophy and of the child subservient to a discourse that breathes the spirit of the learning society and its logic of bare life, we hope that a little frown may be aimed at the dark side of the educator's heartfelt intention, which, it must be acknowledged, we share. It is, after all, for philosophers, for children, and for educators one of the harshest, if not the most difficult and contradictory thing to aspire to, to be oblivious, to be forgetful, to be helpless: to believe, then, that less can indeed be more.

NOTES

1. Looking for places where childhood forms an important object of study, one finally arrives at areas such as developmental psychology, sociology of childhood, or history of childhood. In educational sciences itself this interest is rather limited. In fields such as philosophy for/with children, the concept of the child is mostly unquestioned, and the publications in this field more often than not prefer to emphasise practical applications. Notable exceptions are the work of David Kennedy (2006) and Andrew Stables (2008).

2. See Masschelein, 2000, 2001; Simons, 2000a, 2000b; Simons and Masschelein, 2008a, 2008b; Masschelein, Simons, Bröckling and Pongratz, 2006.

3. Lyotard has also used the concept of 'enfance' in his work in relation to a notion of questioning or resistance. See for instance *Lectures d'enfance* (1991) and Masschelein and Smeyers, 2000. Of course, there is a long history of thought in which the concept of the child refers to something more, or other, than a diachronic referent, in which the semantic connection of the figure of the child to innocence, purity, creativity, beginning anew, etc. can be traced throughout areas such as the arts or religion (e.g. Kennedy, 2006).

4. In his early work on the discourse of the learning society, Jan Masschelein (2001) drew mainly on Hannah Arendt's analysis of the present, whereas in later work he has abandoned the normative position Arendt takes for a more a-normative Foucauldian perspective.

5. This immediate 'translation' of what is new and other into competences and assets, is also seen in the widespread conviction that the solution for economic crises is to be found in the promotion of a knowledge society in which we continuously have to be creative and innovative. We should all put our creative resources to work, more than we already do, to help to safeguard the continuation of the existing, productivity-based economy.

6. This supposedly inexhaustible learning capacity is defined in terms of a rationality in view of which learning is considered to be a process of reflexive problem solving (e.g. Masschelein, 2001, p. 12). In later work Simons and Masschelein have shown the subject of the learning society to have an entrepreneurial relation to the self. This entrepreneurial attitude is evident in the interlacing of 'learning', 'living', and 'investment' (Simons, 2006, p. 532). Also see Masschelein and Simons, 2002 and Vlieghe, 2010 who elaborates a similar point of view from the standpoint of human embodiment in relation to the recent work of Judith Butler.

7. The concept of omnipotentiality is taken from a short passage in Agamben's *Idea of Prose* (where he comments on the idea of power (Agamben, 1995, p. 71). The concept is here not necessarily used completely in line with Agamben's own idea.

8. Neoteny is a specific form of what biologists call 'pedomorphism', which occurs in both fauna and flora. Neoteny, as the acquisition of adult features (such as the capacity for reproduction) whilst remaining in juvenile form (such as the larval stage), is of particular interest here because it is in this notion that maturity and infancy are no longer in opposition to each other, and thus no longer seem to derive meaning from one another. Pedomorphism, then, challenges the distinctions that biologists or zoologists classically make between immaturity and maturity. Other forms of pedomorphism are, for instance, a delayed maturation (postdisplacement), or a halt of maturation itself (progenesis).

9. See Desmond Morris' *Naked Ape* (1967) or Gould's *Ontogeny and Phylogeny* (1977) for a short list of neotenic traits.

10. In this respect Masschelein has argued for a 'poor pedagogy' where the focus lies on 'e-ducating the gaze'. He argues for a distinction between education and e-ducation, where the first stands for 'leading in' (learning) and the second for 'leading out'. In this view of a poor pedagogy, '[e]-ducating the gaze is not about arriving at a liberated or critical view, but about liberating or displacing our view. It is not about becoming conscious or aware, but about becoming attentive, about paying attention.' Such a view on e-ducation is 'not dependent on method, but relies on discipline; it does not require a rich methodology, but asks for a poor pedagogy, i.e. for practices which allow us to expose ourselves, practices which bring us into the streets, displace us' (Masschelein, 2010, p. 44).

11. As we stated earlier, the Greek notions of *bios* and *zoé* derive their meaning *only in relation to one another*. The Agambian suspension is then not only a suspension of the logic of bare life, but also a suspension of the oppositional structure of *form of life* and *bare life*, without which the logic of bare life would not work.
12. Cf. Agamben, 1995, pp. 31–34.
13. Deleuze and Guattari go to great lengths to make this point, and to differentiate philosophy from science and the arts. See Deleuze and Guattari, 1994, pp. 117–200.
14. See e.g. Lipman, Sharp and Oscanyan, 1980.

REFERENCES

Agamben, G. (1995) *The Idea of Prose*, M. Sullivan and S. Whitsitt, trans. (New York, Sun).
Agamben, G. (1993) *Infancy and History. The Destruction of Experience*, L. Heron, trans. (London, Verso).
Agamben, G. (1999) *Potentialities. Collected Essays in Philosophy*, D. Heller-Roazen, trans. (Stanford, CA, Stanford University Press).
Arendt, H. [1951] (1973) *The Origins of Totalitarianism* (New York, Harcourt Brace Jovanovich).
Arendt, H. (1958) *The Human Condition* (New York, Doubleday).
Deleuze, G. (1983) *Nietzsche and Philosophy*, H. Tomlinson, trans. (New York, The Athlone Press).
Deleuze, G. and Guattari, F. (1994) *What is Philosophy?*, H. Tomlinson and G. Burchell, trans. (New York, Columbia University Press).
Gould, S. J. (1977) *Ontogeny and Phylogeny* (Cambridge, MA, Belknap Press of Harvard University Press).
Kennedy, D. (2006) *Changing Conceptions of the Child from the Renaissance to Post-Modernity: A Philosophy of Childhood* (Lewiston, NY, Edwin Mellen Press).
Lyotard, J. F. (1991) *Lectures d'enfance* (Paris, Galilée).
Lipman, M., Sharp, A. M. and Oscanyan, F. S. (1980) *Philosophy in the Classroom* (Philadelphia, PA, Temple University Press).
Masschelein, J. (2000) Can Education Still be Critical?, *Journal of Philosophy of Education*, 34.4, pp. 603–616.
Masschelein, J. (2001) The Discourse of the Learning Society and the Loss of Childhood, *Journal of Philosophy of Education*, 35.1, pp. 1–20.
Masschelein, J. (2010) E-ducating the Gaze: The Idea of a Poor Pedagogy, *Ethics and Education*, 5.1, pp. 43–53.
Masschelein, J. and Simons, M. (2002) An Adequate Education in a Globalised World? A Note on Immunisation against Being-Together, *Journal of Philosophy of Education*, 36.4, pp. 589–608.
Masschelein, J., Simons, M., Bröckling, U. and Pongratz, L. (eds) (2006) *The Learning Society from the Perspective of Governmentality* (Oxford, Carfax Publishing).
Masschelein, J. and Smeyers, P. (2000) *L'enfance*, Education and the Politics of Meaning, in: P. A. Dhillon and P. Standish (eds) *Lyotard, Just Education* (London, Routledge), pp. 140–156.
Morris, D. (1967) *The Naked Ape: A Zoologist's Study of the Human Animal* (New York, McGraw-Hill).
Parr, A. (ed.) (2005) *The Deleuze Dictionary* (Edinburgh, Edinburgh University Press).
Simons, M. (2000a) De school in de ban van het leven. Unpublished PhD thesis, KU Leuven.
Simons, M. (2000b) Quality-Assurance and Biopower in Education, Bare Essentials of Professional and Organisational Life, *Proceedings of the Annual Conference of the Philosophy of Education Society of Great Britain*, Oxford, pp. 363–374.
Simons, M. (2006) Learning as Investment: Notes on Governmentality and Biopolitics, *Educational Philosophy and Theory*, 38.4, pp. 523–540.
Simons, M. and Masschelein, J. (2008a) The Governmentalization of Learning and the Assemblage of a Learning Apparatus, *Educational Theory*, 58.4, pp. 391–415.

Simons, M. and Masschelein, J. (2008b) From Schools to Learning Environments: The Dark Side of Being Exceptional, *Journal of Philosophy of Education*, 42.3, pp. 687–704.

Stables, A. (2008) *Childhood and the Philosophy of Education. An Anti-Aristotelian Perspective* (London, Continuum).

Vansieleghem, N. (2009) Children in Public or 'Public Children': An Alternative to Constructing One's Own Life, *Journal of Philosophy of Education*, 39.1, pp. 101–118.

Vlieghe, J. (2010) Judith Butler and the Public Dimension of the Body, Education, Critique and Corporeal Vulnerability, *Journal of Philosophy of Education*, 44.1, pp. 153–170.

2

Philosophy for Children and its Critics: A Mendham Dialogue

MAUGHN GREGORY

INTRODUCTION

The dialogue that follows was inspired by one that took place in May 2008 at a convent in Mendham New Jersey, during an eight-day seminar of the Institute for the Advancement of Philosophy for Children (IAPC). The theme for that seminar was 'Philosophy as a Way of Life',[1] and the dialogue followed a presentation made by our late colleague, and IAPC co-founder, Ann Margaret Sharp. Some of what follows comes from the transcript of that dialogue; some comes from my recollection of other conversations, with Ann and others; some is a report of internal dialogues with authors I have read. I have condensed the number of participants to five, organised ideas thematically, put words in people's mouths, and rounded out some of the arguments with ideas taken from published material. What follows bears little resemblance to the original dialogue that inspired it, and the characters here should not be taken to represent the original participants.

The purposes of this reconstructed dialogue are: to present a particular, normative account of the work of Philosophy for Children (P4C),[2] to situate that account in relation to a number of different kinds of criticism the programme has attracted, to illustrate the complex interactions among these normative positions, and to indicate where these positions have been taken up in the literature over the past 40 years. Rather than respond to particular criticisms in depth, I indicate the general nature of my position regarding them and provide references to published material where they have been made and responded to. In that regard, this paper is more a review of the literature of P4C advocacy and criticism than a defence of the programme against any particular criticism.

Philosophy for Children in Transition: Problems and Prospects, First Edition. Nancy Vansieleghem and David Kennedy. Chapters © 2012 The Authors. Editorial organization © 2012 Philosophy of Education Society of Great Britain. Published 2012 by Blackwell Publishing Ltd.

THE DIALOGUE

Rosario: Ann, I met you some years ago when you spoke about how philosophy can help children develop critical and creative thinking, and a kind of ethical awareness you called 'caring thinking'. But this week, at this seminar, we've been discussing philosophy as a way of life—as the study and practice of how to live well, to live wisely—as opposed to 'academic philosophy', which most of us have experienced as learning a history of ideas, and learning to become 'intellectual' in ways that have little to do with how we live. So my question is: do you see Philosophy for Children as having moved away from a focus on thinking, toward a more practical or applied approach to philosophy?

Ann: No, I think the emphasis on wisdom has always been there. That's what Mat [Lipman] had in mind from the very beginning. You know, he comes out of the pragmatic tradition, that pays close attention to everyday experience and the art of making judgments that might improve that experience.[3] When I first met Mat in 1974 and asked him what he was trying to do, he said something like, 'I want to introduce children to philosophy because I think that's the way to improve their judgment.'[4] And when I asked him, 'What is philosophy, to you?' he said, 'Philosophy is the search for wisdom'. Mat saw the whole conversation of philosophy, going back to Socrates, as a quest to help us to lead qualitatively better lives.[5]

Rosario: Better, how?

Ann: Well, if we're talking about Western philosophy, then we're going to focus on aspects of our experience that have ethical, or aesthetic, or political, or logical or even metaphysical meaning. And when we learn to become more conscious of those kinds of meaning, you see, we have the opportunity to inquire into them, and to make judgments that, hopefully, can make our experiences more just, more free, more beautiful, or what have you. Mat's idea was to use philosophy to help children learn to do that. It's very explicit, for example, in *Suki*, which he wrote in 1978—over 30 years ago. *Suki* is an attempt to help children become conscious of the aesthetic dimension of their experience, and to make judgments that enhance or stabilise, or diversify the aesthetic qualities they value in their experience—and also to avoid what is petty, or mediocre, or downright ugly or offensive. But also, of course, to problematise what it means to *find* something attractive or repulsive, and hopefully to be more careful about making judgments like that. As I say, it's very explicit in *Suki*, but this emphasis on the meaning of experience is just as strong in *Pixie*, and in fact, it runs throughout the IAPC curriculum.[6]

Joe: But Rosario is right, isn't she, that P4C has always emphasised thinking and thinking skills?

Ann: Well, yes. I would say that in the early days, especially, my friend [Lipman] had a reputation of being very fascinated with the logical component of the programme, and he probably had more to say about critical thinking than about its other aspects. Remember, he started working on Philosophy for Children in the 1960s, after his experiences teaching philosophy to college students and adult education students at Columbia, and the political upheaval he saw there and on other university campuses around the country convinced him that learning to think critically, to inquire about philosophical questions and to form reasonable judgments should begin much earlier in life.[7] But then, even in those days, all you had to do was to open the curriculum and you would see it there—the search for wisdom. Mat didn't separate the skills—the thinking and concept-forming and inquiry skills, the creative and caring skills, and the dialogical skills—from that project of living a meaningful life. Do you see? Because to do that you've got to be awake, or sensitive to all these kinds of meaning; to know how they feel. But you've also got to see them as full of ambiguities and problems and opportunities. You've got to be curious and questioning about them, and know how to think about them carefully, and to dialogue about them with others who think and feel differently. And you've got to live with them and experiment with them, to see what you can make of them.

Maughn: I suspect that P4C's emphasis on meaning, experience and judgment is one reason that parents and teachers haven't been afraid of it—because they don't think of it as 'Teaching Children Plato'—but then that's the same reason that philosophers haven't been enthusiastic about it, until recently. I think it's significant that the way we practice philosophy with children—with self-examination, a certain ethics of dialogue, communal caring, and a focus on how to live—is in some ways a return to the philosophical practices of some of the ancient schools.[8]

Megan: Actually, a number of educational theorists, like Noddings (2005), Nussbaum (1997 and 2010), Rose (2009) and Sternberg (2003), have been drawing attention to the moral and political danger of education that aims exclusively at socio-economic advancement, and not also at living well, or wisdom. A student might be very successful in terms of getting the disciplinary knowledge, the intellectual, social and technological skills, and the cultural capital she needs to compete in the economic market, without having considered whether her life has any meaning or purpose beyond that, and without knowing how to cultivate personal or collective wellbeing. In fact, Sternberg (2003, p. 163) and Nussbaum (2010, pp. 73–6) have recommended Philosophy for Children precisely because it prioritises critical, emotional, political and ethical know-how over getting ahead. Of course, that distinction goes back to Socrates.[9]

Ann: We've even been accused of 'corrupting the youth'. I remember the bumper-stickers that one mid-western school district had printed up, saying 'Get *Harry Stottlemeier*[10] out of our schools!'

Joe: They were afraid it would inoculate their children against their own indoctrination. It's like a parent once said to me, 'No one should talk to my children about right and wrong, or about death, but me'. Some parents and educators don't trust children to be 'the guardians of their own virtue', as you and Mat wrote (Lipman and Sharp, 1980, p. 181).

Megan: That's one kind of criticism the programme has attracted, from the political right; and what Maughn just said about academic philosophers not taking it seriously is another.

Ann: That one, I think, has to do with lingering institutional chauvinism about the intellectual work of teachers—who are mostly women—and of children.[11]

Maughn: It also comes from the 'pure versus applied' distinction,[12] that still haunts some of the disciplines. Real philosophy is supposed to be the discourse (the thinking and talking and writing) of professional philosophers; and anything we do to put that discourse to work—in our friendships or our politics, say—isn't, unless it results in more professional discourse.[13] But of course that distinction has been challenged for some time now, by pragmatism, feminism and continental philosophy. They put the work of philosophy on par with the work of other disciplines, as caught up in all kinds of political, economic and cultural agendas.

Megan: It's not just philosophers, though, who have said that children's discourse can't be philosophical. We've heard that from developmental psychologists—the ones who read Piaget as ruling out certain kinds of cognitive functioning at certain ages.

Joe: I'd say that line of criticism has been mostly deflected by social learning theorists. I just finished reading Mat's *Natasha: Vygotskian Dialogues* (1996a), and it made me realise how formative social learning theory was to P4C. I knew the pragmatist genealogy of 'community of inquiry', from Dewey and Peirce,[14] but I hadn't paid much attention to this strand of educational psychology in Lipman's theory, from Vygotsky and Davydov. It helped me to understand what's at stake in the Piaget versus Vygotsky debate,[15] and it made me look at our work in the schools in a whole new way: as a pedagogy of 'cognitive cooperation with . . . peers and mentors' (Lipman 1996a, p. 45).

Ann: Mat developed a strong interest in 20th-century Soviet psychology, partly because of parallels he found with the pragmatist social psychology of Mead, Dewey and Buchler.[16] He was something of a pioneer in the way he implemented that theory in a practice of classroom dialogue.[17] Today, of course, Vygotsky's 'zone of proximal development' and Davydov's 'ascent to the concrete', are more influential in educational theory than when Mat was working.[18]

Rosario: As a matter of fact, some of the strongest proponents of P4C these days are educational researchers, who have shown how the programme can be instrumental in achieving educational objectives like critical thinking and reading comprehension.[19] But then that very instrumentalism is the target of some of the harshest criticism the programme faces today, from the political left—from critical and cultural theory and postmodernism.

Ann: Say more.

Rosario: Well, of course critical theory, coming out of Marxism, the Frankfurt School and feminist philosophy, has to do with human oppression and liberation. Critical theorists are concerned with how cultural practices that presume to be morally and politically neutral, are in fact oppressive. A lot of their work focuses on race- class- and gender-based oppression, especially as these are integral to the institutions and ideological frameworks of Western culture. Critical theorists of education look at how education often perpetuates, but can also subvert those kinds of oppression. So, for example, today we have colleges of education offering courses in cultural responsiveness, race consciousness and social justice, to prepare teachers to use 'critical pedagogy'.[20]

Joe: The faculty in our college has debated 'critical thinking versus critical pedagogy'. Some who defend critical thinking say that education should be politically and even morally neutral; that it shouldn't take sides. They say critical thinking is about *how* to think, and they worry that critical pedagogy teaches children *what* to think. In fact, the thinking skills component of P4C is something that some conservative parents and some professional philosophers have supported: the parents, because it's content-neutral—it doesn't impose any particular ideas or values on the children that might compete with what they get at home—and the philosophers because informal logic is a recognisable philosophical practice.

Rosario: But for a critical theorist there's no such thing as value-neutral education—or any other kind of cultural production. And since education that pretends to be neutral winds up being oppressive, they say education should be deliberately emancipatory. It should be explicitly anti-racists and anti-sexist and anti-heteronormative and even anti-capitalist. It should wake students up to the oppression they participate in, and give them tools to intervene against it. So, from that perspective, teaching critical thinking, without also doing some kind of consciousness-raising with them, is politically suspect.

Ann: What's the suspicion?

Rosario: Well, it's that if our consciousness hasn't been raised to recognise the systems of oppression we live with, critical thinking could end up being just a tool we use to chase after desires that have been manipulated by our patriarchal home lives and the capitalist media and so on. Or worse: if we get some power we might use our critical thinking to oppress others. Also, I think many people outside of P4C think of critical thinking as an individual thing—something we do alone, inside our own heads, whereas consciousness-raising typically involves understanding our connections to others, and aims at solidarity. I think these are well-founded suspicions.

Maughn: But philosophy has always been culturally critical and even subversive, going back to Socrates. Think of Nietzsche's call to do philosophy with a hammer. Think of Jane Addams' work in Hull House. And this element has been emphasised by many of our colleagues, who see P4C as a way of getting children, not merely to think critically, but to be critical of the world.[21]

Ann: That's just what I was saying: you have to be awake to the ethical and political meaning of your experience—emotionally as well as conceptually—before you can sense, and then articulate that there's something wrong with it. That's why the philosophical content of the programme is so important. It's not incidental; it's not just something we use to practice thinking; it's chosen deliberately to help children recognise those kinds of meaning. That's an indispensable part of the search for wisdom.

Joe: There is also the method. A lot of work has been done by feminists and others who see the community of inquiry in P4C as a method of critical pedagogy, because of how it distributes power and brackets the teacher's content expertise; and also how it nurtures timid voices and brings traditionally marginalised voices forward; how it makes adults take children's ideas and perspectives seriously, and how it works by collaboration.[22] Wasn't there an exchange between Mat and Paulo Freire, and didn't the two of them see their work sharing a kind of liberatory agenda?

Rosario: I can see that, but there is still an ongoing debate about whether getting children to pay attention to ethical and political meaning, inviting them to criticise the world as they experience it, and giving them practice in reasoning and egalitarian dialogue is enough, without also teaching them about racism and class oppression—teaching them to 'read the world' in those terms. How else can we prevent those philosophical practices from being co-opted by oppressive systems? That's especially of concern to critical theorists who suspect that rationality itself is a practice of domination.

Megan: But that's a problem for critical theory, isn't it? The theory needs a grounding conception of human flourishing on which to base its diagnosis of oppression; but the suspicion that all theory is ideology undermines the attempt to find such a conception, doesn't it? Even the Frankfurt school ran into that cul-de-sac. The part of critical theory that points to a more enlightened society or a more self-determined human subject is in tension with the part that sees rational autonomy as a liberal contrivance. Also, inasmuch as the method of critical theory involves empirical observation and means-end rationality, it becomes another science, in need of political deconstruction. So then, 'critical pedagogy' is just as much in need of 'a pedagogy of interruption'[23] as is 'Socratic pedagogy'.[24]

Rosario: Yes, and that's why people like Terry Eagleton have argued for cultural theorists to pay more attention to suffering, objectivity and human nature: to maintain the relevance of their work to real-world struggles.[25]

Ann: I want to step back a bit. I have my doubts about some of these distinctions, like individual versus community, and critical thinking versus critical consciousness. I'm thinking about Dewey's recommendation that education in each subject explain the processes of inquiry that produced the 'textbook knowledge' in that subject, including all the failures and reconstructions along the way, rather than presenting it as a finished product that came out of nowhere and is above critique.[26] I don't see why concepts like tolerance and equality and diversity can't be shared with children as products of inquiry into sexism and racism and etc.—as concepts that have taken on certain meanings and been shaped in certain ways, in response to certain problems. To do that, you see, is to invite children into the ongoing conversation about the meaning of those ideas, and to bring their own experiences to bear on them. It's no different from having them focus on concepts like person, friendship and fairness, that they use every day in a conventional way, but in philosophy they discover that these concepts have a wide range of meanings they may not have considered, some of which might help them make more sense of their experience, and find ways to enhance it. Coming up with a new understanding about what fairness means—let's say, in relation to race, class or gender—could have profound, immediate consequences in the life of a child.

Joe: I wonder if that approach makes P4C less vulnerable to conservative critics who say that values like 'social justice', 'feminism', 'social democracy', 'environmentalism', or even 'tolerance' are too partisan, too leftist to be taught in schools.[27] They say they want schools to be left out of the American culture wars.

Rosario: I notice they don't mind involving schools in culture wars over school prayer, or teaching creationism and nationalism.

Maughn: The kind of thing Joe is talking about—parents who don't want schools teaching their children what to believe about certain religious or moral or political issues—hasn't been a problem for P4C. Parents who investigate the programme can see we don't have that kind of agenda.[28] But Rosario is pointing to something quite different and not so easy to deal with: that some parents don't want their children to question, or even to think critically about the religious or political beliefs the parents teach them. They believe in their own exclusive right to shape their children's beliefs.[29]

Rosario: But can P4C really be value-neutral, in the way that Ann was suggesting? Did I understand you correctly, Ann? How can it be value-neutral, and at the same time be a normative practice in so many ways?

Ann: No, you're right, it's not value-neutral, or, I should say, not entirely. We are committed to procedures of inquiry, and practices of political and ethical interdependence that we take to be normative; and, as I said, to the aim of practical wisdom, or better ways to live. But these commitments aren't dogmas. If someone wants to challenge them, we should give that challenge a fair hearing. But there's a presumption, let's say, in favour of these aims and these procedural norms, based on how well they have served us in the past. We don't pretend to be neutral about them, and we don't pretend they are compatible with every idea we might discuss. But of course, they *are* neutral with regard to all kinds of other questions. So I guess I'd say our practice is *relatively* value-neutral[30]—if that makes sense.

Joe: It's really a priority of commitments, isn't it? Aren't you just saying that our commitment to these practices is prior to, or more solid than our commitment to the outcomes? In the way that we would find it easier, in most cases, to question the outcome of a science experiment or a trial by jury, than to question the norms of experimental research or the rules of evidence? I mean, we would ask ourselves if we followed the method carefully enough before we asked if there were something wrong with the method.

Maughn: That puts me in mind of what some of the philosophers we've been reading at this seminar have written about what it means to be a philosopher, or to live philosophically. There seems to be a norm or an ideal of a kind of personhood at work here, and I'm now wondering if that ideal isn't integral to the practice of P4C.

Ann: What kind of ideal are you thinking of?

Maughn: Well, it has the same kind of priority of commitments Joe just described. I would say the most basic commitment is to continually seek out the true, the beautiful and the good as categories of existential meaning—the kind of meaning that can be lived. I don't think it actually matters very much whether we talk about them as universal, essential or evolutionary, non-transcendent categories of meaning. In any case, the philosophical person yearns for, and works for those *kinds* of meaning. The secondary commitment is to the methods we've evolved for doing that—including analytic thinking and cultural criticism and hermeneutic dialogue and contemplative exercises.[31] The next level would be a lesser commitment to whatever ideas and values and ways of life we've found to be meaningful. And Joe's right: to say we prioritise the last one least is just to say that we are more fallibilistic or humble about specific beliefs or values than we are about the methods we used to get to them, or than we are about our self-understanding as meaning-seeking creatures. That's close to what Rorty meant by being an 'ironist',[32] about our beliefs, and it's close to what Ann often says about learning to hold our beliefs more tentatively.[33]

Megan: Yes, I think something like that is the 'hidden curriculum' of P4C, and it also has to do with what you were saying earlier, Ann, about the ethical, the aesthetic, the political, and so on, as the aspects of experience that we find, or ought to find, to be most meaningful.

Ann: Why, or how do you think it's been hidden? It seems pretty overt, to me. That kind of 'existential meaning', as Maughn calls it, was what Mat thought philosophy could bring to education, with his understanding that many children find school quite meaningless.[34]

Megan: Maybe what I mean is that there is a kind of humanism assumed here, an idea of what it means to live well, or to be a full-fledged person. But, then, that idea is the target of the most recent theoretical critique of P4C, from postmodernists and posthumanists.

Ann: What does that mean—'posthumanist'?

Megan: Well, as I see it, postmodernists, poststructuralists and post-humanists mistrust the very attempt to find objective or trans-cultural foundations for knowledge or for values, or for what it means to be a human being.[35] The possibility of such foundations has been undercut by anti-realist and anti-rationalist theories of the fragmented subject, the slipperiness of meaning, the inescapability of discourse, and the ubiquity of power. So there have been postmodern critics of P4C who have noticed this hidden curriculum of the 'reasonable' or 'philosophical' child, and critiqued it as just one normative model of human subjectivity among many, without any objective or foundational reasons to privilege it over others.[36]

Ann: Yes, I know that line of critique. People have been raising it against our work almost from the beginning, and there have been a number of responses.[37] In fact, you know, some have analysed P4C as a post-colonial, postmodern practice.[38] I wonder if 'posthumanism' is just a new vocabulary for the very old—in fact, maybe the oldest—philosophical problem of scepticism. In any case, I would say that yes, there is some kind of ideal of personhood at work in P4C, though it would be wrong to accuse Mat or me of claiming any kind of absolutist foundations for it. Mat, after all, sided with Dewey's (1997 [1910]) Darwinian arguments against the idea of a fixed human nature, and my dissertation was on Nietzsche's view of the teacher as liberator! And while, on the one hand, I think it's good to be sceptical—to remember to hold our theories lightly and be willing to give up our favourite certainties—scepticism alone doesn't give us a method for deciding what to believe or how to live. It just isn't sufficient to the project of human flourishing.

Joe: I think it's important to distinguish different kinds of scepticism. Ann, you're describing what I would call a Socratic scepticism,[39] which is just ordinary fallibilism, as Maughn mentioned before: not taking our beliefs or values to be final; being willing to self-correct.[40] That's quite different from the more radical scepticism I think Megan is referring to, that is not just cautious but actually *anti*-foundational, which, I think, can become paralyzing.

Maughn: That depends on whether the claim that there aren't foundational reasons to choose a certain belief or a way of life over others is meant to imply that, therefore, there's no way to choose—that foundational reasons are the only kinds of reasons we could use. For me, that would be a false dichotomy: to say that either we know for certain or we don't know at all. Just because we know enough to be sceptical, ironic, tentative about our beliefs, doesn't mean we have reasons to stop believing them. For one thing, how do we know which ones need to be reconstructed before they get us into trouble? And in the mean time, it seems to me we can have plenty of non-foundational reasons for preferring certain ways of life over others.

Megan: Like what?

Joe: How about, for instance, that I have made myself accountable to a community of my peers, who have challenged my ideas; that I have double-checked my reasons for believing—the methods of inquiry or the authorities I've relied on; that I've been willing to self-correct; that my current beliefs help me cope with experience—help me understand it in ways that enable me to act intelligibly; and that I have no other reasons for doubting them now, though I'm open to finding reasons to doubt them later. What more is there to knowing, or even to being certain, than that?

Maughn: Just one thing I would add: we know, on the level of qualitative experience, what it means to live with a political culture of civil rights, to participate in collective decision-making, to do the kind of self-work that moves us from avarice and animosity toward humility and compassion.[41] Even if we can't justify this way of life on absolutist grounds, we *can* say why we prefer it to certain other ways we know of. I agree with Ann: we need to be fallibilistic, but it's only our positive beliefs, values and practices—our vision of what it might mean to be human, even just for here and now—that constitute meaning and make life worth living. Education is just as much about sharing that kind of vision with the next generation, as it is about equipping them to escape it or take hammers to it.[42] I'd say it's every bit as risky *not* to socialise our children in the ways of life that we have found most ennobling and enchanting as it to socialise them so completely that they can't see their way out.[43] The fact that our vision isn't transcendent doesn't mean that it must be naïve or politically sinister.

Megan: But then, as you say, we have to worry that educating children into the humanistic ideal behind P4C might make them resistant to alternative ideals. For instance, many postmodernists mistrust the attempt to distinguish inquiry as a type of discourse that aims at certain kinds of objectivity, from other types of discourse like interest-group politics or consciousness-raising.[44] So there have been critics of P4C who have said that its criteria for 'reasonableness'—like maintaining relevance, uncovering assumptions, . . .

Joe: . . . identifying fallacies, evaluating evidence . . .

Megan: . . . right, and making valid inferences—thanks, Joe—that all of that is just another way of exercising power—the Eurocentric, or even the Anglo-American way. They see argumentative inquiry, with its scientific forms of reason and its drive toward even provisional concords of perspective, as another machinery of dominance,[45] and they worry that by imposing these structures on children, P4C will colonise their thinking and their desires, and make it next to impossible for them to offer radical alternatives—which, some say, is what is most precious about childhood, and about philosophy.[46]

Joe: But that construal of rationality misses the point of all those philosophers of politics and science and ethics who have shown us that what's important and efficacious about rationality is not, or not only certain logical structures, but a family of social and ethical practices like curiosity about alternative views, freedom of expression, account-ability to peers, non-dogmatism and self-correction, that sometimes result in 'unforced agreement.'[47] Certainly the practice of community of inquiry makes us aware that there are many points of view, and different kinds of thinking going on, even in communities that seems heterogeneous.

Ann: And also, isn't the argument that learning one way of thinking—like learning one language, or one tradition of music, or one method of agriculture—makes it difficult to learn alternative ways, at least contest-able? I mean, is it a theoretical argument or something we can observe? I don't see why, on the contrary, the more ways of thinking you learn, shouldn't make it easier to learn others.

Maughn: Of course we can't step outside our own beliefs and values to get a glimpse of Truth Itself—but that doesn't mean we're trapped inside our own perspectives, either. As long as we're able to read widely, and travel some, and get into hermeneutical circles with people who see and feel things differently, there's every chance we will find reasons to alter our beliefs, adopt new values, learn to practice different kinds of subjectivity, and otherwise change our vision of human flourishing.

Rosario: But let's be careful. There's a difference between 'going visiting', in Arendt's sense (1978, p. 257), and going shopping.[48] The postmodernist emphasis on novelty, uniqueness, heterogeneity and radical otherness—the categorical mistrust of the collective and the normative—seems to me like a dangerous (and typically capitalist) distraction from political struggle and solidarity.

Ann: And also, what's the alternative? To act as if children are born outside of culture? Give them nothing to try out, build on or rebel against? Talk about oppressive! If children don't grow up with some kind of language and rationality, and with minimal nutrition and hygiene and literacy and human relationship, they aren't going to be fit to articulate the ugliness or injustice they experience, much less a new vision of the kind of life they want to live. I mean, it's one thing to want to treat children as ends in themselves, and not just as means to our own cultural imperatives;[49] but I can't make any sense of what that would mean—to treat children as ends—if I didn't take them to be capable of thinking and speaking for themselves and taking intelligent action. And those capabilities don't happen in a vacuum.

Maughn: Besides that, I think to find your own voice you have to have something to struggle against.[50] Or, as Dewey put it more positively, human individuality and uniqueness does not precede socialisation, but is actually a result of certain kinds of association.[51] He thought a process of social inquiry—in which multiple voices are heard, meanings are clarified, sympathies are formed, traditions are reinterpreted, compromises are considered, and new accommodations are created—was as necessary for meaningful individuality as for political solidarity.

Rosario: I wouldn't go that far, but I agree that we can't afford *not* to educate children to be literate and critical, because people—including children—who aren't capable of problematising and critically analysing what they are told and what happens to them and all the media they consume are so easily victimised. They are far more likely to become 'true believers' of other people's political agendas, or else completely diverted and neutralised from serious thought—in either case they have suffered a loss of agency. That's why I lose patience with deconstructionists who act like their work has no political consequences. If postmodernism under-mines education for critical rationality, or norms of human liberation that come from the experiences of the underprivileged, we know who will benefit and who will suffer as a consequence!

Joe: So the attempt to distinguish inquiry from negotiation, truth from ideology, right from wrong, and being treated as an end from being treated as a means, has political and moral consequences.

Megan: Still, that's not to say that Western culture has a corner on any of those ideals. Another criticism of P4C has been its lack of multi-culturalism, even just philosophically speaking. For one thing, the nearly exclusive focus on dialogue eclipses other kinds of philosophical practice, like exegetical and contemplative. And as for content, many people have pointed out the lack in the IAPC curriculum of ideas from continental or Asian philosophy, and all the American colloquialisms and cultural norms portrayed in the novels—which, after all, were written for US schools.[52] I believe P4C has to work harder to incorporate more philosophical traditions, especially non-Western traditions; otherwise all the talk about broadening our perspectives and being open to challenge are empty platitudes.

Ann: I've been saying that for a long time now, and I'll give you three reasons. One is what we've just been saying: we need radical alternatives to be shocked out of our habitual ways of seeing, so that we can appreciate an idea or a practice that is more beautiful than anything we might have—and also sometimes just to re-discover the meaning of our own ways. Second, if philosophy is a way of life, as many of us here believe, then these alternatives are actually 'existential options', in Hadot's sense.[53] And third, we have to do our best to sympathise with options we don't take ourselves, in order to avoid violent conflict and to become citizens of the world.[54]

Joe: But there's a big difference in multiculturalism as a more thorough, more open-minded search for greater truth, beauty and goodness—that's what I hear Ann describing—and multiculturalism as a postmodern playground of ideas and arts and kinds of government, with no normative comparison, which is actually the repudiation of those regulative ideals for meaningful life.[55]

Maughn: And let's not lose sight of how the globalisation of P4C, almost from the beginning, has changed the programme. There have been many, very successful cultural adaptations of the novels. And people from many different parts of the world have adapted the programme to blend with local methods,[56] have written new curriculum that draws on local cultural themes or incorporates regional children's literature, and have brought the work of a wide range of philosophers to bear on P4C practice.[57] The early emphasis on critical thinking has been transformed by theorists who see the community of philosophical inquiry as a political laboratory,[58] a method of wisdom training,[59] an operational application of social learning theory,[60] a means of raising philosophical questions across the school subjects,[61] a method of religious exegetics and education,[62] and even a contemplative or spiritual practice.[63] I'd say the programme has had little chance of being culturally or theoretically insulated.

Ann: In fact, all these criticisms we've been discussing today have been discussed for most of P4C's 40-year history—a fact that often goes unnoticed. Thousands of academic books, articles, and doctoral dissertations contending with P4C have been published, from scores of countries. Pre-college philosophy is the topic of dozens of academic conferences and special conference sessions every year, in every part of the world. It's been the primary focus of four academic journals, and a frequent focus of other leading journals in philosophy and education. The published literature includes both philosophical and empirical research on myriad aspects of engaging children and adolescents in different kinds of philosophical practice. I find it very troubling that so many new pre-college philosophy programmes and new rounds of critique against ours lack an honest review of this literature.

Joe: I think the nuns are about to ring the lunch bell, and before we stop I'd like to try to summarise what we've been saying. First, we've been uncovering—some of us, and others I guess are just reiterating—that P4C, as conceived by Mat and Ann, is a practice or a set of practices that derive from, and re-inscribe a particular norm of what it means to be human. That norm has roots in the Hellenistic tradition of philosophy as a way of life given to the search for, and the experience of certain kinds of meaning, and also in American pragmatism—especially its emphasis on qualitative experience and its theory of inquiry—and in American and Soviet social learning theory. This normative account of P4C attracts at least five kinds of overlapping and conflicting criticism that we've identified: from religious and social conservatives who don't want their children to question traditional values; from educational psychologists who believe certain kinds of thinking are out of reach for children of certain ages; from philosophers who say it's not real philosophy because it focuses on meaning and how to live, rather than on theory and exegesis; from critical theorists who think it's too value neutral and politically compliant; and from postmodernists who worry that it's imperialistic and hegemonic: training the minds of children on the trellises of scientistic, bourgeois Western liberalism. Is that about right?

Ann: As Pixie would say, that's the story of how the story happened!

NOTES

1. The seminar included sessions discussing chapters from Dewey, 1989; Hadot, 1995 and 2002; Shusterman, 1997 and 2000; Sharp, 1998; and Lipman, 1978 and 1980.
2. Those not familiar with the program may consult the IAPC website at www.montclair.edu/iapc (accessed 11 January 2011) and Gregory, 2008.
3. John Dewey wrote, e.g., that '[P]hilosophy is love of wisdom; wisdom being not knowledge but knowledge-plus; knowledge turned to account in the instruction and guidance it may convey in piloting life through the storms and the shoals that beset life-experience as well as into such havens of consummatory experience as enrich our human life from time to time' (1991, p. 389). Similarly, Shusterman sees pragmatism as a contemporary revival of the ancient Hellenistic 'idea of philosophy as a deliberative life-practice that brings lives of beauty and happiness to its practitioners[;]' of philosophy having the 'crucial, existential task: to help us lead better lives by bettering ourselves through self-knowledge, self-criticism and self-mastery' (1997, pp. 3 and 21).
4. Lipman describes the aim of philosophical inquiry as 'ethical, social, political, and aesthetic judgments ... applied directly to life situations' (2003, p. 279).
5. Lipman *et al.*, recommended 'philosophical inquiry—not as an end in itself but as a means for leading a qualitatively better life', (1980, p. 84).
6. Lipman wrote a series of philosophical novels for children and adolescents, including *Elfie* (1987), *Kio & Gus* (1982), *Pixie* (1981), *Nous* (1996b) and *Harry Stottlemeier's Discovery* (1969), for elementary school, *Lisa* (1976) and *Suki* (1978) for middle school, and *Mark* (1980) for high school. Each novel, titled for a principle character, shows young people exploring philosophical dimensions of their experience—especially logical, ethical and aesthetic dimensions—and dialoguing about them with and without adults. In Philosophy for Children, these novels are used to help students recognise and problematise philosophical dimensions of their own experiences, and to dialogue about these together as a 'community of inquiry', facilitated by an adult with philosophical training.
7. See Lipman's autobiography, *A Life Teaching Thinking* (2008).
8. See Hadot, 2002, pp. 29, 33-6, 71-3, 124, and 138; and 1995, pp. 92-3, 163, and 274.

9. Socrates famously critiqued education that focused on materialistic and mundane objectives to the detriment of wisdom. See Hadot, 2002, p. 59, and Gregory and Laverty, 2010.
10. Referring to *Harry Stottlemeier's Discovery* (see Note 6).
11. See Sharp, 1989.
12. See Shusterman, 1997, pp. 4–5.
13. George Pollack, for instance, writes that 'to apply philosophy is not thereby to do it. Application of philosophy is exogenous to philosophical activity itself; it comes after the fact' (2007, p. 246).
14. See Lipman, 2004 and Gregory, 2002a.
15. Lipman drew on Piaget's ideas of active learning and constructivism, but also on Vygotsky's social construal of those ideas. See Arkady A. Margolis' afterward to Lipman, 1996a, p. 124; Lipman, 1991; and Lim, 2004.
16. 'The conclusions I found in Vygotsky ... showed me how to apply, specifically to the relationship between teaching and mental development, the views I had arrived at earlier as a result of repeatedly dipping into Peirce and Dewey, as well as more sustained examinations of Buchler ... .'(Lipman, 1996a, p. xiii).
17. As Nussbaum observes, Dewey 'never addressed systematically the question of how Socratic critical reasoning might be taught to children of various ages ... But teachers who want to teach Socratically ... can find very useful and yet nondictatorial advice about Socratic pedagogy in ... Philosophy for Children developed at the Institute for the Advancement of Philosophy for Children ...' (2010, p. 73).
18. See Reznitskaya *et al.*, 2008.
19. See e.g. Topping and Trickey, 2007 and Soter *et al.*, 2008.
20. See e.g. The Paulo and Nita Freire International Project for Critical Pedagogy, http://freireproject.org, accessed 18 November 2010.
21. See e.g. Morehouse, 1994; Vigliante, 2006; and Sharp, 2009.
22. See e.g. Reed, 1992; Daniel, 1994; Glaser, 1994; Lone, 1997; Gregory, 2004; Turgeon, 2004; and Laverty, 2009.
23. See Biesta, 2007, p. 790.
24. See 'Socratic Pedagogy', chapter 4 of Nussbaum, 2010.
25. See 'The Politics of Amnesia', chapter 1 of Eagleton, 2003.
26. See 'The Child and the Curriculum', in Dewey, 1990a, pp. 181–209.
27. See, e.g. Caleb Warnock: 'BYU Drops Controversial Education Program', *The Daily Herald* article posted 2 July, 2010, and Erik Eckholm's article, 'In School Efforts to End Bullying, Some See Agenda', *TheNew York Times*, 7 November, 2010, p. A-16.
28. 'No course in philosophical thinking ... can succeed if used as a means for implanting the teacher's values in the vulnerable minds of the children in the classroom .... One goal of education is the liberation of students from unquestioning, uncritical mental habits, in order that they may better develop the ability to think for themselves .... There is no study that can more effectively prepare children to combat indoctrination than philosophy' (Lipman *et al.*, 1980, p. 85).
29. See 'On Philosophy, Children and Taboo Topics', in Gregory, 2008, pp. 35–36; and Law, 2008.
30. See Gregory, 2000a.
31. On the latter see Hadot, 1995 and Zajonc, 2008.
32. See Rorty, 1989, especially essays 3 & 4. Rorty's notion of philosophical irony, of course, derives from Socrates and other Hellenistic philosophers, for whom, as Hadot observes, '"irony" ... is a kind of humor which refuses to take oneself or other people entirely seriously; for everything human, and everything philosophical, is highly uncertain, and we have no right to be proud of it' (2002, p. 26).
33. See Sharp, 1987. Elsewhere I have explained that, 'The attitude toward our knowledge that follows from the pragmatist model of inquiry is not skepticism but fallibilism .... It does not follow from the expectation that we will need to revise our beliefs at some point, that we can or ought to make ourselves doubt them in the meantime, before we discover what's wrong with them by implementing them. In fact, it is only by trusting our beliefs enough to use them that we can find out their errors and limitations' (Gregory, 2000b, p. 47).

34. 'It was my hunch that children were primarily intent on obtaining meaning—this is why they so often condemned school as meaningless—and wanted meanings they could verbalize ... . Philosophy might be indispensable for the redesign of education, but to make this happen it would itself have to be redesigned' (Lipman, 1996a, p. xv). Judith Suissa (2008, p. 139) argues similarly that for adolescents in particular, their 'struggle to find meaning is a struggle not just to understand the concrete aspects of experience with which they are confronted in their everyday lives, but to make sense of the human knowledge, ideas and concepts reflected in ... social knowledge and cultural meanings.' Howard Gardner (1993, pp. 203–4) recommends Philosophy for Children for introducing what he calls the 'foundational (or existential) entry point [which] examines the philosophical and terminological facets' of a subject and provides the opportunity for students 'to pose fundamental questions of the "why" sort associated with young children and philosophers ...'.

35. 'Humanism specifies what the child, student, or newcomer should become, before giving them an opportunity to show who they are and who they will be. Humanism thus seems to be unable to open to the possibility that newcomers might radically alter our understandings of what it means to be human' (Biesta, 2007, p. 795).

36. See e.g. D'Angelo, 1978; Murris, 1994; Wilks, 1995; Coppens, 1998; and Yorshansky, 2007.

37. See Lardner, 1991; Benjamin and Echeverria, 1992; Weinstein, 1994; and Kennedy, 2002.

38. Fabian Gimenez (1997), for instance, argues that P4C's practice of the community of philosophical inquiry is a postmodern approach to alterity. See also Sharp, 2008.

39. 'American students whose parents are affluent enough to send them to reasonably good colleges find themselves in the hands of teachers [who] do their best to ... make them a little more conscious of the cruelty built into our institutions; of the need for reform, of the need to be sceptical of the current consensus ... . [O]ur hope that colleges will be more than vocational schools is largely a hope that they will encourage such Socratic scepticism' (Rorty, 1999, p. 116).

40. 'Communal philosophical dialogue is the discursive space where the subject's fundamental assumptions about self, world, knowledge, belief, beauty, right action and normative ideals enter a dialectical process of confrontation, mediation, and reconstruction' (Kennedy, 2004, p. 203).

41. See Gregory, 2006.

42. '[T]he word "education" covers two entirely distinct, and equally necessary processes—socialization and individualization' (Rorty, 1999, p. 117). 'It would be well for the colleges to remind us that 19 is an age when young people should have finished absorbing the best that has been thought and said and should have started becoming suspicious of it' (ibid., p. 124). Compare Biesta's argument (2007, p. 789) that 'good education should always consist in a balanced combination' of three functions: qualification, socialisation and interruption, and my own similar arguments in Gregory, 2001 and 2000b. Roger Scruton (2007, p. 20) argues, in fact, that one of the purposes of education is to preserve cultural knowledge: 'True teachers do not provide knowledge as a benefit to their pupils; they treat their pupils as a benefit to knowledge'.

43. I make this argument in greater detail in Gregory, 2002a and 2002b.

44. For more on the distinctive characteristics of inquiry discourse, see Walton, 1998 and Robertson, 1999.

45. Nancy Vansieleghem (2006, p. 179) argues, for instance, drawing on Bakhtin, that 'The community of inquiry turns the dialogue into an argumentative game in which every movement is being converted into a specific code system[; and] this concept of dialogue can't listen to the voice of the other because it operates in function of the reproduction of a certain communication system'. She argues, in fact (p. 180), that 'The attempt to understand everything is exactly what leads to totalitarianism and oppression'.

46. See e.g. Kohan, 1999 and 2002. In response to the latter, see also Guin, 2004.

47. The phrase is from Rorty (1991), p. 38. He argues (p. 37) that 'Another meaning for "rational" is ... something like "sane" or "reasonable" rather than "methodical." It names a set of moral virtues: tolerance, respect for the opinions of those around one, willingness to listen, reliance on

persuasion rather than force . . . . On this construction, to be rational is simply to discuss any topic—religious, literary, or scientific—in a way which eschews dogmatism, defensiveness, and righteous indignation.' Others who construe rationality in this way are Eagleton (2003, ch. 5); Appleby *et al.* (1995, pp. 271–309); Longino (1990, pp. 62–82); Dewey (1986 [1938]) and Peirce (1878).

48. See also Sharp, 2007a.
49. See Cassidy, 2004.
50. '[I]t is as necessary to be immersed in existing knowledge as it is to be open and capable of producing something that does not yet exist' (Freire, 1998, p. 35). Compare Rorty (1999, p. 118): 'Socialization has to come before individualization, and education for freedom cannot begin before some constraints have been imposed.'
51. 'Liberty is that secure release and fulfillment of personal potentialities which take place only in rich and manifold association with others: the power to be an individualized self making a distinctive contribution and enjoying in its own way the fruits of association' (Dewey, 1990b, p. 150).
52. See e.g. Reed, 1991; Jesperson, 1993; and Rainville, 2000.
53. See note 8.
54. See Sharp, 1995; Slade, 1997; and Nussbaum, 2010, pp. 79–94.
55. '[T]his postmodern world . . . is a playground world, in which all are equally entitled to their culture, their lifestyles, and their opinions' (Scruton, 2007, p. 83).
56. See e.g. Palsson, 1988; Zelman, 2004; and Martens, 2008.
57. See e.g. Curtis, 1985; de la Garza, 1990; Martens, 1990; Kohan, 1996; Glaser, 1998; and Lim, 2003.
58. See Johnson, 1997; Cevallos-Estrellas and Sigurdardottir, 2000; and de la Garza, 2006.
59. See De Puig, 1994; Gregory and Laverty, 2009; and Sternberg, 2003.
60. See note 15.
61. See Weinstein, 1986, and Knight and Collins, 2000.
62. See Du Puis, 1979, and Deitcher and Glaser, 2004.
63. See Vallone, 1987; Sharp, 1994a, 1994b, and 2007b; and Mendoca, 1996.

REFERENCES

Appleby, J., Hunt, L. and Jacob, M. (1995) *Telling the Truth About History* (New York, W.W. Norton & Co.).

Arendt, H. (1978) *The Life of the Mind* (New York, Harcourt).

Benjamin, M. and Echeverria, E. (1992) Knowledge and the Classroom, in: A. Sharp and R. Reed (eds) *Studies in Philosophy for Children: Harry Stottlemeier's Discovery* (Philadelphia, PA, Temple University Press), pp. 103–22.

Biesta, G. J. J. (2007) What is at Stake in a Pedagogy of Interruption?, in: T. Lewis, J. Grinberg and M. Laverty (eds) *Philosophy of Education: Modern and Contemporary Ideas at Play* (Dubuque, IA, Kendall/Hunt), pp. 788–806.

Cassidy, C. (2004) Children: Animals or Persons?, *Thinking*, 17.3, pp. 13–16.

Cevallos-Estrellas, P. and Sigurdardottir, B. (2000) The Community of Inquiry as Means for Cultivating Democracy, *Inquiry: Critical Thinking Across the Disciplines*, 19.2, pp. 45–57.

Coppens, S. (1998) Some Ideological Biases of the Philosophy for Children Curriculum: an Analysis if *Mark* and *Social Inquiry*, *Thinking*, 14.3, pp. 25–32.

Curtis, B. (1985) Wittgenstein and Philosophy for Children, *Thinking*, 5.4, pp. 10–19.

D'Angelo, D. (1978) The Ideological Nature of Teaching Philosophy to Children, *Revolutionary World*, 26, pp. 55–60.

Daniel, M. (1994) Women, Philosophical Community of Inquiry and the Liberation of Self, *Thinking*, 11.3–4, pp. 63–71.

de la Garza, T. (1990) José Ortega y Gasset and Eduardo Nicol: Alternatives for Philosophical Foundation of Philosophy for Children in Latin America, *Analytic Teaching*, 10.2, pp. 22–26.

de la Garza, T. (2006) Education for Justice, *Thinking*, 18.2, pp. 12–18.

De Puig, I. (1994) Beyond Knowledge, Wisdom: A Revindication of the Practical Character of Philosophy, *Thinking*, 11.2, pp. 22–24.

Deitcher, H. and Glaser, J. (2004) Modalities of Theological Reasoning, in: H. Alexander (ed.) *Spirituality and Ethics in Education* (Brighton, Sussex Academic Press), pp. 140–151.

Dewey, J. (1986) [1938] *Logic: The Theory of Inquiry (LW 12)* (Carbondale, IL, University of Illinois Press).

Dewey, J. (1989) [1934] *Art as Experience (LW 10)* (Carbondale, IL, University of Illinois Press).

Dewey, J. (1990a) [1915] *The School and Society and The Child and the Curriculum* (Chicago, IL, University of Chicago Press).

Dewey, J. (1990b) [1927] *The Public and its Problems* (Athens, OH, Ohio University Press).

Dewey, J. (1991) [1949–52] *Essays, Typescripts, and Knowing and the Known (LW 16)* (Carbondale, IL, Southern Illinois University Press).

Dewey, J. (1997) [1910] *The Influence of Darwin on Philosophy and Other Essays* (Amherst, NY, Prometheus Books).

Du Puis, A. (1979) Philosophy, Religion and Religious Education, *Thinking*, 1.3–4, pp. 60–63.

Eagleton, T. (2003) *After Theory* (New York, Basic Books).

Eckholm, E. (2010) In School Efforts to End Bullying, Some See Agenda, *The New York Times*, 7 November, p. A-16.

Freire, P. (1998) *Pedagogy of Freedom: Ethics, Democracy and Civic Courage* (Lanham, MD, Rowman & Littlefield).

Gardner, H. (1993) *Multiple Intelligences: The Theory in Practice* (New York, Basic Books).

Gimenez, F. (1997) Community, Alteridad* and Difference: The Voices of Difference, *Analytic Teaching*, 17.2, pp. 77–85.

Glaser, J. (1994) Reasoning as Dialogical Inquiry: A Model for the Liberation of Women, *Thinking*, 11.3–4, pp. 14–17.

Glaser, J. (1998) Thinking Together: Arendt's *Visiting Imagination* and Nussbaum's *Judicial Spectatorship* as Models for a Community of Inquiry, *Thinking*, 14.1, pp. 17–23.

Gregory, M. (2000a) Care as a Goal of Democratic Education, *Journal of Moral Education*, 29.4, pp. 445–61.

Gregory, M. (2000b) The Status of Rational Norms, *Analytic Teaching*, 21.1, pp. 43–51.

Gregory, M. (2001) The Perils of Rationality: Nietzsche, Peirce and Education, *Educational Philosophy and Theory*, 33.1, pp. 23–34.

Gregory, M. (2002a) Constructivism, Standards, and the Classroom Community of Inquiry, *Educational Theory*, 52.4, pp. 397–408.

Gregory, M. (2002b) Uma éticapragmatista da socialização [A Pragmatist Ethic of Socialization], in: W. Kohan (ed.) *Ensino de Filosofia: Perspectivas [Teaching Philosophy: Perspectives]* (Minas Gerais, Brazil, AutênticaEditora de Belo Horizonte).

Gregory, M. (2004) Being Out, Speaking Out: Vulnerability and Classroom Inquiry, *The Journal of Gay and Lesbian Issues in Education*, 2.2, pp. 53–64.

Gregory, M. (2006) Pragmatist Value Inquiry, *Contemporary Pragmatism*, 3.1, pp. 107–128.

Gregory, M. (ed.) (2008) *Philosophy for Children Practitioner Handbook* (Montclair, NJ, IAPC).

Gregory, M. and Laverty, M. (2009) Philosophy and Education for Wisdom, in: A. Kenkmann (ed.) *Teaching Philosophy* (London, Continuum International), pp. 155–73.

Gregory, M. and Laverty, M. (2010) Introduction to Special Edition: Philosophy, Education and the Care of the Self, *Thinking*, 19.4, pp. 3–9.

Guin, P. (2004) The Political and Social Ends of Philosophy, *Thinking*, 17.3, pp. 41–46.

Hadot, P. (1995) *Philosophy as a Way of Life: Spiritual Exercises from Socrates to Foucault*, M. Chase, trans (Malden, MA, Blackwell Publishing).

Hadot, P. (2002) *What is Ancient Philosophy?* M. Chase, trans (Cambridge, MA, Harvard University Press).

Jesperson, P. (1993) Problems with Philosophy for Children, *Analytic Teaching*, 14.1, pp. 69–71.

Johnson, S. M. (1997) Critical Pedagogy and Civic Ideals: Liberating Our Students (and Selves) from False Dilemmas, *Thinking*, 13.3, pp. 17–21.

Kennedy, D. (2002) The Child and Postmodern Subjectivity, *Educational Theory*, 52.2, pp. 155–167.

Kennedy, D. (2004) Communal Philosophical Dialogue and the Intersubject, *International Journal for Philosophical Practice*, 18.2, pp. 201–216.

Knight, S. and Collins, C. (2000) The curriculum transformed: philosophy embedded in the curriculum areas, *Critical and Creative Thinking*, 8.1, pp. 8–14.

Kohan, W. (1996) Heraclitus and the Community of Inquiry, *Analytic Teaching*, 17.1, pp. 34–43.

Kohan, W. (1999) What Can Philosophy and Children Offer Each Other?, *Thinking*, 14.4, pp. 2–8.

Kohan, W. (2002) Education, Philosophy, and Childhood: The Need to Think an Encounter, *Thinking*, 16.1, pp. 4–11.

Lardner, A. T. (1991) Philosophy for Children Internationally: A Response to the Post Modern and Multi-Culturalist Critiques, *Analytic Teaching*, 12.1, pp. 17–24.

Laverty, M. J. (2009) The Bonds of Learning: Dialogue and the Question of Human Solidarity, in: R. Glass (ed.) *Philosophy of Education 2008* (Urbana, IL, Philosophy of Education Society), pp. 120–28.

Lim, T. K. (2003) Introducing Asian Philosophy and Concepts into the Community of Inquiry, *Thinking*, 16.4, pp. 41–44.

Lim, T. K. (2004) Piaget, Vygotsky and the Philosophy for Children Program, *Critical and Creative Thinking*, 12.1, pp. 32–38.

Law, S. (2008) Religion and Philosophy in Schools, in: M. Handand and C. Winstanley (eds) *Philosophy in Schools* (London, Continuum), pp. 41–57.

Lipman, M. (1969) *Harry Stottlemeier's Discovery* (Montclair, NJ, IAPC).

Lipman, M. (1976) *Lisa* (Montclair, NJ, IAPC).

Lipman, M. (1978) *Suki* (Montclair, NJ, IAPC).

Lipman, M. (1980) *Mark* (Montclair, NJ, IAPC).

Lipman, M. (1981) *Pixie* (Montclair, NJ, IAPC).

Lipman, M. (1982) *Kio & Gus* (Montclair, NJ, IAPC).

Lipman, M. (1987) *Elfie* (Montclair, NJ, IAPC).

Lipman, M. (1991) Rediscovering the Vygotsky Trail, *Inquiry: Critical Thinking Across the Disciplines*, 7.2, pp. 14–16.

Lipman, M. (1996a) *Natasha: Vygotskian Dialogues* (New York, Teachers College Press).

Lipman, M. (1996b) *Nous* (Montclair, NJ, IAPC).

Lipman, M. (2003) *Thinking in Education*, 2nd edn. (Cambridge, Cambridge University Press).

Lipman, M. (2004) Philosophy for Children's Debt to Dewey, *Critical and Creative Thinking*, 12, pp. 1–8.

Lipman, M. (2008) *A Life Teaching Thinking* (Montclair, NJ, IAPC).

Lipman, M. and Sharp, A. (1980) *Writing: How and Why* (Montclair, NJ, IAPC).

Lipman, M., Sharp, A. and Oscanyan, F. (1980) *Philosophy in the Classroom* (Philadelphia, PA, Temple University Press).

Lone, J. M. (1997) Voices in the Classroom: Girls and Philosophy for Children, *Thinking*, 13.1, pp. 9–11.

Longino, H. E. (1990) *Science as Social Knowledge* (Princeton, NJ, Princeton University Press).

Martens, E. (2008) Can Animals Think? The Five Most Important Methods of Philosophizing with Children, *Thinking*, 18.4, pp. 32–35.

Martens, E. (1990) Philosophy for Children and Continental Philosophy, *Thinking*, 9.1, pp. 2–7.

Mendoca, D. (1996) The Religious Dimension of Philosophy for Children, *Critical and Creative Thinking*, 4.2, pp. 48–54.

Morehouse, R. (1994) Cornel West and Prophetic Thought: Reflections on Community Within Community of Inquiry, *Analytic Teaching*, 15.1, pp. 41–44.

Murris, K. (1994) Not Now, Socrates, Part II, *Cogito*, 8.1, pp. 80–86.

Noddings, N. (2005) *Happiness and Education* (Cambridge, Cambridge University Press).

Nussbaum, M. (1997) *Cultivating Humanity: A Classical Defense of Reform in Liberal Education* (Cambridge, MA, Harvard University Press).

Nussbaum, M. (2010) *Not for Profit: Why Democracy Needs the Humanities* (Princeton, NJ, Princeton University Press).

Palsson, H. (1988) Educational Saga: Doing Philosophy with Children in Iceland. PhD Dissertation, Michigan State University.

Peirce, C. S. (1878) How to Make our Ideas Clear, *Popular Science Monthly*, 12, pp. 286–302. Available at: www.peirce.org/writings/p119.html; accessed 17 December 2010.

Pollack, G. (2007) Philosophy of Education as Philosophy: A Metaphilosophical Inquiry, *Educational Theory*, 57.3, pp. 239–260.

Rainville, N. (2000) Philosophy for Children in Native America: A Post-Colonial Critique, *Analytic Teaching*, 21.1, pp. 65–77.

Reed, R. F. (1992) Discussion and the Varieties of Authority, in: A. Sharp and R. Reed (eds) *Studies in Philosophy for Children: Harry Stottlemeier's Discovery* (Philadelphia, PA, Temple University Press), pp. 61–73.

Reed, R. F. (1991) Philosophy for Children: Some Problems, *Analytic Teaching*, 8.1, pp. 82–5.

Reznitskaya, A., Anderson, R. C., Dong, T., Li, Y., Kim, I. and So-young, K. (2008) Learning to Think Well: Application of Argument Schema Theory, in: C. C. Block and S. Parris (eds) *Comprehension Instruction: Research-Based Best Practices* (New York, Guilford Press).

Robertson, E. (1999) The Value of Reason: Why Not a Sardine Can Opener?, in R. Curren (ed.), *Philosophy of Education Society Yearbook 1999*. Available at: www.ed.uiuc.edu/EPS/PES-Yearbook/1999/robertson.asp; accessed 24 November 2010.).

Rorty, R. (1989) *Contingency, Irony, and Solidarity* (Cambridge, Cambridge University Press).

Rorty, R. (1991) *Objectivity, relativism and truth* (Cambridge, Cambridge University. Press).

Rorty, R. (1999) *Philosophy and Social Hope* (New York, Penguin Books).

Rose, M. (2009) *Why School? Reclaiming Education for All of Us* (New York, The New Press).

Scruton, R. (2007) *Culture Counts* (New York, Encounter Books).

Sharp, A. M. (1987) What is a Community of Inquiry?, *Journal of Moral Education*, 16.1, pp. 37–45.

Sharp, A. M. (1989) Women and Children and the Evolution of Philosophy, *Analytic Teaching*, 10.1, pp. 46–51.

Sharp, A. M. (1994a) The Religious Dimension of Philosophy for Children, *Critical and Creative Thinking*, 2.1 (1994), pp. 2–14.

Sharp, A. M. (1994b) The Religious Dimension of Philosophy for Children, Part II, *Critical and Creative Thinking*, 2.2, pp. 1–18.

Sharp, A. M. (1995) The Role of Intelligent Sympathy in Education for Global Consciousness, *Critical and Creative Thinking*, 3.2, pp. 13–37.

Sharp, A. M. (1998) The Aesthetic Dimension of the Community of Inquiry, *Inquiry: Critical Thinking Across the Disciplines*, pp. 67–77.

Sharp, A. M. (2007a) Let's Go Visiting: Learning Judgement-Making in Classroom Community of Inquiry, *Gifted Education International*, 23.3, pp. 301–312.

Sharp, A. M. (2007b) The Classroom Community of Inquiry as Ritual: How We Can Cultivate Wisdom, *Critical and Creative Thinking*, 15.1, pp. 3–14.

Sharp, A. M. (2008) Postmodernilapsi [The Postmodern Child], in: T. Tomperi and H. Juuso (eds) *Sokrateskoulussa. Itsenäisenjayhteisöllisenajattelunedistäminen opetuksessa [Socrates at School: Encouraging thinking for oneself and together]* (Tampere, Eurooppalaisenfilosofian seurary/niin& näin), pp. 121–129.

Sharp, A. M. (2009) The Child as Critic, in: E. Marsal, T. Dobashi and B. Weber (eds) *Children Philosophize Worldwide: Theoretical and Practical Concepts* (New York, Peter Lang).

Shusterman, R. (1997) *Practicing Philosophy: Pragmatism and the Philosophical Life* (New York, Routledge).

Shusterman, R. (2000) *Pragmatist Aesthetics: Living Beauty, Rethinking Art*, 2ⁿᵈedn. (Lanham, MD, Rowman & Littlefield Publishers, Inc.).

Slade, C. (1997) Conversing Across Communities: Relativism and Difference, *Analytic Teaching*, 17.2, pp. 67–76.

Soter, A.O, Wilkinson, I., Murphy, P., Rudge, L., Reninger, K. and Edwards, M. (2008) What the Discourse Tells Us: Talk and Indicators of High-Level Comprehension, *International Journal of Educational Research*, 47, pp. 372–391.

Sternberg, R. J. (2003) *Wisdom, Intelligence, and Creativity Synthesized* (Cambridge, Cambridge University Press).

Suissa, J. (2008) Philosophy in the Secondary School—a Deweyan Perspective, in: M. Hand and C. Winstanley (eds) *Philosophy in Schools* (London, Continuum), pp. 132–44.

Topping, K. J. and Trickey, S. (2007) Collaborative Philosophical Enquiry for School Children: Cognitive Gains at Two-Year Follow-Up, *British Journal of Educational Psychology*, 77, pp. 781–796.

Turgeon, W. (2004) Multiculturalism: Politics of Difference, Education and Philosophy for Children, *Analytic Teaching*, 24.2, pp. 96–109.

Vallone, G. (1987) Entering, Deepening and Furthering the Dialogue: Relaxation as a Preparation for Doing Philosophy, *Analytic Teaching*, 7.2, pp. 8–9.

Vansieleghem, N. (2006) Listening to Dialogue, *Studies in Philosophy of Education*, 25, pp. 175–190.

Vigliante, T. (2006) Effective Anti-Racism Education in Australian Schools: The Need for Philosophical Inquiry in Teacher Education, *Critical and Creative Thinking: The Australasian Journal of Philosophy in Education*, 13.1–2, pp. 90–113.

Walton, D. (1998) *The New Dialectic: Conversational Contexts of Argument* (Toronto, University of Toronto Press).

Warnock, C. (2010) BYU Drops Controversial Education Program, *The Daily Herald* 2 July. Available at www.heraldextra.com/news/local/article_452b4496-2eca-536c-9643-cfeca6c806b7. html; accessed 12 October 2010.

Weinstein, M. (1986) Philosophy and the General Curriculum: The Map of Knowledge, *Metaphilosophy*, 17.4, pp. 239–49.

Weinstein, M. (1994) How to Get from Ought to Is: Postmodern Epistemology and Social Justice, *Inquiry: Critical Thinking Across the Disciplines*, 13.3–4, pp. 26–32.

Wilks, S. (1995) Thinking Well? According to Whom?, *Analytic Teaching*, 16.1, pp. 50–54.

Yorshansky, M. (2007) Democratic Education and the Concept of Power, *Critical and Creative Thinking: The Australasian Journal of Philosophy in Education*, 15.1, pp. 15–35.

Zajonc, A. (2008) *Meditation as Contemplative Inquiry* (Great Barrington, MA, Steiner Books).

Zelman, T. W. (2004) Community Dynamics and the Ethics of Learning: Russian and American Models, *Analytic Teaching*, 24.1, pp. 1–8.

3

The Play of Socratic Dialogue

RICHARD SMITH

'For it is impossible to learn the serious without the comic, or any one
of a pair of contraries without the other, if one is to be a wise man.'
(Plato, *Laws* 816e, R.G. Bury, trans., 1926)

INTRODUCTION: YOUNG PEOPLE AND PHILOSOPHY

Two things can be said with reasonable certainty about 'P4C', as
its proponents call Philosophy for (sometimes with) Children.[1] First, its
practice is avowedly Socratic in style. Karin Murris (2008) in a wide-
ranging overview writes that the pedagogy of P4C is 'inspired by
Socrates' (p. 669) and begins her article with the famous image, from the
Meno, of the philosophy teacher as a kind of stingray, reducing her pupils
to numbness and perplexity. Murris approves of this: it 'can start to shake
the habitual certainty with which people take for granted the meaning of
everyday abstract concepts' (p. 670). P4C commonly conceives its
purpose as less for children to learn *about* philosophy than to learn to
philosophise (p. 675). Accordingly it is helpful, and perhaps even
necessary, for the teacher to be familiar with philosophy that is written
in dialogue form (p. 676). Matthew Lipman, writing at the beginning of
the P4C movement, writes in similar vein:

> For children to find these matters out for themselves in a community of
> enquiry setting is for them to experience afresh the robust exuberance
> exhibited by Socrates and his companions in their conversations about the
> nature of the True, the Beautiful and the Good (Lipman, 1991, p. 248).

Robert Fisher writes about 'thinking' rather than specifically about P4C, but
ch. 6 of his (1990) book *Teaching Children to Think* has the title
'Philosophy for Children'. It is prefixed with Socrates' famous remark that

Philosophy for Children in Transition: Problems and Prospects, First Edition. Nancy Vansieleghem and
David Kennedy. Chapters © 2012 The Authors. Editorial organization © 2012 Philosophy of Education Society
of Great Britain. Published 2012 by Blackwell Publishing Ltd.

'The unexamined life is not worth living', and Fisher notes that 'Ever since the time of Socrates the search for wisdom has meant dialogue' (p. 157).

Secondly, Murris, along with many other proponents of philosophy for children, links children's aptitude for philosophising with their capacity for play (quoting Harris, p. 668). This makes them at home with the 'willingness to experiment and play with new ideas' (p. 678) that characterises the community of enquiry that is P4C. Lipman and Sharp (1978) observe that 'Children's philosophical practice may take many forms', notably the casual and spontaneous 'play of ideas', and that 'the playing of games comes very easily to children' (p. 90), so that they can easily be encouraged to compare the ways that rules function in a game and the way that they apply to moral conduct. Elsewhere Lipman notes that although we may think of play rather than intellectual exercise as natural to childhood, still the intellect offers 'its own forms of play' (Lipman, 1991, p. 2). He writes that 'children may be even more moved by ideas than adults are', and is critical of discussion of children's play that does not do justice to its cognitive/affective dimension (p. 248).

Now if P4C is distinctively Socratic there is a problem, for Socrates, or 'Socrates'—that is the character of the dialogues whom Plato calls 'Socrates' (or perhaps it is Plato himself)—urged caution in the matter of introducing young people to philosophy. A well-known passage in *Republic* VII (539 a–d) reads as follows[2] (Socrates in discussion with Glaucon, with Socrates speaking first):

'. . . if you want to avoid being sorry for your thirty-year-olders, you must be very careful how you introduce them to such discussions'.

'Very careful'.

'And there's one great precaution you can take, which is to stop their getting a taste of them too young. You must have noticed how young men, after their first taste of argument, are always contradicting people just for the fun of it [hōs paidiai]; they imitate those whom they hear cross-examining each other, and themselves cross-examine other people, like puppies who love to pull and tear at anything within reach'.

'They like nothing better', he said.

'So when they've proved a lot of people wrong and been proved wrong often themselves, they soon slip into the belief that nothing they believed before was true; with the result that they discredit themselves and the whole business of philosophy in the eyes of the world'.

'That's perfectly true', he said.

'But someone who's a bit older', I went on, 'will refuse to have anything to do with this sort of idiocy; he won't copy those who contradict just for the fun of the thing, but will be more likely to follow the lead of someone whose arguments are aimed at finding the truth. He's a more reasonable person and will get philosophy a better reputation'.

'True'.

The problem seems to be compounded by the fact that it is the very *playfulness* of the young, who behave like puppies, that is said here to make them unsuitable for philosophy. The important distinction is spelled out at *Theaetetus* 167e: between playfully (*en men tōi paizēi*) scoring points and engaging in serious dialectic (*en de tōi dialegesthai spoudazēi*).[3] In the first you delight in tripping your opponent up, while in the second you apply yourself to setting him back on his feet. The young become carried away by their first taste of 'reason itself' (*tōn logōn autōn*) and the immediate outcome is that they become confused and muddled (*Philebus* 15d). We return to the contrast between play (*paidia*) and seriousness (*spoudē*) below.

Of course these texts do not refer to children: the passage from *Republic* specifies thirty year-olds, and elsewhere it is 'young men' who are indicated. Here there seems to be something of a paradox: in many of the early and middle-period dialogues it is precisely young men—such as Phaedrus, Theaetetus and Euthyphro—that Socrates engages in dialectic. Protarchus in *Philebus* takes the matter to heart: 'Considering, Socrates, how many we are, and that all of us are young men, is there not a danger that we and Philebus may all set upon you, if you abuse us?' (*Philebus* 16a, Jowett's translation). The oddity is compounded by the fact that the philosophical outcomes, so to speak, of these dialogues are seldom entirely satisfactory. Euthyphro is not deflected from his self-righteous prosecution of his own father; Theaetetus is no more able to give an account of what knowledge is by the end of the dialogue than he was at the beginning; the sparkling and impressionable Phaedrus, at the end of the dialogue that bears his name, imagines that a delightful day sitting at Socrates' elbow makes him a philosopher too,[4] just as at the start he was an uncritical disciple of the sophist Lysias. Most attempts in the dialogues to reach a definition—of courage, friendship and so on—fail resoundingly (see Hyland, 1995, p. 117 n. 123). Do these failures, if this is what they are, and the generally poor quality of philosophical argument—as we might put it today—confirm the wisdom of the advice not to engage in dialectic with the immature? This of course would be a difficulty for any version of philosophy for children that took Socratic dialectic as its model. Or is there some other conclusion that we should draw?

THE LAYERS OF THE TEXT

The thought that we might draw any *conclusions* from Plato's texts comes up against the fact that they seem remarkably well designed to prevent us from doing any such thing:[5] from assuming that any, still less every, sentence or set of sentences written by Plato reports a view that Plato held. First, of course, almost every significant view expressed is put into the mouth of Socrates, who may or may not historically have held these views or ones like them. There is a widespread view that the early Plato is more faithful to Socrates, the later Plato less so. This 'developmental' view, which sees the dialogues as tracing Plato's steady discovery of his own philosophical voice, relies on chronological dating of the dialogues, which cannot be firmly established, and is often circular, taking the supposed development of Plato's own thinking as evidence for the chronology (see, e.g., Howland, 1991).[6] In any case, we might do better to think of Socrates more as 'Socrates'; and since this character of the drama often reports on what he said and did we have a further member of the cast, the "'Socrates'" whom 'Socrates' talks of, the character that this character creates. Thus what might seem in these dialogues to be the dependable voice that talks to us about courage, beauty or truth, is often strangely second- or third-hand, transmitted rather than direct. Always, of course, it is written of as having been spoken. Sometimes, as in *Phaedrus*, writing things down is said (of course it is in fact written) to be second-rate by contrast with the directness of speech. There is a layeredness and irony that, if we are sensitive to it, make the authorial voice, however we are to identify it, seem less than completely authoritative. *Theaetetus* supplies a good example, not least because the central question of the dialogue is generally supposed to be 'what is knowledge?'

To summarise the opening of *Theaetetus*, Euclid and Terpsion meet to have read to them the dialogue, the text of a conversation which took place many years before: Socrates told Euclid of the conversation, and Euclid wrote notes down and 'filled them up from memory', and then had Socrates check them over on more than one occasion. On the basis of this Euclid produced a corrected text. We should note that the text does not pretend to be complete: 'I have nearly the whole conversation written down', says Euclid. Two further framing devices are that Euclid says 'I *believe* that he had seen him a little before his own death, when Theaetetus was a youth, and he had a memorable conversation with him', as if the truth of the whole event is in doubt, and that a slave reads the dialogue to Euclid and Terpsion. 'Memorable' of course carries a sense of *worth* being remembered, something one ought to remember, perhaps, rather than something that one in fact does. Thus we have here a complex text, a philosophical text as we now call it, nuanced and abstract. It is read by a slave: this must be an unusual slave. Plato writes that a slave reads an incomplete text which Euclid wrote on the basis of notes about what Socrates told him—supplementing the notes from his own confessedly unreliable memory ('I asked Socrates about any point which I had forgotten')—about a conversation Socrates only probably had with Theaetetus and some others. If this text is going to tell us what knowledge is, then we are from the beginning alerted to the idea that there will be no straightforward answer—as if the answer might be, neatly, that knowledge is sense-perception, or true judgement (and of course these and other answers are indeed shown in the dialogue to be inadequate).

Republic too offers us layers behind layers. We read, as if we were hearing the voice of Socrates, that he went down (the famous first word of the text, *katebēn*) to the Piraeus to pray and watch the celebration of a festival. This seems at first refreshingly direct, but things quickly become complicated. Socrates and Glaucon turned back towards the city, but 'Polemarchus the son of Cephalus chanced to catch sight of us from a distance as we were starting on our way home, and told his servant to run and bid us wait for him. The servant took hold of me by the cloak behind, and said: Polemarchus desires you to wait' (Jowett's translation). The Greek here is *perimeinai he keleusai* —and the verb that Jowett translates with 'bid' and 'desires' is repeated three times. It is the standard Greek word for telling someone to do something. (Lee's translation has 'sent his slave running on ahead to tell us to wait for him . . . "Polemarchus says you are to wait"'). Socrates is taken against his will to the house of Cephalus because the old man has expressed a desire to hear some entertaining conversation. The conversation that he gets (but does not listen to very much of) is what we now call the *Republic*: is this less a philosophical dialogue, then, than just entertainment to gratify the whim of a rich, elderly businessman, something like an ageing *mafioso*? Here Plato presents us with a philosopher who is stopped—and so by implication is prevented from doing his business, which is philosophical dialectic—and who nevertheless does thus philosophise, or has been interpreted for several thousand years as doing so. However, even leaving aside the concern that the setting implies that the *Republic* might be little more than intellectual cabaret, its logic is notoriously weak. It includes what might seem, from a modern philosophical perspective, flights of fancy such as the allegory or simile, as it is variously called, of the cave (the beginning of Book VII) and the myth of Er at the very end of the *Republic*. These are less philosophical than poetic. The plot of the dialogue (and of course after the first Book it is a dialogue in little more than name) rests on the analogy between the human soul and the *polis* (we started, after all, by wondering about the nature of justice and the just person), which hardly amounts to rigorous reasoning. Do we find here the thought that philosophical dialectic may be less powerful and less productive of understanding than a kind of poetry? The layers of irony are reminiscent of the *Phaedrus*, where Plato writes a dialogue—a narrative of what was said—in which Socrates, a philosopher who never wrote, tells the story of the invention of writing, in which this great invention is declared to be inferior to speech: and of course—to overstate the obvious, perhaps—all of this is set out in a written text of great literary artistry. At any rate the reader of *Republic* might pause, as Socrates too is forced to pause, and not rush on to what might be thought of as the philosophical meat of the *Republic*, the Forms, perhaps, or Sun, Divided Line and Cave; or of course the Theory of Education.[7]

To give a third and final example, the opening of the *Symposium* describes Apollodorus as being stopped (another stopping: a *topos* that we really should pause and mark) by Glaucon, who wanted to 'hear about the discourses in praise of love, which were delivered by Socrates, Alcibiades, and others, at Agathon's supper' (Jowett's Introduction, p. 489). Glaucon is under the impression that this supper occurred recently, but Apollodorus corrects him: it was 'in our boyhood', and thus a long time ago. Nor was it Socrates who reported these discourses to Apollodorus, but Aristodemus. Apollodorus says 'I asked Socrates about the truth of some parts of his narrative, and he confirmed them'. Thus he can tell the whole story to Glaucon as they walk to Athens. But *this* opening is framed within another one: Apollodorus begins the dialogue by saying to an unnamed companion that he (Apollodorus) is in a good position to tell the story again, since he has already rehearsed it with Glaucon.[8] Of course a story is not more true for being well-rehearsed (it might need more rehearsing if it was false).

Two further points might strike us about this introduction. First, the 'companion' makes reference to Apollodorus' nickname as 'the madman', which Apollodorus confirms: 'I am mad (*mainomai*) and get things wrong (*parapaiō*, literally 'strike beside', 'hit the wrong note'). His credentials as a reliable witness are far from secure. Secondly, the first sentence of this dialogue, spoken to the 'companion' reads, in Jowett's translation, 'I believe I am prepared with an answer' (i.e. to the request for an account of the speeches at Agathon's supper). It is hard to suppose we are to skip over the introduction, as if it was mere stage-setting, when the very first words promise an answer. Bury translates as 'I believe I have got the story you inquire of pretty well by heart', Shelley as 'I think that the subject of your enquiries is still fresh in my memory'. None of these captures the double negative: Apollodorus says, literally, 'I believe I am not unpractised (*ouk ameletētos*) concerning what you are enquiring about'.[9] This is wonderfully ambiguous: is it diffident or self-deprecating, casting immediate doubt on the story he goes on to tell? Or is it a way of claiming all the greater authority by way of understatement?

READING PLATO

Commentators seldom make much of these and other complex openings to the dialogues—they tend to be philosophers after all, and keen to get onto the philosophy which it is their business to expound. But if we read Plato without sensitivity to the introductions and their framing of what follows them then, like the commentators, we are reconstructing Plato as a modern philosopher, someone who has a substantial thesis to expound, a set of doctrines to pass on (as if the dialogues might be thought of as a palatable way of dressing them up for the reader), a philosophical standpoint to represent. The introductions however repudiate the claim to *represent* any determinate philosophical position, partly because they set up such a distance between any such thing and the text that might be supposed to articulate it. The witnesses are unreliable, their memory faulty, their accounts second- or third-hand.

Statkiewicz (2009) reads the introductions as rendering problematic any attempt to distinguish between the 'dialogue proper' and what he calls the 'rhapsodic frame', that is the essentially poetic nature of the text, in the sense that poetry is a making (*poiesis*) rather than a mirroring or representing. He writes that 'any attempt to save the representational structure while still reading the dramatic prologues seems doomed to failure' (p. 56). To write dialogue at all is to resist the ideal of what Statkiewicz calls 'univocal intention' (p. 24), and cuts through the logic of representation. (p. 3).

To read Plato in this way is to read him, in terms of Richard Rorty's distinction (Rorty, 1979), not as a systematic philosopher but more as an edifying one. Systematic philosophers aim to solve philosophical problems so that they can move on to other such problems that need solving. Twentieth century analytical philosophy is broadly of this kind. It sees itself as having removed particular confusions in the sense that, say, Ryle's *The Concept of Mind* should have cured us of thinking of the mind as a 'ghost in the machine'. 'Edifying' philosophy on the other hand returns again and again to addressing issues that always seem to have the power to bewilder us: how we are to talk about the value of goodness or justice (or education) 'for itself' and apart from its consequences, for instance; or how to resist the spell that science seems to hold over epistemology. In Rorty's words, it works 'by substituting the notion of *Bildung* (education, self-formation) for that of "knowledge" as the goal of thinking' (Rorty, 1979, p. 359). Although this comparison can be illuminating of course it does not mean that we should think of Plato as (so to speak) committed to a *system* of edification or as having a worked-out theory of himself as a 'protreptic' philosopher, that is as one who aims to reorient the soul of the pupil or disciple. It does not mean that the dialogues are to be read as exemplifying any kind of philosophical *method*, as proponents of philosophy for children sometimes seem inclined to do.

The problem here is in thinking of Plato as a philosopher at all, where philosophy as a kind of writing is conceived as essentially different from other kinds, such as poetry (or, to use Statkiewicz's term, 'rhapsody'). It has to be said that philosophers of education, and those writing about Plato from the point of view of education, have not always been sensitive to the distinctive nature of Plato's texts. To take only one recent example, Williams (2010) begins a chapter on 'Plato and Education' by writing 'Plato invented the philosophy of education as we know it today . . . Plato is almost unique among philosophers, and certainly among political philosophers, in taking so much interest in the topic of education' (p. 69). Williams seems to see nothing strange in writing of 'Plato's curricular recommendations' as if the *Republic* was a simple blueprint. Neither the word 'dialectic', nor the point that the text takes dialogue form, appear at all in his chapter.[10] One paragraph (p. 79) notes that the *Republic* 'should be read with considerable caution. Plato is a seductive writer, well capable of enticing the reader into assuming that he intends us to believe everything to which he gives Socratic voice ... his own work is often playful and ironic'. But these caveats are not brought to bear on the text as a whole: the next paragraphs return to talking of 'Plato's theory of the tripartite soul, his 'model of human mentality' and his 'conception of human society as divided into three distinct classes'.

SERIOUSNESS AND PLAY

Those who come to Plato with an interest in education today require their Plato to be serious. Otherwise how could he be taken to have anything to say to the urgent and practical concerns of education in the twentieth or twenty-first century? Williams (ibid.), while acknowledging (above) that Plato is often 'playful and ironic', insists in the same sentence that Plato would have wanted to raise discussion 'to the highest level of rigour and seriousness'. There is a problem here, at least at first sight, in reconciling playfulness on the one hand and rigour and seriousness on the other. If Williams is right then there seems to be a further problem for anyone who thinks that children's natural inclination to play especially suits them for philosophising. And there is yet another problem because play and seriousness are in Plato's texts set in a distinctive relationship that seems to give comfort neither to those who read the philosophising there as 'serious', nor to those who read it as 'playful'. Since there are clearly important implications here for philosophy for children the issue is worth discussing in some detail.

Shortly before the passage, quoted near the beginning of this chapter, in which we read that we should be wary of introducing 'young men' to philosophy because of their puppyish playfulness, Socrates sets out in detail what kind of people are to be chosen to have an education suitable for the Guardians of the future. They must be the steadiest and bravest we can find, as well as the best looking (535a); they must have 'good memories, determination and a fondness for hard work' (535c). This sounds as systematic as the literal reader could want (though she might wonder why they have to be good-looking). But then the text sounds a rather different note. If we choose those who are sound in body and mind, Socrates says, and give them an appropriate and substantial course of education and training,

> Justice itself can't blame us and we shall preserve the constitution of our society; if we make any other choice the effect will be precisely the opposite, and we shall plunge philosophy even deeper in ridicule than it is at present ... But I'm not sure I'm not being slightly ridiculous myself at the moment ... I was forgetting that we are amusing ourselves [*epaizomen*: literally, 'we were playing'] with an imaginary sketch, and was getting too worked up. I had in mind as I spoke the unjust abuse which philosophy suffers, which annoyed me, and my anger at the critics made me speak more seriously [*spoudaioteron*] than I should (536b–c).

Philosophy is in ridicule, and unless we carefully specify who is to be selected for training as Guardians we shall make it look more ridiculous: the implication is that philosophy is seen as ridiculous because its practitioners pay too little attention to practicalities (an implication confirmed by the caricature of Socrates in Aristophanes' *Clouds*). And Socrates here in *Republic* is being ridiculous:[11] not by being insufficiently serious and practical, however, but by forgetting that all this talk of the imaginary state is a game, a form of playing. And yet it seemed to be this tendency to playfulness that was responsible for philosophy's reputation as ridiculous. Reverting immediately to what might seem his more serious tone, Socrates rejects Solon's maxim that people can learn a lot as they grow old: 'the time for all serious effort is when we are young',[12] he concludes, so that 'arithmetic and geometry and all the other studies leading to dialectic should be introduced in childhood'. No sense here, then, that preparation for philosophy will be at all playful, yet directly after this we read 'Then don't use compulsion', I said to him, but let your children's lessons take the form of play' (536e–537a: ... *tous paidas en tois mathēmasin alla paizontas trephe*). Whether Socrates is to be understood as speaking seriously or playfully in these injunctions to both seriousness and play, he draws important conclusions in what remains of Book 7. The young Guardians will lack the stabilising influence of parents, not least because of the 'noble lie' that they like all the citizens of the state have sprung from their native soil as natural members of their particular class. They risk turning into moral relativists, sceptical of tradition (538d). Hence the importance of not introducing them to the intoxication of philosophy too early. The Book ends with the importance of sending all citizens over the age of ten away to the country, to make it easier for the guardians to indoctrinate the children who are left. Glaucon does not pause to wonder whether this is a serious or playful recommendation, any more than most modern commentators do. He finds it all quite clear, and the Book finishes with his conclusion that 'there's no more to be said' (Lee).

Jowett observes that Plato naturally mingles 'jest and earnest' in the same work: he is writing of the *Symposium*, but the point can be made more generally. James Adam in his commentary on *Republic* 536c (where Socrates says he forgot that he and his interlocutors were supposed to be playing rather than deadly serious) writes that 'Jest and earnest are never far apart in Plato'. Numerous passages are regularly cited to this effect by commentators, including the passage from *Laws* that is the epigram to this paper. The discussants in *Laws* ought to proceed by indulging in an old man's sober play with laws (*peri nomōn paizontas paidian presbutikēn sōphrona*, 685a). People ought to be 'in serious earnest about serious things, and not about trifles. ... thus I say that every man and woman ought to pass through life in accordance with this character, playing at the noblest of pastimes' (*Laws* 803c).[13] In an especially paradoxical passage in *Laws* the Athenian criticises the popular view that work is to be endured for the sake of play: it's rather that natural, spontaneous play is the most serious thing there is:

> Now they imagine that serious work should be done for the sake of play; for they think that it is for the sake of peace that the serious work of war needs to be well conducted. But as a matter of fact we, it would seem, do not find in war, either as existing or likely to exist, either real play or education worthy of the name [*out'oun paidia pephukuia out'au paideia pote hēmin axiologos*], which is what we assert to be in our eyes the most serious [*spoudaiotaton*] thing (803d).

It might seem reasonable to ask, then, particularly in the context of philosophy with children, whether Plato's dialogues represent philosophy or dialectic as in the end fundamentally playful, as fundamentally serious, as neither, or perhaps in some other way—possibly as a tension between the serious and the playful, or as a constant dialectic between them, even a Hegelian *Aufhebung* in which each is both preserved and yet changed by the apparent opposition. However this question encounters a far-reaching difficulty with the very idea of representation. There is to be no representation in the ideal state painted in the *Republic*. The artist, who undertakes *mimesis*, representation or imitation, is several stages removed from the reality of what he depicts. The user of a flute knows all about the merits and defects of his flute, and instructs the flute-maker accordingly; but those who represent flutes by drawing them or painting pictures of them have the knowledge of neither the flute-player nor the flute-maker. 'So the artist has neither knowledge nor correct opinion about the goodness or badness of the things he represents' (*Republic* 602a). *Mimesis* is a form of play and not to be taken seriously (*einai paidian tina kai ou spoudēn tēn mimēsin*, 602b). Lee translates 'the art of representation has no serious value', Jowett 'Imitation is only a kind of play or sport'. The conclusion, to continue with Jowett's translation, is that 'the tragic poets . . . are imitators in the highest degree'. Poetry, of course, is for the most part to be banned in this ideal state. Presumably Plato's own writing would fall to the same proscription if he were making the mistake of *representing* dialectic.

UNSTABLE CONCLUSIONS

Of course this does not have to be taken at face value: does not have to be taken seriously, as we might say. For the *Republic* is itself heavily representational. Plato represents Socrates as having said 'I went down yesterday to the Piraeus', and so on. In fact Socrates too is representing: representing the conversation that is supposed to have taken place the day before. As Hyland (1995, p. 88) notes, 'In short, the *Republic* itself is a written imitation of a spoken imitation, an "imitation of an imitation", or precisely the characterisation of art which gets so severely criticised within its own pages'. Things don't seem entirely stable here. *Mimesis*, which is a form of play (above) is both proscribed and everywhere evident in the dialogues: and the more layered and complex the contexts of those dialogues are, as we have seen in the cases of *Republic*, *Theaetetus* and *Symposium*, the more *mimesis* is going on. (We might have put matters a little differently above, noting that in the *Symposium* Apollodorus represents to an unnamed companion the various discourses about love that Aristodemus had represented to him; formally speaking, he is representing the version of all this that consists in his conversation with Glaucon.)

The other significant instability here concerns seriousness and play. They do not form a fixed binary, with the rigour and steadiness of *spoudē* holding authority over the unruliness and lability of art and play (cf. Statkiewicz, 2009, p. 7). As soon as one term seems to be prioritised in the text the binary is quickly inverted, as we have seen. This is the effect of the play of *mimesis* throughout the dialogues. For once we give up the assumption that Plato is presenting the reader with a philosophical treatise, it becomes possible for us to read the dialogues not very differently from the way we would read poetry: with an ear for its resonances, obliquities, occlusions; for its turnings-back on itself, its rueful confessions, its many ways of saying more or otherwise than it seems to say. This means in turn the end of any attempt to achieve univocal interpretation, based on 'what Plato means' or 'what we are to understand him to mean'—any more than it is sensible to talk of a poet in this way, of 'what Keats is trying to say'. As if for either Plato or Keats there could be a detachable message, a content (that expectation of a treatise or theory again) separable from the text. As if we could skip over the Introductions, and the scene-setting—all those things that alert us, if we are reasonably sensitive, to the textuality of the dialogues—and get down to the real business of discussing (dialectically, of course, since we like to think we are the heirs of Socrates) Plato's metaphysics, ontology and epistemology.

Here we have a particularly strong way of expressing the difficulty of supposing that Socratic dialectic can be a model for philosophy with children. For that supposition is based on a vision of the dialogues as pointing to the philosophical possibilities of live, face-to-face conversation. But my discussion in this paper leads to the conclusion that we wholly misconceive the Platonic or Socratic dialogues if we fail to register that they are, first, vividly textual by nature, and that Plato must be thought of as a textual artist—a poet or, as Statkiewicz prefers, a kind of rhapsody. Secondly we must make sense of their multi-layeredness, as I have called it above, and the distinctive quality of the irony that is in play here. I have not explored this latter point to any degree here since it does not bear particularly on the topic in hand, which is philosophy for children. I discuss the irony of the dialogues and their connection with philosophy conceived as a kind of therapy in my 'Re-reading Plato: The Slow Cure for Knowledge' (forthcoming).

Nothing that I have written above implies that philosophy for or with children is misguided. In its various versions it seems to offer children a space for the free play of ideas that can be intellectually exhilarating, and a release from the tyranny of jumping through educational hoops in the effort to reproduce the correct answers. It may even have the effect of delivering the serious pay-offs in terms of performance and test results to recommend it to head-teachers and other education managers. All that I have argued here is that it cannot be readily identified with, or draw its justification from, what we find in the dialogues of Plato.

There is a temptation to finish on what might seem to be a more positive note: to draw substantial educational conclusions for instance regarding the importance of attentiveness to language, and from there perhaps to imagine how philosophy for young people, if not philosophy itself— whatever such a phrase might mean—could be conceived in the spirit of a greater attunedness, a readiness to listen, to other people as well as to texts. Listening to oneself, so to put it, would be included: a readiness to attend to nagging doubts, uncertainties and ambivalences, and to distrust puppyish impulses towards the cross-examination of others and simplistic analysis, delight in breaking things down and pulling them apart. If I am not drawn in this direction here it is partly because I am sceptical of the widespread tendency readily to deduce 'educational recommendations', as if nothing could be educationally significant or interesting unless it came out in that kind of way. It is also partly because, having in this paper and elsewhere (e.g. Smith, 2008) questioned the easy separation of philosophy from other ways of thinking and writing, I am not wholly clear just what I would be recommending. Of course to first be seduced by the thought, even the assumption, of the possibility of that separation is a precondition of coming to have the disturbing and exhilarating sense that philosophy both demands and refuses to be said and practised: a sense which moves its distinctively educational or edifying power to a level that Plato allows us to glimpse even as he seems to ask us not to expect it to be disclosed, as if like wine or water such wisdom as is to be found here could be poured from vessel to vessel, from one person to another.[14,15]

NOTES

1. Where I do not refer to 'P4C' below I talk of 'philosophy for children', in lower-case.
2. All translations from the *Republic* are by Lee (Plato, 1974) unless indicated otherwise.
3. The transliterated Greek may please the eye of neither the Greek-less reader nor anyone who can read the original Greek. Perhaps this defamiliarisation of what may be over-familiar is no bad thing. At any rate, attention to the *words* is central to any engagement with the dialogues as *text*. A paraphrase or summary of the text is a different text.
4. I take this to be the implication of the final interchange in *Phaedrus*. Socrates offers up a prayer to Pan and all the other gods of the place where he and Phaedrus had been sitting. Phaedrus

says, 'Offer it for me too, Socrates; friends should share everything' (Hamilton's translation; Plato. 1973). The off-handedness of the claim to intimacy with Socrates is pointed up by the solemn context.

5. Hyland (1995, p. 117 n. 123) goes so far as to wonder whether the regular failure of the dialogues to reach definitions constitutes a kind of therapy of our obsession with the 'closure' they provide.

6. There is no space here to provide even an overview of the many theories of how we are to read Plato's dialogues. Hyland (1991, Introduction) supplies an excellent summary.

7. Elements of these paragraphs on *Republic* are adapted from my 'Half a Language: Listening in the City of Words' (2009).

8. An interesting response to the complexities of this scene-setting can be found in Griffith's (1989) translation. He lists 'The Speakers in the Dialogue' first in Greek and then in English (no page numbers) but omits altogether Apollodorus, Glaucon, Aristodemus and the anonymous 'companion'. Jowett includes all the names under 'Persons of the Dialogue', but three are relegated from the main list: 'APOLLODORUS, who repeats to his companion the dialogue which he had heard from Aristodemus, and had already once narrated to Glaucon' (Plato, 1892). Shelley in his translation of *The Banquet* includes them all in order of appearance as *dramatis personae* (Plato, 1985).

9. Benardete comes close, in the slightly stiff 'In my own opinion I am not unprepared for what you ask about' (Plato, 2001).

10. The very last sentence uses the word 'dialogue' for the first time, to assert that Plato's arguments represent 'a serious and challenging voice in the ongoing dialogue of philosophy of education' (p. 80). It is therefore all the odder that Williams makes nothing of the formally dialogical structure of the *Republic*.

11. More than 'somewhat': Jowett translates 'in thus turning jest into earnest I am equally ridiculous'. There is some dispute over the Greek text here.

12. *Neōn de pantes hoi megaloi kai hoi polloi ponoi*, 536 d: more literally, in Adams' translation, 'To the young belong all heavy and frequent labors' (Plato, 1902). The term of art for seriousness, *spoudē*, is not used here.

13. All translations from *Laws* are by Bury (Plato, 1926).

14. '"How fine it would be, Agathon", he said, "if wisdom were a sort of thing that could flow out of the one of us who is fuller into him who is emptier, by our mere contact with each other, as water will flow through wool from the fuller cup into the emptier"' (*Symposium* 175d, Bury's translation [Plato, 1909]).

15. I am grateful to Nancy Vansieleghem for prompting the thoughts that led to this final paragraph.

REFERENCES

Adams, J. (ed) (1902) *The Republic of Plato*, with critical notes, commentary, and appendices. 2 vols. (Cambridge, Cambridge University Press).

Fisher, R. (1990) *Teaching Children to Think* (Oxford, Blackwell).

Howland, J. (1991) Re-reading Plato: The Problem of Platonic Chronology, *Phoenix*, 45.3, pp. 189–214.

Hyland, D. A. (1995) *Finitude and Transcendence in the Platonic Dialogues* (Albany, NY, State University of New York Press).

Lipman, M. (1991) *Thinking in Education* (Cambridge, Cambridge University Press).

Lipman, M. and Sharp, A. M. (1978) Some Educational Presuppositions of Philosophy for Children, *Oxford Review of Education*, 4.11, pp. 85–90.

Murris, K. M. (2008) Philosophy with Children: The Stingray and the Educative Value of Disequilibrium, *Journal of Philosophy of Education*, 42.3–4, pp. 667–685.

Plato (1926) *Laws*, R. G. Bury, trans. (London, W. Heinemann).

Plato (1973) *Phaedrus* W. Hamilton, trans. (Harmondsworth, Penguin).

Plato (1985) *The Banquet*, P. B. Shelley, trans. (London, Concord Grove Press).

Plato. (1892) *The Dialogues of Plato*, B. Jowett, trans., 5 vols (Oxford, Oxford University Press).

Plato (1974) *The Republic*, D. Lee, trans. (Harmondsworth, Penguin).

Plato (2001) *The Symposium*, S. Bernadete, trans. (Chicago, IL, University of Chicago Press).

Plato (1909) *The Symposium*, R. G. Bury, trans. (Cambridge, W. Heffer and Sons).

Plato (1989) *The Symposium*, Greek text; T. Griffith, trans. (Berkeley, CA, University of California Press).

Rorty, R. (1979) *Philosophy and the Mirror of Nature* (Princeton, NJ, Princeton University Press).

Smith, R. (2008) To School with the Poets: Philosophy, Method and Clarity, *Paedogogica Historica*, 44.6, pp. 635–645.

Smith, R. (2009) Half a Language: Listening in the City of Words, in: M. Depaepe and P. Smeyers (eds) *Educational Research: Proofs, Arguments, and Other Reasonings* (Dordrecht, Springer), pp. 149–160.

Statkiewicz, M. (2009) *Rhapsody of Philosophy: Dialogues with Plato in Contemporary Thought* (University Park, PA, Pennsylvania State University Press).

Williams, I. (2010) Plato and Education, in: R. Bailey, R. Barrow, D. Carr and C. McCarthy (eds) *The SAGE Handbook of Philosophy of Education* (London, Sage).

4

Childhood, Philosophy and Play: Friedrich Schiller and the Interface between Reason, Passion and Sensation

BARBARA WEBER

INTRODUCTION

When we examine Philosophy for Children or other philosophical programmes inspired by it, one characteristic seems to be persistently present: they tend to remain tied to the effort to define philosophy in terms of a peculiar form of idealism, and appear to be aiming at the production of a form of subjectivity—the perfectly reflexive and rational self—associated with the ancient Greek notion of a *zoon logon echon* or later *animal rationale*—that actualises its true nature through reasoning, and has access thereby to an unchanging truth. Inspired by the ideas of Friedrich Schiller, I will suggest in this article that we often assume an unspoken nexus between the notion of philosophy and the concept of *zoon logon echon*. This assumption can stay hidden as long as philosophy remains an 'artificial discipline' exiled in the ivory tower of academia, but once it becomes a social activity or an educational programme, its anthropological implications can no longer be concealed. In the case of Philosophy for Children, this tacit connection suggests an inherent pedagogical prejudice that may even *contradict* the basic intention of the whole programme and those like it: that because humans are mainly rational beings, and because children are not yet capable of reason,[1] the latter must be 'defective creatures'; in short, the extreme prejudice that children are both different in kind *and* inferior in value.[2]

The literal meaning of *zoon logon echon* or *animal rationale* is 'the *animal* that is capable of language and reason'. This means that humans are not merely 'disembodied rational brains' but rather that their

Philosophy for Children in Transition: Problems and Prospects, First Edition. Nancy Vansieleghem and David Kennedy. Chapters © 2012 The Authors. Editorial organization © 2012 Philosophy of Education Society of Great Britain. Published 2012 by Blackwell Publishing Ltd.

rationality is rooted in 'animality', and therefore cannot be separated from the human as sensuous, embodied and passionate. This more complex image of humanity has been emphasised by many philosophers and thinkers. Among them is Friedrich Schiller, for whom 'sensible sensitivity', a 'new form of sensuous reason', was crucial for disclosing the full potentiality of being human.[3] He proposed a way of thinking that might complement the existing philosophical and anthropological grounding of Philosophy for Children, which in large part goes back to John Dewey's work as well as to the analytic tradition.

Schiller's work *On the Aesthetic Education of Man* ([1795] 2009) can be read as both a theory of education and as a philosophical anthropology. It represents the effort to overcome the dichotomy between reason and passion through the notion of 'moving beauty' (*bewegte Schönheit*) or 'ludic drive' (*Spieltrieb*). On this account, reality is not 'discovered' solely by reason or perceived passively through the senses, but rather is actualised by the power of beauty—the joyous interplay between substance and form. Consequently, reason and passion are unified in the sensitivity of embodied life. However, even such an expanded anthropology calls for the necessity to educate each aspect; that is, the raw powers and abilities of children need to be cultivated and refined rather than suppressed. My final aim is to apply Schiller's anthropology of humanity and reason to Philosophy for Children, and to suggest that we understand the community of philosophical inquiry as a 'playground of thought'—a public space where children can reconstruct and recreate their own interpretations of reality within a community; or, using Schiller's terms, to form a 'ludic[4] chiasm' between passions and rationality. In opposition to a reduced concept of humanity, this more complex, expanded anthropology allows us to acknowledge children in their otherness. It regards childhood[5] as a necessary aspect of society because children remind adults of a more sensuous and passion-oriented way of being in the world. In this sense, it serves as a basis for intergenerational dialogue. Before introducing Schiller's anthropology as a possibility to rethink Philosophy for Children, I will give a short overview of the way Philosophy for Children is currently conceived. I will do so by introducing some characteristics of Philosophy for Children in the Anglo-Saxon as well as the German tradition.

PHILOSOPHY FOR CHILDREN AS A CRITICAL THINKING PROGRAMME: IMPLICATIONS AND PROBLEMS

The 'Logical' Dimension of Philosophy for Children

Philosophy for Children began primarily as a critical-thinking programme in the early 1970s, which was an era of huge protests and student movements. The programme's founder, Matthew Lipman, was shocked by students' inability to reason, communicate and resolve conflicts that had arisen between them and the administrators of the university. He blamed this situation at least partly on the fact that logic is taught to university students much too late, and that many other critical-thinking programmes concentrated only on the outcomes and results of critical thinking without discussing its real meaning (Lipman, 2003, p. 209f.). In ensuing years, he explored a variety of remedies for this situation, and finally argued that children needed to learn to give 'good reasons' for their own beliefs and likewise distinguish between good and bad reasoning in others, correct their opinions if necessary, and modify their judgment-making accordingly (Lipman, 2003). Nevertheless, Lipman was careful to also identify meta-criteria within critical thinking itself—e.g. coherence, precision, consistency and values such as true, false, good, bad, just and beautiful (Lipman, 2003, pp. 201f.); that is, all the criteria that remain unquestioned.

Most of these characterisations come from analytic philosophy, which is concerned to provide logical and epistemological criteria such as sensitivity to logical fallacies, and the systematic application of logical principles (e.g. syllogisms). Lipman held that from a methodological point of view, philosophy provides all the tools needed to learn critical thinking: 'It cannot be sufficiently emphasised however, that there is nothing in the practice of critical thinking that does not already exist in some form or other in the practice of philosophy ...' (Lipman, 2003, p. 229). For Lipman, there are precise criteria, such as relevance, precision, consistency, sufficiency, etc., which have to be followed in order to achieve 'good reasoning'. Every fallacy can be detected, and one can specify which criteria have been violated. However, while the definition of critical thinking is based on logic, the dialogic method of Philosophy for Children—known as the community of inquiry—has its philosophical roots in the American pragmatist tradition.

Philosophy for Children presumes to argue for an active and practical understanding of philosophy that is clearly distinguished from a knowledge-based 'history of philosophy.' However, its intensive focus on critical thinking seems to suppress other approaches—such as phenomenology, hermeneutics or speculation[6]—and thus favours a methodological monism. Specifically, critical thinking emphasises 'making good judgments' or even 'good thinking', although it admits that its founding concept rests upon 'unquestionable criteria' such as 'good', 'true' or 'beautiful'.[7] This kind of 'exclusive thinking' can be interpreted as a form of Western epistemological colonisation and in fact, as I have argued elsewhere, often leads to a rejection of the programme.[8] I will refrain from repeating here the main postmodern arguments against this constraining definition of reason. Rather, I want to investigate the attitude that stands behind this constraint and to explore how it leads to a constricted and one-sided image of the human.

The Problems of a One-Dimensional Anthropology

Lipman believes that being a child is an inevitable aspect of being human, and he criticises any images of childhood that reduces the child to a 'pre-form' of the human being. 'Moreover, just as the differences between male and female perspectives constitute no insuperable barrier to their being experientially shared, so the differences between child and adult perspectives represent an invitation to the shared experience of human diversity rather than an excuse for intergenerational hostility, repression and guilt' (Lipman, 2003, p. 143). Therefore, Lipman makes the case for engaging with children in philosophical dialogues about sense and meaning. In arguing against Piaget's argument for delaying the education of thinking skills until adolescence (p. 376), he observes: 'Children are treated as if they were incapable of philosophical deliberation; therefore they behave as if they were incapable of philosophical deliberation' (p. 378). This is why he argues for the early teaching of 'good thinking skills.' Accordingly, the overall aim of Philosophy for Children is often *reduced* to teaching children 'thinking skills' instead of teaching other modes of being in the world, such as feeling and perceiving. And although 'creative thinking' and 'caring thinking' were subsequently introduced into the programme, these are classified as 'modes of thinking'.

However, if we *only* teach thinking skills based on the 'right' and 'wrong' application of logical operations, the content of children's statements remains secondary or even irrelevant. Consequently, Philosophy for Children would then implicitly reduce childhood to a deficiency (since children are not yet capable of reasoning, although they are able to learn to reason) and also reduce humanity to a 'disembodied head' that is able to speak and to apply reason, but is disconnected from any emotional or sensuous aspects. In my view, this implicit analytic background is why the later and important variations of 'creative' and 'caring thinking' have always remained somewhat detached: because they do not fit into the overall analytic and language-based philosophical concept. Specifically, 'caring thinking' has been reduced to a 'thinking mode' by linking it *inter alia* to Martha Nussbaum's concept of emotions (Nussbaum, 1992). Thus, my inference is that Philosophy for Children was forced to reduce emotions to a thinking mode, because—based as it is on an analytic and pragmatist background—it regards itself mainly as a 'thinking programme' and as such, only thinking modes can be fostered by the programme. However, and on the other hand, Lipman's collaborator, Ann Sharp, developed a number of pedagogical exercises that address *all* the senses and emotions—not only as thinking modes—although it remains unclear how these exercises can be philosophically justified, given the analytic-pragmatist orientation of the programme along with the idea that emotions are mainly thinking skills.

A broader and more complex understanding of philosophy, creativity and emotions not only resolves these unnecessary reductions, but also opens to a more complex and holistic understanding of being human. It reveals a horizon of existential questions that cannot be answered solely by reason. Philosophical dialogue, then, engages pedagogues and children alike in a horizontal and playful discourse, where neither presumes to a definite answer, above all given that every generation develops a new set of solutions in an exchange of ideas with previous generations. This understanding of philosophy offers a platform for intergenerational dialogue about meaning and existence itself—a platform on which children and adults can think their own conceptions of humanity, which includes who they themselves want to become.

Images of Humanity: Between Logos and Pathos

In his treatise on reason and sensation, Wolfhardt Henckmann asks which kind of reason we are talking about when we try to defend or justify our special status in nature. In other words, what sets the *zoon logon echon* or the *animal rationale* apart from other species? Is it a neo-positivistic concept that reduces reason to logical operations? Is it a reanimated metaphysical reason in Husserl's sense? Or is it the intuition of an epiphany, as Friedrich H. Jacobi and Gottfried Herder argued against the Kantian distinction between practical and absolute reason? In considering these very different interpretations, Henckmann asks if we could also think of a 'sensuous reason' or 'reasonable sensuousness' when we try to come to grips with ourselves and our human situation through philosophical deliberation (Henckmann, 2003, p. 12).

As mentioned above, Aristotle defines the human as *anthropos zoon logon echon*: the animal that speaks and is capable of reason. However, and as is well-indicated in the later Latin translation (*animal rationale*) of the Greek term, this expression implies that humans are first of all animals, who are characterised by their use of 'abstract language' as well as by their ability to use reason. Hence, humans are both sensuous *and* reasonable beings. This leads to two very different understandings of reason: a) reason as a form of agency that leads the sensitive-emotional nature of humans forward in the best possible way and b) reason as a form of agency that opposes sensation and emotion (see Simon-Schaefer, 2001). Plato can be seen as an advocate of a purely reason-based anthropology. His psychological *tricotomism* lays the foundation for the traditional Western interpretation of the emotions, which holds that emotions are excluded from the *logistikon* and belong to the lower parts of the soul (Kaufmann, 1992, p. 41). For Plato, affects disturb calm contemplation and thus impede progress toward human perfection.

Aristotle neither adopts Plato's trisection nor the absolute suppression of the emotions, but argues instead for the 'golden mean' or 'happy middle' (*mesotes*). Humans should avoid excessive emotions while simultaneously not completely suppressing them. Nevertheless, for Aristotle, humans are primarily characterised by the ability to use language and to apply reason. This is why only the philosophical life (*bios theoretikos*) leads to fulfilment and happiness (*eudaimonia*).

From Plato and Aristotle onward, there evolved a long history of discourses dealing with the reason-emotion conflict. Two images have tended to determine these discourses: either the emotions are seen as modes of thinking and thus are subordinated to reason, or they are seen as contradictory to reason and thus need to be suppressed. Very rarely do we find a third image, whereby emotions and sensations are seen as different in kind, but equal in value—that is, as a necessary part of being human. Schiller's anthropology may be regarded as encouraging us to think that third image.

FRIEDRICH SCHILLER: TOWARDS A 'SENSIBLE SENSITIVITY'

Problem: A Critique of Enlightenment

Schiller's *Über die ästhetische Erziehung des Menschen*[9] (*On the Aesthetic Education of Man in a Series of Letters*) ([1795] 2009) pursues an anthropological approach, and explores to what degree passions and reason are intertwined, even though they embody very different modes of being. In what follows, I will suggest how his formulation might serve as an element or as the beginning of a theoretical foundation that anchors the creative and the emotional pedagogical tools of Philosophy for Children in an overarching and more complex image of humanity.

Schiller begins with an honest appreciation and at the same time a severe critique of enlightenment: 'Utility has become the great idol of our time'[10] (Schiller, [1795] 2009, p. 9). In opposition to Kant's practical reason, Schiller rejects the dominance of reason as well as the instrumentalisation of passions. His critique re-invokes the traditional dichotomy between freedom and morality: How can we act with moral goodness and simultaneously follow our free will? How can we emotionally will the reasonable?

As the embodied creatures that we are, the force of necessity throws us into the world of utility: 'Nature doesn't begin with the human differently than with the rest of her work: she acts for him where the free intellect cannot yet do that for himself'[11] (p. 11). However, as reasonable creatures, we reconstruct the work of necessity backwards and transform it into a work of free will: necessity becomes morality. 'Reason has done what it can, once it has found the law or maxim, now it is up to the courageous will and the vivid sensitivity to actualise and perform and act accordingly'[12] (p. 31). But how can we harmonise our passions with our reasonable decisions? In this seemingly paradoxical dichotomy, Schiller sees the grand tragedy of being human.

Humans are both in and beyond time. Our nature calls for manifoldness, the presence of sensations, necessity and change, whereas our inner ideal and free will strive to transform the manifoldness of the world into one ideal law, logical rule, and infinite truth. Consequently, humans bear within themselves an ideal and inalterable unity that they are compelled to actualise in a multitude of different expressions. Because of this contradictory nature, humans can be at odds with themselves in two different ways: they either become 'savages' or a 'barbarians'. The 'savage' symbolises for Schiller the dominance of the passions and the appreciation of nature, but the savage becomes enslaved to his emotions and impulses. The 'barbarian' represents the dominance of rational maxims which destroy the passions and disregard nature. 'Where the man of nature uses his arbitrariness without any limits or laws, we may not show him his freedom; but where the artificial human is not yet using his freedom, we may not take away his arbitrariness'[13] (p. 3). Thus the goal for the cultivated human is to befriend and honour nature by tempering her arbitrariness[14] (p. 17). In his social criticism, Schiller foresees the devastating effect of a culture that relies solely on the power of reason and utility, and he warns that it will finally destroy the holistic character of human nature.[15] This imbalance will lead to a separation of passions and morality, pleasure and work, means and ends, effort and reward (see p. 23).

The Paradoxical Nature of Humanity

Schiller's criticism leads him to distinguish between two aspects of being human: *personhood* and *becoming*. The first is the person's enduring and stable aspect; the second is his changing condition. As embodied entities, we are separated from the world and we are our own foundation. Consequently, we pursue an ideal of being self-grounded and absolute, which is expressed by our notion of freedom. However, our body is exposed to time and open to the world through the senses, which influence our momentary condition. This is why humans embrace the extremes of being in time: on the one hand, they flow through time and change; on the other hand, they consist of an unchangeable essence that defies time. The essence itself cannot change, because it would result in the deconstruction of the entity in itself. We are like the flower that grows, blossoms and withers: the flower itself is the essence, which moves through different stages of actualisation. Just so does the human unfold his potentiality in the flow of time by his free will—and in the process we become who we already are.[16] For Schiller, this human dichotomy[17] leads to the extremes of the 'savage' consumed by the cyclic time of a changing nature; or the 'barbarian' disconnected from nature and fleeing into the eternal and unchangeable world of thought and reason. Both routes lead to the breakdown of the human capacity to be both reasonable and passionate, nature and person, connected with the world and capable of free will.

In invoking this dichotomy, Schiller is referencing Kant's *Critique of Pure Reason*: 'Thoughts without content are empty, intuitions without concepts are blind' (Kant, 1781, p. A 51, B 75). However, Schiller sees it under another aspect, and applies it to his anthropology by suggesting that as long as the barbarian is not submerged in the sensuous world, he will remain an empty form and potentiality only, i.e. a concept without life. But, the 'savage' has no concepts, no personhood, no form to actualise the continuously floating perceptions from the sensuous world and, as a consequence, he is swept away by impressions, passions and instincts. As a consequence, his freedom remains abstract. This is why humans must combine the actuality of all possibilities (sensuous world) with the necessity of actuality (world of reason). 'In order to not only be world (sensuousness, impressions, etc.) he has to give matter a form through reason and concepts; however, in order to not only be form, he must actualise his ability to be sensuous'[18] (p. 46). This leads Schiller to formulate two fundamental aspects of the human. The first aims for absolute reality: the human has to transform everything into world that is only form. The second aims for absolute form: it shall absorb everything that is only world and bring it into con-formity. In other words: humans shall realise everything that is within themselves and shall in-form everything that is outside of themselves.[19]

Sensuous Drive, Form Drive and Ludic Drive

In keeping with this double nature, humans are dominated by two contrary drives. Schiller calls the first one the 'sensuous drive' (*sinnlicher Trieb*). It is rooted in the physical nature of the human, i.e. his embodiment. As embodied entities, we are thrown into 'matter', which means that a part of the world has become aware of itself and has started to communicate with itself from within itself: we can feel our hand, but at the same time we feel our hand being felt.[20] As this sensuous being, we are linked to the world through our senses. Being embodied as substance also means to be submerged in time, change and an outside reality, which equally follows the laws of time (see pp. 47ff). However, being in time means to constrain what is to the actualisation of one aspect of what is at each moment. A human who is driven by his 'sensuous drive' lives in the moment only, and his personhood is abolished as long as the stream of time ties him to the presence of sensory input only. The second instinct is the 'form drive', i.e. the maintenance of personhood. It transcends change, nullifies time and strives for truth and justice. It seeks stability, essence and unity.

The difference between passions/sensations and reason arises from these two drives: sensitivity can only confirm that something is true for this particular person and moment. This is why Kant stresses the necessity of a practical reason that constitutes maxims which are good and true in all situations, independent of the passions. Nevertheless, Schiller criticises Kant's emphasis on practical reason only: he claims that if we are solely dominated by pure or practical reason, we lose our individuality and become mere members of a species, because we are divested from our particularities. Therefore Schiller does not see the form drive and the sensuous drive as opposed instincts, but rather states that both have their proper tasks and areas of expertise: the form drive aims for unity and stability, and its subject is the *Gestalt* (shape)—but a form without content remains empty. The sensuous drive aims for change and its subject is 'life'; it doesn't affect the essence of personhood itself, but only the stream of consciousness, i.e. the way a person moves through time.

Schiller derives his educational recommendations from this theory: we need, he suggests, to protect sensuousness against the interventions of reason and freedom, while simultaneously protecting personhood against the power of the senses. The first can be achieved by the cultivation and usage of the senses; the second, through the cultivation and usage of reason (pp. 48ff.). Through the passivity of the senses, humans are exposed to as much of the world as possible. Cultivation of the senses includes exposure to the world and the deepening of experience. However, by means of personhood, humans have the potentiality to be independent of their passions and to become active agents in a world of mere impressions. These two potentialities involve two dangers: either reason is overly strong and disconnects us from our sensations, in which case the person cannot experience something 'else', i.e. an otherness; or, in the second case the person is dominated by his passions and sensations and will never become himself (see p. 52). 'Only insofar as we are an essence and independent from change, is there is a reality outside of us and are we receptive to it; and only insofar as we are receptive to it is there is a reality inside of us and are we a thinking force'[21] (p. 54). Hence, the sensuous drive must be controlled by the person and the form drive must be guarded by sensitivity. However, and like every balance, this equilibrium is never definite or stable, but has to be actively maintained every moment, in the sense of a continuous flow of energy.

Nevertheless, for Schiller, this tension between the form drive and the sensuous drive remains static and conflict-laden. This is why he introduces a third and interlinking instinct, which he calls the 'ludic drive'. The sensuous drive wants to be determined and to receive its object; the formal drive wants to determine and to create the object itself; and the ludic drive wants to receive what it itself has created and will create it in the way that the senses want to receive it. The sensuous drive excludes all freedom; the formal drive strips us of all dependencies. The exclusion of freedom is a physical necessity; the exclusion of the passions is a moral necessity (with regard to Kant's categorical imperative). This is why the ludic drive addresses and forces both, the passions and reason: it suspends chance as well as all its necessity, and simultaneously frees the human physically and morally.

Play is genuinely human, because it allows us to distance ourselves from the instinctive impulses through reason. Nevertheless, we always remain part of the sensuous force of the world too, although without being overwhelmed by it (mere sensuous drive). We remain distanced from these sensuous calls that come towards us from the things, but still perceive them. At the same time, we have not yet fallen completely into the form drive, because we are still 'just playing with the world' without any 'end-oriented' intention. Thus, in a way, we are free and connected from and with both instincts *and* habits. As a consequence, we re-enter the realm of potentiality and become creative by unfolding our own unusual and unique usages and meanings. Through this expansion of meanings, and in the process of finally choosing one, the chosen becomes our very own one. This is why, for Schiller, we are only free when we play and we only play when we are free (see p. 58). The body plays a core role in this meaning-making process.[22]

The subject of the formal drive is *Gestalt* and the subject of the sensuous drive is 'life.' This leads to the content of the ludic drive, which is 'vivid form' (*lebende Gestalt*) or, in other words, 'beauty' (p. 31). Therefore beauty is neither pure life nor is it mere gestalt, but rather it occurs between the two. Pure gestalt is dead and abstract, and accordingly pure life remains impression only, without being recognised by anyone—it is swept away by the flow of time. 'Only if form lives in our sensations and our life is being formed, following our reason, do we ourselves become a vivid form'[23] (p. 59). In this moment, when reason and sensation are unified by the ludic drive, nature becomes aware of itself from within itself—it is given a gestalt through the formal drive and thus is uplifted and rescued from the sensuous stream of continuous change.

This is why, for Schiller, the harmony between reason and passion, the true and the good, can be only be found when both pairs of opposites are anchored in beauty, i.e. in the play with form and substance. As a result, instead of the idea of 'the good' (which Plato ranked as the highest of all three ideas), Schiller—and, incidentally, also the German poet Hölderlin—regard 'beauty' as the most important idea, because it links the material world, which can be perceived through the senses, with the world of the mind, i.e. the true and the good, which eludes the perception of the body. In other words: beauty is the only idea that reaches down into the world of substance and embodiment.[24] As such, beauty precedes the true and the good, and is the only idea that can elevate us into the realm of truth and goodness.[25]

Play and Beauty

But what does Schiller mean by 'play'? In another chapter, he emphasises that 'play' is by no means 'mere play'. He writes: 'with the pleasant, the good and the perfect, he [the human] is only serious, but with beauty, he plays'[26] (p. 61). Thus, 'play' has nothing to do with 'gambling.' Rather, reason sets up an ideal for beauty, and this ideal is what the ludic drive aims for. Therefore, beauty is not merely gestalt or life; rather, it is absolute formality and absolute reality. This is why Schiller finally proclaims that 'the human should only play with beauty and he should play only with beauty ... Because ... the human only plays when he is in its full meaning human and he is only fully human when he plays' (p. 62).[27]

Schiller's thought shines a completely new light on sensitivity and passion, which suddenly become crucial for the spheres of politics and cultural criticism. The task of political education is to accept the importance and the role of sensitivity on the one hand, and to protect people against supremacy of the sensations on the other hand. However, if reason is not subordinated to sensation and sensations are not subordinated to reason, then each aspect inhabits its own space of action. As a result, Schiller argues for a balanced cultivation of sensations, emotions and reason in order to actualise the 'true nature of humanity'[28]:

> It ought to be equally difficult to determine whether our practical philanthropy[29] will be more disturbed and chilled by the tempestuousness of our desires or by the rigidity of our fundamental principles, by the egoism of our senses or by the egoism of our reason. Feeling and character must unite to sculpt us into sympathetic, helpful and actively participating people, just as the openness of the senses must encounter the energy of reason to create experience. Notwithstanding the praiseworthiness of our maxims, how can we be kind, benevolent and humane toward others if we lack the capacity genuinely and truly to accept alien nature in ourselves, to adopt alien situations and to make alien feelings into our own? (13th letter, second footnote).[30]

CONCLUSION

Philosophy for Children between Ideal and Reality

Humans are born with the ability to perceive and connect with the world, as well as with the ability to think rationally and to distance themselves from the world. This is why reason without passion remains meaningless and valueless, and passions without reason are blind and abulic. Only if both are linked will our passions have a content, direction and meaning. Schiller tries to achieve a harmony between those two poles through the notion of play, through which we free ourselves from the immediacy of the passions as well as the necessity of reason, and thus enter that playful state of suspension which represents the realm of possibilities. Through play, we open up the given, distance ourselves and explore various interpretations of the world. In so doing, we begin to play with the world and with our concepts. Through this hermeneutic reconstruction of the given, we internalise the world as ours—we respond and thus are responsible;[31] we are responsible because we respond to the given and choose a momentary interpretation of the world. By choosing one, we actualise this one possibility, but at the same time suppress the actualisation of every other possibility. However, in order to freely choose and actualise one interpretation, humans first have to distance themselves from the necessity of the given, their instinctive impulses, and start to play *with* the world as an independent entity.

Hence, we are within the world and at the same time we act upon the world by finding new shapes, forms and concepts through which we possess the world and understand ourselves in relation to the world; we gain a reality and an identity. The notion of play becomes so central because when we play we become creative—we acquire reality in an act of passive perception *and* active form-giving (see Winnicott, 2005, p. 72), which Schiller calls the 'vivid form'. Through this process, reality becomes 'our' reality. And if we understand Schiller correctly, then he claims that 'we are only human when we play and we only play when we are human.' This is to say that we are an entity, separate from the world, but the world becomes 'our world' when we handle it, play with it, perceive it and give it a form. In other words: we are moved by the world and the world is moved by us.

In a very similar manner, the infant psychoanalyst D. W. Winnicott suggests in *Playing and Reality* that 'it is in playing and only in playing that the individual child or adult is able to act creatively and to use the whole personality, and it is only in creativity that the individual discovers the self' (p. 73). This is because we interpret the world and give it a shape hermeneutically, and this is the reconstructive force appropriated by children who play with reality. A very basic example is the creative use of objects by younger children, who use, for example, a table as a cave or a fork and a spoon as puppets. Older children also begin to play with words, concepts and meanings and thus to create their own interpretations of reality; they abandon their immediate instincts or leaned habits and re-enter the realm of possibilities and creativity (alternative meaning and usage of the world).

Similarly to Schiller, Winnicott sees the human as embracing the two extremes of being fully immersed in the world and simultaneously separate from it. Accordingly, we are in danger either of being only world or of being disconnected from it. And also like Schiller, creative play, for Winnicott, symbolises the effort to be both connected with the sensuous world and simultaneously to construct concepts and interpretive structures that lift the continuous stream of being into the world of ideas and reason. Play with the world becomes play with concepts.

However, a few questions remain unanswered. For one, why should we and how can we cultivate the sensations, emotions and reason through philosophy? Aren't other disciplines more powerful or more appropriate for the cultivation of passions? How can we locate the notion of play in philosophy for/with children? Schiller's philosophical anthropology and

Winnicott's psychological deliberations give a clear and appropriate answer to the first question: reason can only be cultivated when it remains connected with the passions, and the linking force between the two is the 'ludic drive', which energises the creative play with concepts that relate to actual problems from children's life-world.

Children reconstruct and re-acquire reality through the creative act of philosophising together. The community of philosophical inquiry, as modelled in Philosophy for Children, may be described as the intertwining of an inner sensuous perception of things on the one hand, and an 'objective' shared reality with others, which is based on concepts and forms. And in keeping with Kant's proposition as altered by Schiller, concepts remain empty if they are not filled by subjective sensuous experiences; and experiences remain blind if they are not conceptualised and shared with others. This is why the community of inquiry can be described as a chiasmic space between sensations and reason. The dialogue that emerges there may be identified as a form of creative play because the participants try out various concepts and share experiences. Different possibilities are explored and a reality takes shape through the linkage of concepts/forms and subjective experiences, passions and sensations. This makes the individual acquisition and thus a reconstruction of meaning available to children. In turn, this process becomes one of self-realisation as children transform their own identity through deliberating with others, and thereby reconstructing their connection with the experienced world. This is why I suggest calling the community of philosophical inquiry a 'playground of thought.'

Philosophy for Children as a Playground of Thought

This article began with a criticism of Philosophy for Children's main philosophical background, which lies in the analytic and pragmatist tradition. As a consequence, Philosophy for Children has often been reduced to a critical-thinking programme. Lipman later introduced two other modes of thinking—the creative and the caring. However, the reduction of creativity and caring to 'thinking modes' led to a diminution of the phenomena in themselves. This reduction was probably a reaction to the problem of whether or not the cultivation of passions and sensations can be regarded as 'philosophical.' But I have tried, through my exploration of Schiller's anthropology, to suggest that if we are to cultivate reason, we need to address the passions/sensations at the same time (and not only as thinking modes). The notion of play is the link between those two aspects. In the case of Philosophy for Children, the community of philosophical inquiry remains rooted in sensations because it derives its examples from the children's life-world. Dialogue represents the playful application of various ideas and concepts in order to reconstruct and reinterpret reality as our very own worldview.

Hence, if Philosophy for Children is no longer reduced to a 'critical-thinking programme', then philosophical deliberation offers an opportunity to cultivate a playful and creative dialogue, especially between generations: a space for pondering, a realm in which not only pedagogues teach children, but where new sense and meaning is generated and where all modes of being human have their rightful place (senses, emotions, reasons etc.). Thus, it becomes a 'playground of thought' where meaning emerges on the cusp between our perceptions of the world and the playful application of ideas.

NOTES

1. Certainly, the appearance of postmodernism, multiculturalism and ethnocentrism casts doubt on the Western concept of rationality and demands that its claim of a universal purview be justified. However, I am not so much suggesting that Philosophy for Children practitioners consciously try to do that, than that there are unresolved assumptions hidden in the theoretical background of the programme.
2. Of course, this is exactly opposite to the goals of philosophy for children programs. In fact they want to see children in their abilities and not in their inferiorities. However, the implicit pragmatist and analytic orientation of most philosophy for children programmes might easily lead to such a misunderstanding, especially in countries that are dominated by a more continental philosophical tradition (e.g. Germany or France). This perceived prejudice has actually led to severe criticism in Germany (e.g. see Martens, 1999, 2003).
3. In what follows, I will use the word 'reason' as a translation for *Vernunft*. To denote the other dimension, Schiller uses different words such as *Gefühl* (emotions, passions) or *Wahrnehmung* (perception, sensitivity). However, for Schiller both expressions mean something similar, i.e. our ability to feel and perceive and thus to be in the present moment and connected with the world through our body. To translate the intended meaning, I will stay close to the German text and use these terms largely synonymously.
4. This term refers to Friedrich Schiller's three drives: the form drive, the sensuous drive and the ludic drive. These will be explained in greater detail later.
5. And, we might add, senescence as well.
6. A philosophical method that Martens included in his 'Five-Finger-Model' (see Martens, 2003) and which can be found in ancient Greek philosophers, i.e. the dialogues of Plato, as well as in more contemporary thinkers, e.g. Ernst Bloch.
7. This aspect has often led to severe misunderstandings. However, if one reads Lipman carefully, it becomes evident that he relies on a pragmatist understanding of truth—that is, he does not intend to provide a method for finding an absolute truth. Rather, for Lipman, truth is intersubjectively constructed (with a sideward glace at Charles Peirce). Consequently, the more people we involve in our quest, the broader our picture will become. Furthermore, Lipman's aim is to gain consensus for pragmatic communal actions. Accordingly, critical thinking can be understood as a pragmatic tool to make one's own contribution better understandable to others: coherent, precise and consistent. However, those criteria are *only* relevant for the actual aim of mutual understanding. In that way, 'critical thinking' in a community of inquiry resembles Habermas' ideal dialogue situation. I have explored this parallel in another article (see Weber, 2008).
8. Philosophy for Children has, for example, long been rejected in Germany because *Harry Stottlemeier's Discovery* focuses mainly on logic, and logic and language are considered to be overrepresented in the programme's manuals.
9. Translations of the German original are the author's, with the help of Howard Fine; the original German text can be found in the footnotes.
10. 'Nutzen ist das grosse Idol unserer Zeit.'

11. 'Die Natur fängt mit dem Menschen nicht besser an, als mit ihren übrigen Werden: sie handelt für ihn, wo er als freye Intelligenz noch nicht selbst handeln kann.'

12. 'Die Vernunft hat geleistet, was sie leisten kann, wenn sie das Gesetz findet und aufstellt; vollstrecken muss es der muthige Wille, und das lebendige Gefühl.'

13. 'Wo der Naturmensch seine Willkühr noch so gesetzlos missbraucht, da darf man ihm seine Freyheit kaum zeigen; wo der künstliche Mensch seine Freyheit noch so wenig gebraucht, da darf man ihm seine Willkühr nicht nehmen.'

14. 'Der gebildete Mensch macht die Natur zu seinem Freund, und ehrt ihre Freyheit, indem er bloß ihre Willkühr zügelt.'

15. A criticism that was later picked up by philosophers such as Max Weber and Jürgen Habermas, who claim that feasibility becomes the main reason, whereas the question of value or aim is relegated to the background.

16. Hannah Arendt enlarges this image and claims that humans have the capacity to break out of the of nature's cyclic time, which revolves around consumption and production. By the force of free will, humans can become 'beginners' in linear time or, like Prometheus, they can create their own stable world outside of the rise and fall of nature's time (see Arendt, 1998, especially chapters on *Homo faber* and the *vita activa*).

17. That is, becoming and personhood, essence and change.

18. 'Um also nicht bloß Welt zu seyn, muss er der Materie Form ertheilen; um nicht bloß Form zu seyn, muss er der Anlage, die er in sich trägt, Wirklichkeit geben.'

19. See p. 46: 'Er soll alles Innere veräußern und alls Äußere formen.'

20. For this 'double sensation' see Merleau-Ponty, 2002.

21. 'Nur insofern er selbständig ist, ist Realität außer ihm, ist er empfänglich; nur insofern er empfänglich ist, ist Realität in ihm, ist er eine denkende Kraft.'

22. For example, we cut with a knife, we fold paper or we enter a house through the door. Meaning arises always in relation to the body and its movement through the world. This becomes even clearer when we think about 'broken' or 'meaningless' objects or sites that 'rob us of our breath': e.g. a house without a door, a guitar without strings or the breathtaking experience of a site in nature (e.g. Niagara Falls). These examples don't make sense; they transcend our capacity for meaning-making because they are either useless to or beyond comparison with our body.

23. 'Nur indem seine Form in unserer Empfindung lebt, und sein Leben unserm Verstande sich formt, ist er lebende Gestalt, und dies wird überall der Fall seyn, wo wir ihn als schön beurtheilen.'

24. Many stories and myths play with this important distinction: *Hurqualia*, for example, is a place where things and people that are outwardly beautiful are also inwardly good and truthful, i.e. you can immediately 'see' what is good and true. A similar strategy is pursued in many Hollywood movies: e.g. in *The Lord of the Rings* a mere glance dispels any doubt that elves are good and orcs are evil.

25. A similar argument can be derived from Plato himself, when he talks about the 'erotic ascent of the soul' in the *Symposium*.

26. '[M]it dem Angenehmen, mit dem Guten, mit dem Vollkommenen ist es dem Menschen nur erst, aber mit der Schönheit spielt er.'

27. 'Der Mensch soll mit der Schönheit nur spielen, und er soll nur mit der Schönheit spielen. Denn, um es endlich auf einemal herauszusagen, der Mensch spielt nur, wo er in voller Bedeutung des Worts Mensch ist, und er ist nur da ganz Mensch, wo er spielt.'

28. Of course, the idea of a 'true nature of humanity' has been extensively challenged by postmodernism and other philosophical currents. However, Schiller's thesis can also be regarded as a possible metaphor for thinking about the 'human' without claiming epistemological and absolute validity.

29. Here used in its original etymological sense: the one who loves fellow human beings.

30. 'Ebenso schwer dürfte es zu bestimmen seyn, ob unsere praktische Philanthropie mehr durch die Heftigkeit unserer Begierden, oder durch die Rigidität unserer Grundsätze, mehr durch den

Egoism unserer Sinne, oder durch den Egoism unserer Vernunft gestört und erkältet wird. Um uns zu theilnehmenden, hülfreichen, thätigen Menschen zu machen, müssen sich Gefühl und Charakter miteinander vereinigen, so wie um uns Erfahrung zu verschaffen, Offenheit des Sinnes mit Energie des Verstandes zusammentreffen muss. Wie können wir bey noch so lobenswürdigen Maximen, billig, gütig und menschlich gegen andre seyn, wenn uns das Vermögen fehlt, fremde Natur treu und wahr in uns aufzunehmen, fremde Situationen uns anzueignen, fremde Gefühle zu den unserigen zu machen?'

31. Of course, I refrain here from saying anything about 'philosophy as a discipline *per se*' and focus only on 'philosophy as a praxis when doing Philosophy for Children'.

REFERENCES

Arendt, H. (1998) *The Human Condition* (Chicago, IL, University of Chicago Press).

Henckmann, W. (2003) Über Vernunft und Gefühl, in: C. Bermes, W. Henckmann and H. Leonardy (eds) *Vernunft und Gefühl: Schelers Phänomenologie des emotionalen Lebens* (Würzburg, Königshausen & Neumann).

Kant, I. [1781] (1998) *Kritik der reinen Vernunft* (Hamburg, Meiner Verlag).

Kaufmann, P. (1992) *Gemüt und Gefühl als Komplement der Vernunft* (Frankfurt am Main, Peter Lang).

Lipman, M. (2003) *Thinking in Education*, 2nd edn. (Cambridge, Cambridge University Press).

Marsal, E., Weber, B. and Dobashi, T. (eds) (2009) *Children Philosophize Worldwide* (Frankfurt am Main, Peter Lang).

Martens, E. (1999) *Philosophieren mit Kindern. Eine Einführung in die Philosophie* (Stuttgart, Reklam).

Martens, E. (2003) *Methodik des Ethik- und Philosophieunterrichts: Philosophieren als elementare Kulturtechnik* (Hannover, Siebert).

Merleau-Ponty, M. (2002) *Phenomenology of Perception* (New York, Routledge).

Nussbaum, M. (1992) Emotions as Judgments of Value, *Yale Journal of Criticism*, 5.2, pp. 205–210.

Schiller, F. [1795] (2009) *Über die ästhetische Erziehung des Menschen [On the Aesthetic Education of Man]* (Frankfurt am Main, Suhrkamp).

Simon-Schaefer, R. (2001) Die Anthropologie der Sinne—Zur Dialektik von Emotionalität und Rationalität, in: J. Mauthe (ed.) *Affekt und Kognition* (Sternenfels, Wissenschaft und Praxis).

Weber, B. (2008) J. Habermas and the Art of Dialogue: The Practicability of the 'Ideal Speech Situation', *Analytical Teaching*, 28, pp. 2–10.

Winnicott, D. (2005) *Playing and Reality* (New York, Routledge).

5

Transindividuality and Philosophical Enquiry in Schools: A Spinozist Perspective

JULIANA MERÇON AND AURELIA ARMSTRONG

The reality of individuals seems incontestable. We tend to perceive the world as consisting of discrete things, units of cohesive matter which we identify as clearly bounded objects or living beings. Traditionally, individuality has been theorised either via a substantialist perspective, whereby being is considered consistent in its unity, given to itself, and resistant to what it is not,[1] or through a hylomorphic[2] approach, whereby the individual is conceived as the perfecting form or *telos* of matter. The self-centred substantialism of individuals is here opposed to the bipolarity of the hylomorphic schema. In both cases, however, the existent individual is the starting point of investigation, and an ontological privilege is granted to the constituted individual (see Simondon, 2005).

What sort of theory would emerge if our inquiry did not focus primarily on constituted individuals, but on the very processes of constitution that enable individuation[3] to occur? The work of Gilbert Simondon represents a recent response to that query. His objective is to understand the system of reality that permits individuals to become separated from the environment—the individual is thus considered as what is to be explained rather than the starting point of inquiry. For Simondon, the individual and the collective correspond to effects in a process of individuation. Individual and collective do not succeed one another, but are, rather, synchronic, participating in the same process that engenders interiority and exteriority. Both individuations, the psychic and the collective, are reciprocal to each other. Their reciprocity defines the transindividual: 'a systematic unity of the interior (psychic) individuation and the exterior (collective) individuation' (Simondon, 2005, p. 23).

The term transindividuality thus refers to the mutual constitution or reciprocal determination of the psychic and the collective. From the notion

Philosophy for Children in Transition: Problems and Prospects, First Edition. Nancy Vansieleghem and David Kennedy. Chapters © 2012 The Authors. Editorial organization © 2012 Philosophy of Education Society of Great Britain. Published 2012 by Blackwell Publishing Ltd.

of the transindividual another key concept emerges in Simondon's theory: that of *relation*. The transindividual understood as relation is not what occurs between individuated terms, but is a dimension of individuation itself. Relation is, according to this perspective, what constitutes individuals and not the reverse. In sum, the concept of the transindividual is characterised by the primacy of processes of individuation over constituted individuals and of relations over *relata*.

Etienne Balibar suggests that Simondon's arguments for transindividuality are 'truly spinozistic' and, indeed, that Spinoza's striking rejection of abstract oppositions is best described in terms of Simondon's notion of transindividuality. Following Balibar's suggestion that Spinoza can be fruitfully understood as a 'theoretician of transindividuality' (Balibar, 1997, p. 11), our objective is to demonstrate that Spinoza's version of transindividuality challenges traditional dichotomies in a way that sheds new light on some of the processes that take place in the philosophical community of inquiry in the classroom. Spinoza is one of the few philosophers to have formulated a consistent critique of the dualisms that form the conceptual infrastructure of post-Cartesian Western thought. In understanding his challenge to the dualisms of mind and body, knowledge and affect, interior and exterior, individual and collectivity through the notion of transindividuality, these classical antinomies are more clearly reconfigured. Given the productive connection between Simondon's notion of transindividuality and Spinoza's philosophy, the suspicion that moves the present paper is the following: if we conceive of philosophical inquiries with children as complex psycho-social or transindividual processes, we will be better able to understand how the aforementioned distinctions are, in fact, not dichotomies, but reciprocally actualised and maintained through a complementary dynamic.

Spinoza is often portrayed as an arch rationalist. The undeniable significance of reason in his philosophy, however, should not blind us to the pivotal role played by the affects[4] and desire in his philosophical system. Reason, like imagination, is a form of knowledge that corresponds to a type of bodily experience. According to Spinoza, body and mind are modes of the attributes of a single substance that express the same individual power. *Conatus* is the name given to this power—it is our striving to persevere in existence, our complex drives and dispositions, which are also identified with our desire. The understanding of an individual's *conatus* as a reciprocal dynamic between the power to affect and to be affected (between productivity and receptivity) will serve as the centrepiece of the discussion of Spinoza's conception of individuality in the first part of the paper.

The second part of the paper examines the relation between two types of knowledge or ways of knowing: imagination and reason. From a Spinozist perspective, *imagination* refers to an immediate, partial and non-causal form of knowledge, whereas *reason* involves adequate ideas about causes.

We argue that the complex rational explanations that occur in philosophical discussions with school children can be understood as a rational transindividual system from which relatively stable singular and collective forms emerge. Philosophical inquiry is thus understood as an individuating process that gives rise to individuals and communities. A paradoxical process emerges from this dynamic system: integration is enhanced (that is, individuation is diminished) while difference is highlighted (that is, individuality is reinforced). Thinking as a social process fosters self-determination or individuality, just as the increase in the intellectual powers of individuals enhances a certain kind of social integration. Since different forms of thinking seem to be directly associated with the formation of distinct types of community, we conclude this paper with reflections on some of the 'political' implications of the practice of philosophy with children.

SPINOZA AND INDIVIDUALITY

Spinoza's philosophy has been subjected to radically different interpretations. Genevieve Lloyd (1996) and Christopher Norris (2006) argue that the fact that significantly different readings may display exegetical thoroughness and argumentative rigour, and that strong evidence can be mustered to support opposing claims, indicates how inassimilable Spinoza's thinking is to mainstream classification. If, for instance, Spinoza is classified as a rationalist on the grounds that he maintains that true wisdom can only be achieved through a reasoned critique of common-sense notions or self-evident ideas,[5] he can equally be considered a radical naturalist or materialist, according to whom such wisdom consists in due recognition of the various physical, causal, and socio-political factors that are the material conditions of knowledge.[6]

In agreement with Balibar (1997), we maintain that the apparent incoherence detected in Spinoza's philosophy indicates the difficulty readers have in comprehending a perspective that challenges some of the most ingrained antinomies of classical metaphysics and ethics. This challenge is nowhere more apparent than in Spinoza's notion of individuality as essentially relational. Spinoza's relational individual is not the originating and sole source of reason or the affects. Rather, it is situated in, and constituted by, social imaginary and rational systems that hamper or promote its powers of action and thought. Spinoza thus invites us to rethink the identity and activity of individuals as correlated with extended interrelations.

What then is a human individual for Spinoza? Our response to this question focuses on three main aspects of Spinoza's theory of individuality: (1) the concept of finite modes; (2) the doctrine of psychophysical parallelism; and (3) the identification of an individual's essence with its *conatus* or desire.

Spinoza conceives of the human individual as a union of body and mind (EII P21 S).[7] In striking contrast to Descartes, body and mind are not defined as separate substances but as finite modes or modifications of the attributes of a single substance or all-encompassing reality.[8] A mode is not self-causing but is 'that which is in another through which it is also conceived' (EI D5)—it is, in other words, existentially and conceptually dependent. A mode is limited by other modes of its kind (bodies limit bodies and ideas limit ideas). The finitude of a mode means that it has no absolute self-sufficiency; it can only be comprehended through its relations with other modes. In short, the concept of a mode indicates a constitutive openness: bodies and minds are not understood as atomic or self-contained, but as constitutively relational.

The totality of bodies and minds corresponds to *natura naturata*—that is, the set of all individuals. All that exists is an effect of *natura naturans*—that is, Nature's immanent and incessant production of existing individuals (EI P29 S). Nature understood as constant production or *natura naturans* is the process of individuation on which this paper focuses. In sum, Substance or Nature (the two are equivalent for Spinoza) is nothing but this infinite process of production of multiple individuals, whereas individuals, being all interrelated, are the necessary existence of substance. The multiplicity of individuals and the unity of substance are reciprocal for Spinoza (Balibar, 1997, p. 8).

As modes of the attributes of Substance, mind and body have not only the same order and connection (EIIP7), but also the same *being*. Moreover, as modes of the autonomous attributes of thought and extension, there can be no causal interaction between them. Instead, their connection is explicated as a union or identity, which is expressed in Spinoza's claim that mind is the idea of the body. In other words, mind or idea and body are the same thing represented from the point of view of either thought or extension. An important consequence of Spinoza's denial of psychophysical interaction is the refusal of the eminence of mind over body, with the result that the agency or action of modes or singular things can no longer be understood in Cartesian fashion as a function of the voluntary power of the mind—or will—over bodily motions. Spinoza's so-called 'parallelism' of mind and body thus challenges the classic dualist dichotomy that divides the human being into the higher faculty of active mind and the passive animal drives and passions. Spinoza replaces this dualistic, hierarchical model of mind-body relations with one that attends to the psychophysical whole.

To define the mind as idea or awareness of an actually existing body (EII P13), is to say that the mind is reflective and expressive of its own body. Its activity (or the activity that it is)[9] corresponds, in the first instance, to the series of states of its body object (EII P11). Since the body, of which the mind is an idea, is continuously affecting other bodies and being affected by them, the mind is the idea not only of the body to which it corresponds, but also of the ongoing relation between the body and its immediate environment. The mind, therefore, is not an isolated unit set against an external world that it apprehends, but is the process of encompassing the relations between body and world in thought.

For Spinoza, the essence of human individuals is their very desire (EIII Def Aff I Exp), which is in turn defined as their appetite or *conatus*—that is, their striving to persevere in existence—together with awareness of their dispositions (EIII P6). For the spinozist individual to maintain its identity—or exist—it must necessarily be connected to other body-minds within a complex network of causal and affective relations. Spinoza's theory of *conatus* explains what it means to exist as the inherent striving of the individual to maintain identity in and through such exchanges with its environment. He understands *conatus* or desire as a principle of determination and differentiation, and not of unification: 'the desire of each individual differs from the desire of another as much as the nature, or essence, of the one differs from the essence of the other' (EIII P57 D). Spinoza thus eschews appeal to a universal human essence, and instead refers to the singularity of individuals—to their multiple forms of affection and striving—in order to define them.

Having briefly characterised the spinozist human individual as a finite mode, a union of body and mind, and a complex network of strivings or desire, it is now important to address Spinoza's understanding of reason. For Spinoza, the more an individual exercises its power of thinking the more it is said to be active. Our 'conative power' finds its maximum expression in reason, that is, in our power to adequately understand the causal order.[10] Adequate understanding is not the same as theoretical knowledge; to understand more adequately is not simply to change one's intellectual perspective. It is, rather, a form of affective therapy that involves a change in one's existential stance, activity and desire. Reason is always affective, necessarily involving a dimension of corporeal assimilation or sensitivity. In fact, affecting and being affected constitute a single power operation for Spinoza. Spinoza claims that a defining characteristic of more complex and powerful bodies is a capacity for 'being acted on in many ways at once' (EII P13 S.). The growing complexity of the body is accompanied by an expansion in the mind's power to assimilate impressions. A body that is capable of being affected in a great number of ways shares a multitude of things with other bodies and is thus more capable of regarding a greater number of things at once and of comprehending the relations of agreement, difference and opposition between them (EII P29 S).

The interdependence of productivity and receptivity may seem paradoxical insofar as it reconfigures the traditional dichotomy between autonomy and heteronomy by affirming the compatibility of self-determination with sensitivity or exposure to the world: any possible separation delineated by individual powers cannot be dissociated from the individual's open and fluid communication with other bodies and minds. In this sense, we can affirm, with Hans Jonas, that 'only by being sensitive can a body and mind be active, only by exposing themselves can they be self-determined' (Jonas, 1973, p. 278). A powerful, productive or active body is not one that is invulnerable to the world's determining causes. Activity is not the result of a process of 'disaffection' or 'desensitisation', but is the expression of a flexible, vigorous, and multiply-determined form of sensitivity.

If we give Spinoza's theory of body-mind correspondence any credit, our desire to develop our intellectual power cannot but imply the cultivation of our corporeal sensitivity. Likewise, since individual bodies and minds are interdependent, the more other individuals increase their sensitive power and their associated power of thinking, the more our capacities expand and vice versa. Sensitivity and productivity, like sociality and individuality are reciprocal processes in the individuation of the body-mind.[11]

Lipman and others have argued in various (and often contrasting) ways for the general idea that sociality informs (and forms) individual identity.[12] Vygotsky's social learning theory, Davidov's theory of activity, the social psychology of George H. Mead, systems and process theories, and hermeneutics, among other theoretical strands, have assisted researchers in constructing a description of philosophical inquiry with children that is neither one-dimensional (precluding the individual or the collective) nor simplistic (refusing to analyse the connections between these two realms). It is generally accepted that individual reasoning results from a complex process of internalisation of collective speech/thinking. Communal discussion implies adjustments in an individual's mode of thinking, just as self-correction and interventions that improve the reasoning applied by an individual in a philosophical dialogue promote the development of the student group as a whole.

Thinking is a process that relies on a system of signs, socially shared meanings and forms of communication. Individual body-minds participate in that system being both its products and partial producers. Turning our attention to individuation or to the transindividual nature of individuals allows us to focus not on what one is or thinks, but on the processes of individual/collective thinking that lead to temporarily stable personal/social forms. From this perspective, the practice of philosophy with children can be interpreted as a unique relational space where personal and communal intellectual transformations are rapidly and intensely experienced. As a systematic communicative process, philosophical dialogues with children can be said to correspond to transindividual systems of thinking that contribute to the formation of individuals. Of course, the same claim could be made about any number of social influences operating on the individual, including for example, groups of friends, the family, various social institutions, and the media. In order to identify what is unique about the formative process of the practice of philosophy with children we need to understand what sort of individuating system it is. The distinction between imagination and reason is central to our response to this question.

IMAGINATION AND REASON AS TRANSINDIVIDUAL SYSTEMS

Imagination and reason are, for Spinoza, forms of knowledge through which we understand the world around us. They are also thinking processes through which distinct kinds of sociality and individuality are engendered. Against the conventional view of imagination as creative, Spinoza defines it as inadequate knowledge that is a function of the various alterations that the body undergoes in its interactions with its immediate environment. It is considered inadequate because the reality that immediate awareness grasps is local, partial, and non-causal.

Spinoza claims that 'as our bodies retain traces of the changes brought about by other bodies, the mind regards the other bodies as present even when they no longer exist' (EII P17 D, C). Imagination consists in the mind regarding bodies in this way. Its inadequacy resides in the confused perception that we have of other bodies and our own since we are aware of the effects of other bodies on our own but not of the true causes of these effects. The contents of imaginary knowledge are, therefore, like 'conclusions without premises' (EII P28 D).

Imaginative knowledge derives primarily from memory, which is a result of the fortuitous order of affections experienced by our bodies (EII P18 S). It operates through accidental and unexamined associations: 'when our body has once been affected by two or more bodies at the same time, when the mind subsequently imagines one of them, it will immediately recollect the others also' (EII P18). Furthermore, in future encounters, when the body is affected by one of the affects that occurred simultaneously in the past, it will also be affected by the others (EIII P14). These associations created by imagination explain, for instance, why we love or hate certain things out of sympathy or antipathy without understanding the causes of our feelings (EIII P15 S). Operating via contiguity or similarity, imaginative associations thus expose us to accidental and arbitrary affects.

Another central mechanism of imaginary life is affective imitation. Spinoza appeals to the notion of affective imitation in order to account for the way in which the resemblances individuals perceive between themselves and others form the basis of imaginary identifications. Spinoza explains that 'if we imagine a thing like us, toward which we have had no affect, to be affected with some affect, we are thereby affected with a like affect' (EIII P27). This affective mimetism is, for Spinoza, an automatic or pre-reflexive mechanism—it does not involve any comparative thought between us and the things we imagine to be similar to us. Moreover, because, for Spinoza, the mind's initial ideas or imaginings are not a reflection of the body's affections, but are these affections under the attribute of thought, it is our whole psychophysical state that is modified as we interact with external bodies. Thus, we cannot help but affectively imitate others because to be affected by the affects of others with whom we identify just is to express a certain state of our body and mind like that of the affecting individual. This mimetic principle constitutes the affective basis of pre-conscious social bonds. Imaginative processes are thus not only the result of personal and idiosyncratic experiences, but also of shared socio-cultural contents, inherited conceptions and collective fictions that are affectively reproduced through sociability.

Spinoza maintains that true or adequate understanding entails a transition from the knowledge of the immediacy of bodily alterations to the knowledge of the corporeal and mental causal order, that is, to reason. This transition is facilitated by the fact that imagination and reason are distinct but not opposed forms of understanding.[13] Rational thinking is considered adequate because causal explanations are produced—this form of understanding offers, for Spinoza, a genetic description of things. Thus, instead of reproducing in idea the body's responses to the immediate surroundings, the human individual can think of the causal extensional order so as to understand the very genesis of its own bodily affects. When the mind incorporates its causes or the genesis of its ideas and bodily modifications, the individual becomes a complete or adequate cause of its thoughts. As Heidi Ravven points out, it is not that one's thinking of reality is then transformed but 'it is the very reality of one's mind that changes' (Ravven, 2002, p. 239). In other words, in thinking adequately, the mind does not mirror or represent an external reality. Rather, the individual really becomes more integrated into the causal order of nature and is able to identify with an increasingly inclusive perspective.

When the mind knows according to reason, it is 'determined internally, from the fact that it regards a number of things at once, to understand their agreements, differences, and oppositions' (EII P29 S). Reason and imagination are ways of relating to the world, and imply different qualities of individual and collective life. In this sense, Balibar (1997, pp. 30–31) suggests that both imagination and reason are not to be conceived as faculties of the mind, but as 'transindividual systems' in which different minds are mutually implicated. Imagination and reason as such are processes and the individuals involved correspond to moments in these processes, at different levels of integration.

In the case of reason, integration is enhanced. As ideas become increasingly adequate, individuation, that is, what separates or distinguishes individuals is correspondingly diminished. Individuals are thus able to understand and experience the world not so much as a series of physical/psychological self-contained units, but from an increasingly expansive, inclusive and common perspective. Nevertheless, as Amelie Rorty argues, it is important to note that in this process individuality is not extinguished, but, indeed, enhanced: in diminishing what separates them; namely, inadequate ideas, individuals do not diminish their individuality

(Rorty, 2001, pp. 289–290). In fact, individuality—one's singularity and self-determining power—is augmented in direct proportion to the decrease of differentiation, as the inadequate ideas that separate individuals are absorbed into the co-determinative system of adequate ideas.

This striking paradox describes what occurs in the most engaging philosophical inquiries with children. When rational thinking is intensely shared and communal understanding allows each individual to expand their own ideas, the group becomes an increasingly integrated whole, with each member participating in a shared thinking process, which is enhanced by the contribution of different individual perspectives. Unity and plurality become complementary. Thinking as a social process fosters self-determination or individuality, just as the increase in individual intellectual power promotes social cohesion through the linking threads of dialogue. Thinking and understanding are actively shared while personal contributions remain noticeably singular. It is in this sense that Ann Sharp asserts that 'the success of the community is compatible with, and dependent on, the unique expression of individuality' (Sharp, 1991, p. 33). On a similar note, Gabriela Traverso suggests that the community of inquiry involves two interdependent dimensions: one refers to 'the development that each individual gains on her or his own thanks to the interaction with the rest of the group', and the other to 'the strengthening of the community as a function of the interpersonal enrichment gained from dialogue' (Traverso, 1997, p. 21).

In a circular manner, the perception and experience of corporeal/mental boundaries is a product of our understanding of reality just as the perception and experience of divisions and continuities (in)form our thinking. In this sense, collective philosophical dialogues with children serve to question and reconfigure conventional limits between interiority and exteriority. As thinking becomes increasingly communal the participation of others functions as an important condition for one's own intellectual empowerment. In other words, one's 'interiority' and empowerment is a result of sociality and can be said to be expanded through shared thinking processes. Conversely, the more one exercises one's own thinking, actively participating in philosophical dialogues, the more 'exterior' dialogues become a part of one's 'interior' processes. Philosophical dialogues foster the externalisation of active thinking, just as shared active thinking is internalised by individuals through philosophical inquiry (see Jenkins, 1988). It is this reciprocal dynamic between individual empowerment and social integration that differentiates philosophical communities of inquiry from other forms of socialisation and sociality. The formative influence of the various social institutions (family, neighbourhood, church and nation) that shape individuality is often not correlated with individual empowerment and the strengthening of individual autonomy. From Spinoza's point of view, this is because such forms of belonging are often parochial, narrow and exclusive and so fail to foster the broadening of individual understanding to encompass the widest possible web of relations. What facilitates the enlargement of individual understanding in philosophical dialogue is the practice and procedure of inquiry.

Laurance Splitter argues that whilst communities—with their bonds of trust, collaboration, risk-taking and a sense of common purpose—can be formed and developed without inquiry, inquiry in schools depends on the formation of a dialogic community in order to occur (Splitter, 2007, pp. 12–13). This is explained by the fact that inquiry as a mode of thinking has a dialogical structure and as such is 'problem-focused, self-correcting, empathetic and multi-perspectival' (p. 13). Moreover, Karin Murris claims that what distinguishes *philosophical* inquiry from similar theme or problem focused forms of collective inquiry is that it entails reflection about thinking itself, that is, about the very procedures of the dialogue (Murris, 2008, p. 670). Meta-thinking, or what Lipman calls 'complex thinking' (Lipman, 1996, pp. 23–24), is an essential characteristic of the type of dialogue that takes place in collective philosophical inquiries with children. Reflecting on dialogue as a process, on how thoughts are being expressed by others and oneself, is a way of reinforcing the rational, non-automatic and open-to-scrutiny nature of inquiry (Murris and Haynes, 2000). Dialogues about the criteria and procedures involved in formulating and choosing a question for discussion, about how speech should be distributed, about the facilitation performed by teachers, and other meta-dialogical issues prevents automatic thinking; that is, thinking that merely passively reproduces authoritative opinion or proceeds by accidental associations. By the same token, meta-dialogical reflection also strengthens active or rational thought; that is, thinking that understands its own mental and material conditions and is, in that sense, self-generated.

CONCLUSION: THE POLITICS OF THINKING

What kind of community is formed in and by the systematic practice of philosophising with children? Due to the social nature of our bodily/mental affects, to our finitude as modes of Nature, and to our limited understanding, imaginative knowledge is an ineradicable dimension of all human communities. On the other hand, knowledge will never be exclusively immediate, reactive or restricted to automatic responses to our physical and psychological environment. A completely irrational community is as unimaginable as a totally rational one. Philosophy with children fosters more rational communities, that is, forms of sociability in which affective reason plays a significant role in the reciprocal dynamic between self-determination and cooperative integration. Philosophy with children can be said to facilitate the transition from more passive and imaginary forms of sociality to more active and rational forms of community. How should we understand this transition?

Let us consider, for instance, the influential role exercised by teachers and facilitators in the classroom. In the traditional classroom teachers are the primary source of authority both with respect to children's behaviour in class and with respect to their thinking. We can say, then, that student's identities are partially shaped by images/ideas that explicitly or implicitly derive from the teacher (who in turn complexly embodies ideas from certain institutions and pedagogical theories). Students respond (either positively or negatively) to what is imagined as the teacher's expectations: identities are constructed in relation to what students perceive as the model they are expected to conform to in thought and action. Modelling and authoritative expectations, often reinforced by rewards and punishments, are an important imaginary and affective component of all classroom communities, including philosophical communities of inquiry.

Although the traditional classroom relies on techniques of external regulation of students in order to promote obedience to authority and cooperative behaviour, and therefore involves a degree of passivity, it would be wrong to construe this passivity as a hindrance to the development of active, rational thought. On the contrary, passivity, that is, the external regulation of student's desires and powers that is achieved by encouraging imaginary identification with a model, serves as an enabling condition for the development of individual and collective power. Imaginary identification and unexamined affective bonds function here to promote a form of non-rational connectivity that serves to strengthen and build cooperative and harmonious relations. From Spinoza's perspective, cooperative and mutually beneficial relations between individuals can be said to accord with reason, even if they don't follow from a rational understanding of one's advantage, because such relations ensure that individuals are more likely to experience joyful passions, and to act on the basis of desires born of joy. Spinoza explains the link between joyful passions and reason in the *Ethics*. Joy, he says,

> . . . agrees with reason (for it consists in this, that a man's power of acting is increased or aided, and is not a passion except insofar as the man's power of acting is not increased to the point where he conceived himself and his actions adequately. So if a man affected with Joy were led to such a great perfection that he conceived himself and his actions adequately, he would be capable—indeed more capable of the same actions to which he is now determined from affects which are passions (EIVP59D).

In this passage Spinoza indicates that there is only a small gap separating joyful passive affections from adequate activity. External material circumstances can bring about a passive increase of our powers, and this passive increase can bring us to brink of more adequate understanding and action. The establishment of cooperative and cohesive relations by passive means nevertheless ensures that individuals have something in common and Spinoza tells us that 'the mind is more capable of perceiving many things adequately as its body has many things in common with other bodies.' (EIIP39). To participate in a community, and to enjoy harmonious relation with others who 'agree with our nature' (EIVAppVII) is to be affected in ways that increase our capacities for rational thought and action. In other words, the degree of activity and independence individuals enjoy depends on supportive interactions and favourable external influences. In short, for Spinoza, passive and active power are complexly related rather than opposed.

On the basis of this general description of the complex interweaving of passive and active power in Spinoza's thinking, we can examine in more detail the relation between the practice of philosophy in the classroom and the imaginative and affective interrelations that are the social basis and condition for this practice. Our claim would be that the practice of philosophy contributes to the creation of more active and rational forms of community by means of an immanent critique of, and reflection on, those imaginary preconditions. The immanent critique of the epistemic and social processes that encompass the practice of philosophy with children is what prevents the community from being predominantly constituted by coercive forms of power, dogmatic opinions, and social automatisms. Moreover, this meta-reflection or complex thinking allows intrinsic rational mechanisms to self-regulate individuals and the group, setting the directions for personal and social transformation. Reason, for Spinoza, is equivalent to the active understanding of the causes that shape one's body and mind. In this sense, thinking about what, how and why we think promotes the understanding of how philosophy individuates at the same time that it participates in the formation of more active and self-determined communities.

From a spinozist perspective, we could affirm that the more rational processes such as 'philosophy for children' are shared, the more the individuals and social groups that are engendered by these processes exert their singular powers in a more compatible way. Breaking from a tradition of ethical and political polarities, Spinoza explicitly advocates for a relational conception in which the individual's rational pursuit of her/his own advantage is not the foundation of conflict or unsociability, but the same movement through which more virtuous communities are formed. In their operation as transindividual systems, philosophical inquiries with children engender forms of integration based on mutual convenience: each individual's striving to expand their own power is reinforced by the *conatus* of others, thus mutually engaging in empowering interactions without suppressing their self-determination. In communities constructed through the practice of philosophy, the growing autonomy of the individual (greater self-determination and singularity) is reciprocal to closer association with other individuals.

In conclusion, we can now note how the epistemological, ethical and political realms are inextricably linked in transindividual systems. Individuals and social formations—their corporeal conducts and associated forms of understanding—are constituted in/by relational networks of imaginary and rational ideas. The practice of philosophical inquiries with children offers us a compelling example of how shared reason operates as an individuating system whereby knowledge and affect, interiority and exteriority, individuality and collectivity can be experienced in action/thought as reciprocal or complementary aspects of the same process. The communities that derive from these philosophical educational experiences are evidence of the interdependent movement between a growing unity and a flourishing plurality: a common world in which many worlds co-exist.[14]

NOTES

1. Plato's archetypal forms (which give priority to the invariants outside the individual) are the inspiration for this long standing tradition.
2. From the Greek ύλο hylo-, which means wood, thus matter, and morphic, from μορφη, morphē, that is, form. The priority given by Aristotle to the inner perfection of the individual is the ancient touchstone for this conception of individuality.
3. By individuation we mean that individuals become separated from the environment, which is made of numerous other inanimate and living individuals.
4. Affect (affectus) is a central concept in Spinoza's philosophy. It is, simultaneously, an affection (affectio) of the body that increases or decreases, aids or restrains its power to act, and the idea of this affection. Extension and intellect, materiality and thought are indissolubly involved in the notion of affect. An affect is thus a passage from a lesser to a greater or from a greater to a lesser corporeal power to act just as it is, at the same time, a transition in our power to think.
5. Some of those who see Spinoza's philosophy as primarily rationalist include G. H. Parkinson (1953), Alan Donagan (1988), and Steven B. Smith (1997).
6. Louis Althusser (1976), for instance, attributes to Spinoza a privileged role in the prehistory of dialectical materialism. Other commentators who understand Spinozism as fundamentally materialist in orientation include Alexandre Matheron (1988); Pierre Macherey (1979); and Antonio Negri (1991).
7. 'The mind and the body are one and the same individual, which is conceived now under the attribute of thought, now under the attribute of extension' (EII P21 S). The following abbreviated notation will be used to refer to Spinoza's Ethics: EI (II, III, IV, V) for Ethics, Part I (Roman numerals refer to the Parts of the Ethics); A for axiom; C for corollary; D for demonstration (or definition if followed by an Arabic numeral); L for lemma; P for proposition; Pref. for preface; S for scholium (Arabic numerals denote the lemma, proposition or scholium number); and, Ap for appendix. Citations from the Ethics are quoted from The Ethics and Other Works. A Spinoza Reader (Spinoza, 1994 [1677]).
8. Substance is what 'is in itself and is conceived through itself, that is, that whose concept does not require the concept of another thing, from which it must be formed' (EI D3). In this sense, there is only one substance for Spinoza, namely God or Nature. The identification of God with Nature entails the rejection of any anthropomorphic projection onto God. Spinoza's God has no will and no goals—it is simply the matrix of law governed relations, or Nature.
9. 'The idea of the mind and the mind itself are one and the same thing' (EII P21 S).

10. Spinoza understands adequate knowledge as Aristotle does: knowing a thing adequately corresponds to knowing its causes. The more we understand how things are determined the more we are able to act effectively within causal networks.
11. For a more detailed discussion about Spinoza's conception of relational individuality and the challenge it poses to the distinction between activity and passivity, see Armstrong, 2009.
12. See, for instance, Lipman, 1996; Margolis, 1996; Kohan, 1996; Kennedy, 1999; Splitter, 2007; and Stoyanova and Kennedy, 2010.
13. It is beyond the scope of this paper to demonstrate how imagination and reason are contiguous forms of knowledge in Spinoza's system. For more on that topic see Genevieve Lloyd's *Spinoza and the Ethics* (Lloyd, 1996), and 'Spinoza and the Education of the Imagination' (Lloyd, 1998).
14. This paper was produced under the auspices of The University of Queensland.

REFERENCES

Althusser, L. (1976) *Essays in Self-Criticism*, G. Lock, trans (London, Humanities Press).
Armstrong, A. (2009) Autonomy and the Relational Individual in Spinoza and Feminism, in: M. Gatens (ed.) *Rereading the Canon: Feminist Interpretations of Benedict Spinoza* (University Park, PA, Penn State University Press), pp. 43–63.
Balibar, E. (1997) *Spinoza: From Individuality to Transindividuality* (Delft, Eburon).
Donagan, A. (1988) *Spinoza* (Chicago, IL, University of Chicago Press).
Jenkins, T. J. O. (1988) Philosophy for Children, *Values*, 2.3, pp. 33–36.
Jonas, H. (1973) Spinoza and the Theory of Organism, in: M. Greene (ed.) *Spinoza: A Collection of Critical Essays* (Notre Dame, IN, University of Notre Dame Press), pp. 259–278.
Kennedy, D. (1999) Thinking for Oneself and With Others, *Analytic Teaching*, 20, pp. 40–49.
Kohan, W. (1996) The Social Aspect of the Mind in *Pixie*, in: R. Reed and A. Sharp (eds) *Studies in Philosophy for Children. Pixie* (Madrid, Ediciones de la Torre), pp. 174–191.
Lipman, M. (1996) *Natasha. Vygotskian Dialogues* (New York, Teachers College Press).
Lloyd, G. (1996) *Spinoza and the Ethics* (London, Routledge).
Lloyd, G. (1998) Spinoza and the Education of the Imagination, in: A. Rorty (ed.) *Philosophers on Education: New Historical Perspectives* (London, Routledge), pp. 157–172.
Macherey, P. (1979) *Hegel ou Spinoza* (Paris, Maspero).
Margolis, A. (1996) A Comparison Between the Philosophy for Children Approach and the Cultural-Historical and Activity Approaches: Psychological and Educational Foundations, in: M. Lipman, *Natasha. Vygotskian Dialogues* (New York, Teachers College Press), pp. 119–135.
Matheron, A. (1988) *Individu et Communauté chez Spinoza* (Paris, Les Éditions de Minuit).
Murris, K. and Haynes, J. (2000) *Storywise: Thinking Through Stories* (Newport, Dialogue Works).
Murris, K. (2008) Philosophy with Children, the Stingray and the Educative Value of Disequilibrium, *Journal of Philosophy of Education*, 42.3–4, pp. 667–685.
Negri, A. (1991) *The Savage Anomaly: The Power of Spinoza's Metaphysics and Politics*, M. Hardt, trans (Minneapolis, MN, University of Minnesota Press).
Norris, C. (2006) Spinoza and the Conflict of Interpretations. Paper presented at the *Wandering with Spinoza Conference* (Melbourne, Victorian College of the Arts).
Parkinson, G. H. (1953) *Spinoza's Theory of Knowledge* (Oxford, Claredon Press).
Ravven, H. (2002) Spinoza's Individualism Reconsidered. Some Lessons from the *Short Treatise on God, Man, and His Well-being*, in: G. Segal and Y. Yovel (eds) *Spinoza* (Aldershot/Burlington, VT, Ashgate/Dartmouth), pp. 237–264.
Rorty, A. (2001) The Two Faces of Spinoza, in: G. Lloyd (ed.) *Spinoza. Critical Assessments of Leading Philosophers*, Vol. II (London, Routledge), pp. 279–290.
Sharp, A. M. (1991) The Community of Inquiry: Education for Democracy, *Thinking*, 9.2, pp. 31–37.
Simondon, G. (2005) *L'individuation à la Lumière des Notions de Forme et d'Information*. Collection Krisis, edn. 2. (Grenoble, Jérôme Millon).

Smith, S. B. (1997) *Spinoza, Liberalism and the Question of the Jewish Identity* (New Haven, CT, Yale University Press).

Spinoza, B. (1994) [1677] *The Ethics and Other Works. A Spinoza Reader*, E. Curley, ed. and trans (Princeton, NJ, Princeton University Press).

Splitter, L. (2007) Do the Groups to Which I Belong Make Me Me? Reflections on Community and Identity, *Theory and Research in Education*, 5.3, pp. 93–114.

Stoyanova, N. and Kennedy, D. (2010) Between Chaos and Entropy: Community of Inquiry from a Systems Perspective, *Complicity: An International Journal of Complexity and Education*, 7.2, pp. 1–15.

Traverso, G. (1997) Community and Hermeneutic Rationality, *Analytic Teaching*, 17.2, pp. 86–92.

6

Community of Philosophical Inquiry as a Discursive Structure, and its Role in School Curriculum Design

NADIA KENNEDY AND DAVID KENNEDY

One of the most notable pedagogical windfalls that followed on the introduction and development of the idea of engaging children in philosophical discourse in a group setting has been the emergence of the notion of 'community of inquiry'. Its location at the intersection of the discourses of argumentation theory, communications theory, semiotics, systems theory, dialogue theory, learning theory and group psychodynamics makes of it a rich site for the dialogue between theory and practice in education. This article is an exploration of those intersections, and a prospectus of its possible role in the formation and reformulation of school curriculum. It will be argued here that, when formulated as community of *philosophical* inquiry in particular, it offers the possibility of 'philosophising' the school curriculum in general, by extending the concept-work that doing philosophy entails to all of the disciplines. We will begin with an attempt at a definition of the term as here understood, move to an analysis of its dynamics, offer an example of its use in a mathematics classroom, and finish with a schematic view of its whole-curriculum and whole-school possibilities.

A WORKING DEFINITION

A community of philosophical inquiry (CPI) is understood here as an intentional speech community in the form of a relatively stable and regularly attending group of people who meet in order to dialogue with each other about philosophical concepts—by which we mean common, central and contestable concepts like truth, justice, friendship, economy,

Philosophy for Children in Transition: Problems and Prospects, First Edition. Nancy Vansieleghem and David Kennedy. Chapters © 2012 The Authors. Editorial organization © 2012 Philosophy of Education Society of Great Britain. Published 2012 by Blackwell Publishing Ltd.

person, education, gender and so forth. A group may be gathered together to investigate philosophical concepts anywhere along a broad range of discursive registers, ranging from highly focused and regulated conversation within disciplinary boundaries that is characteristic of academic settings, and which will be the focus of the second half of this article; to groups that meet with no prespecified agenda, as is the case with Bohmian dialogue groups (Bohm, 2004). Although there is plenty of room for argument over what constitutes philosophical dialogue in a group setting, we can at least begin by characterising it as what happens in an interlocutive space that a group of people enters with the shared intention of undergoing ongoing critical deliberation together about philosophical issues, with the expectation that new meaning or significance will arise from their interaction that will at least be partially shared by everyone; and that they will experience some sort of reconstruction of belief through the challenging and testing of each other's assumptions in the common space of dialogue around which they are gathered.

Even in the most radical forms of CPI there is a set of basic discourse rules, implicit or otherwise, that people tend to abide by, and one or more leaders—we will call them 'facilitators'—who act to clarify and to coordinate the emergent structure of ideas and arguments that the conversation generates.[1] Following Socrates, who gave us the earliest (that we know of) prototype for CPI, we will call this emergent structure 'the argument', which suggests that it is a systemic whole that is involved in a continual process of reconstruction; a process that is triggered and moved forward through a series of critical interventions, or 'moves', such as categorising, classifying and hypothesising, suggesting definitions, identifying and questioning assumptions, offering and evaluating examples, proposing counter-arguments, exploring and evaluating implications, summarising, restating, and so forth.

Most of these moves are, we would suggest, embedded in everyday language and learned through everyday use. In learning to speak I learn to classify ('It's a cat'), to evaluate part whole relations ('I'm not finished'), to make distinctions and comparisons, and to think analogically ('It looks like a dog'), to combine propositions syllogistically (X: 'It's a dog'. Y: But it couldn't be, it doesn't have a tail!') and so on.[2] If someone makes a generalisation ('All cats are black',) I do not have to consult a manual in order to decide to search for a counterexample—it happens reflexively, and the same could be said for analogical comparisons, or for definitional extension. Furthermore, our observation is that the implicit and explicit discourse rules of CPI (for example, 'everyone must give reasons for their opinions', or 'everyone must relate what they say to something that has been said before') create a setting and a framework for the emergence of these moves. The individual's formation of a 'good set of moves' is influenced by the modelling of those moves in the context of communal dialogue—mainly by the facilitator but also by the other participants—and the facilitator's interventions that clarify or even correct participants' moves. As Davydov (1993, 1988) claims, given the setting and the modelling and correction processes, these moves are continually being internalised and then externalised; that is, the participants put into practice what was already internalised, and through this cycle the moves are further transformed and reinforced. Internalisation occurs in an inseparable unity with externalisation as much on the individual as on the group level, through a self-regulative process (Davydov, 1990; Vygotsky, 1978).

Thus the assumption here, which is a pedagogical one, is that it is not necessary to teach directly moves like making a proposition, classifying, making a distinction or an analogy, or reasoning syllogistically; all that is required is a setting, a task, and an interactive feedback-structure for which their use is an intrinsic requirement. But one certainly can become conscious of the moves one is using, and thereby enter another realm of judgment (both logical and ethical) in terms of their use. Our further assumption is that this metacognitive realm—the realm of the 'critical'— and the transition into it is one major epistemological goal of doing philosophy in a group setting, with clear implications for the reconstruction of public discourse, not to speak of the collaborative reconstruction of belief in a public space. In CPI as we practice it, the role of the facilitator is to secure the conditions for the emergence of this realm of judgment, which is a procedural matter, and to model and coach its heuristics.

Procedurally, the facilitator may act to regulate the distribution of turns or the length of a speaker's intervention, call for summarisation or location of the argument, or support calls for group response that are unheeded or over-ridden by the next speaker. Her operative goal is in fact to distribute her procedural authority throughout the group—that is, to promote a system-condition in which *all* participants, including herself, share in regulating the distribution of turns, calling for summarisation or restatement, and so on, as well as in calling for definitions or examples, encouraging alternative hypotheses, identifying unstated assumptions, and so on. As such, the regulative ideals of CPI include both distributed intelligence and distributed agency (Kennedy, 2004a, 2004b).

Genealogically, CPI as understood here is associated with the earlier Socratic dialogues of Plato, and more recently, C. S. Peirce (1966) and John Dewey (1916, 1938), and their understanding of inquiry as ongoing conceptual reconstruction. Psychologically and epistemologically, it is associated with Dewey's collaborator George Herbert Mead (1934); Lev Vygotsky (1978), his colleagues—most particularly Aleksei Leontiev and his 'activity theory' (1978)—and that group identified as neo-Vygotskian (Mercer, 1994), for example Rogoff (1990), Lave and Wenger (1991), Wertsch (1991), and Davydov (1988); with Jean Piaget (1970); and more recently with self-organising systems and communication theory. Mead is important as an influence on CPI theory and practice in his claim that primary meaning arises out of social interaction and is negotiated through language, and that self/subjectivity is an interpersonal construct through and through; Piaget in the sense that cognitive development is an equilibrative process involving the ongoing reconstruction of cognitive schema; Vygotsky, Leontiev, and Davydov in the sense that habits of thought and belief, including the skills and dispositions of critical thinking used in CPI, develop from the interaction between the *inter*psychic and the *intra*psychic planes, and that CPI is in fact a collectively constructed zone of proximal development; systems and communication theory in the sense that CPI can be understood as a emergent dynamic whole in continual self-reconstruction (Lushyn and Kennedy, 2000; Kennedy and Kennedy, 2010).

In terms of pedagogical heuristics, Vygotsky's notion of the group as located in a zone of proximal development probably best matches the working analysis offered above of how the critical moves emerge, are reinforced, and become progressively metacognitive in the development of a CPI; but that analysis is also associated very specifically with the educational programme Philosophy for Children, and the methodology adopted and developed by its founder, Matthew Lipman and his colleagues (Lipman, Sharp and Oscanyan, 1980 and 1984; Lipman, 2003; Splitter and Sharp, 1995; Kennedy, 1997, 1999a and b, 2004a, 2004b). The methodology of Philosophy for Children reprises, in a sense, the implicit Socratic ideal of philosophy as practised communally in the agora as an essential discourse of authentic democracy. But it does so by imagining it in the classroom and among children. As such, it represents a challenge, not just to traditional approaches to curriculum, but to the organisation of power in schools as well. In its understanding of *philosophical* dialogue to be a fundamental educational form—a keystone in fact, of emancipatory educational reform and reconstruction in a democratic polity—CPI shows its connections with the progressive educational ideals of the first half of the 20th century, best represented by Dewey in his notion of the school as an 'embryonic society', and education as the 'midwife' of democracy.

SOME CHARACTERISTICS OF THE DISCOURSE

In a broad sense, it could be said that the mission of a CPI, its task as a working group, is to clarify, to develop and, following Deleuze and Guattari (1994) to *create* concepts—or, more accurately, to assist at their 'becoming', which, they suggest, is a process of shift and reconstruction driven not least by exploring their connective relationships with other concepts. As a dynamic discursive structure, CPI could be described as a non-linear, self-organising communication and argumentation system (Lushyn, 2002; Lushyn and Kennedy, 2000, 2003; Kennedy, 2005) that presents itself as linear, since whatever its emergent and open-ended properties, propositions are offered, claims are argued through standard logical entailment, and the conversation is guided on one level by the classical laws of thought (identity, non-contradiction, and the excluded middle). Analogously, it could also be described in Deleuzian and Guattarian terms as a dynamic interplay between the arborescent and the rhizomatic, or vertical and lateral impulses, of which more later.

CPI's ostensible discursive aim is dedicated to making propositions or structures of propositions that seek to universalise concepts like truth, justice and beauty, self, thinking, animal and so on—that is, to reach a reasoned agreement or disagreement about the necessary and sufficient elements of each concept, and about the criteria through which the concept gets applied, or lived, in the world of objects, persons, and experience. This is often experienced by the participants of a CPI as a process of de- and re-construction of the concept, which has been rendered problematic by the very movement of seeking a consensus about its use and relevance, and what the criteria for applying it in experience are. The felt teleology of CPI, then, is to put back together what, with the attempt to identify and characterise it, has been taken apart. This teleology is double-pronged, in that the deconstruction and reconstruction of the concept is undergone both on an individual and a collective level. The implicit understanding of its practitioners is that through reconstruction the concept or structure of concepts becomes more salient and more visible in its work in human action and interaction, with the implication that it renders our experience more self-aware and reflective. The fact that the process is never completed is in fact a mark of philosophical *praxis*: half-reconstructed, the concept re-enters human practice, where it is challenged by context and experience to justify the new understanding of it. It then re-enters the space of philosophical dialogue—both inter- and intra-subjective— where the work of reconstruction is taken up yet again. The extent to which the process is never completed could be seen as an index of the inherently futuristic character of this form of philosophical praxis. Deleuze and Guattari (1994, p. 108) write, 'The creation of concepts in itself calls for a future form, for a new earth and people that do not yet exist'.

We now list, albeit briefly, some other characteristics of CPI as a discursive system—that is, as a coherent set of communicative, linguistic, and argumentative practices. Whether they are descriptive or normative— that is, whether they are brought to the model by its practitioners as principles of practice or whether the model itself requires them—is not always clear. This ambiguity is perhaps characteristic of any pedagogy, which in its normative sense is not a technology based on a set of scientific formulations, but a *techne* (Greek: skill, art, craft) based on a series of philosophical judgments, and in which the descriptive and the normative are in a chiasmic relationship. Insofar as CPI as here understood is what Robert Corrington (1992) has called a 'community of interpretation'— which, on his account, is always latent within what he calls (after Josiah Royce) 'natural communities'—the normative/descriptive distinction is moot. Natural communities, he suggests, 'remain opaque to themselves and to their own sign material' (p. 95), whereas communities of interpretation embody self-reflexion and an openness to the 'not yet', which makes of them 'communities of expectation' (p. 98). On this account the two forms of community are in a dialectical relation. In any healing community, for example, whether religious or otherwise, the drive for transparency and transformation exists in uneasy relationship with the 'natural man'. As such, the characteristics of CPI that we list here can be interpreted as indices of emancipatory potential—of the possibility of the reconstruction of social and personal habit such that, as Dewey put it, 'habits be formed that are more intelligent, more sensitively percipient, more informed with foresight, more aware of what they are about, more direct and sincere, more flexibly responsive than those now current' (Dewey, 1922, p. 90).

1) As an approach to knowledge, CPI is *fallibilist, inquiry-driven, communal, and dialogical*. That is, we can never be sure that we have the whole truth or the final word, and we could in fact be quite wrong about a number of things; knowledge is never fully and finally accomplished, but is the subject of ongoing construction and reconstruction; knowledge is understood in great part as a social phenomenon—something that we argue, deliberate, and decide to be the case *together*; we arrive at knowledge through 'thinking for ourselves and with others'—a process of self and mutual interrogation.

2) As an approach to agency and intersubjectivity, CPI aspires to a *multilogical, distributed, polyphonic, ideal speech situation*. That is, it operates through the expression and attempted coordination of multiple points of view, multiple styles of thinking, multiple ways of talking, and multiple experiences of the world. It is a distributed intelligence, in the sense that the resources through which the argument is constructed—both cognitive and dispositional—are not located in one person, but are potentially present in each member, and are expressed through interaction and exchange rather than as univocal propositions. The cognitive and emotional work of the group as a whole is implicitly dedicated to the emergence of a democratic collective subject—that is, a collective with a general, shared disposition to dialogue, mediation, collaboration, com-munication, power-sharing, equality, self-organisation and self-correction. The relationship between three levels of subjective activity—a) the individual subject-in-process, b) the collective subject-in-process, and c) the work of reconstruction of belief in and between these two systems—is not a hierarchical or a nesting one, but rather one of mutual influence. For example, the group's deliberation on the concept of gender as it relates to voice, individual power or influence, epistemological style, and possibilities of love and friendship influences and is influenced by my personal process of reconstructing, through my interaction with the group, the concept as it applies to my own life and behaviour and relationships. These two dimensions—the personal and the communal—are in constant mutual process.

CPI's implicit horizonal goal is the complete and equal distribution between roles that involve speaking and listening, and a coordination of philosophical perspectives. Thus, the goal of the facilitator is to become an equal member of the group herself. Her success is measured by the extent to which her regulative function—distributing turns fairly and showing concern for the argument as a whole rather than just her individual perspective—comes to be shared by every other member of the group. In a mature group, each member takes the same care for the procedural and the substantive process itself, which allows the facilitator to become more philosophically, and not just procedurally active.

3) As a cognitive and psychodynamic communal activity, CPI is an open, emergent, self-organising system, in that it is ecological, non-linear and irreversible, only partially predictable, and develops through an equilibrative *process* that steers a course between chaos and stagnation. It is ecological in that the confrontation of perspectives that it entails leads, not to a unilateral imposition of one perspective, but to the transformation of the whole system to a new level of development, which leaves all its elements intact but different. Here we may identify the system (at least on one level) as 'the argument'—a structure of propositions, assumptions, hypotheses in dynamic process of reconstruction. It is irreversible in that it never returns to a previous level of organisation. And because it is epistemologically decentred in the sense that there is no authoritative 'teacher' voice, it is only partially predictable, and characterised by *ambiguous control* (Lushyn and Kennedy, 2003), resulting in a power structure that matches the normative requirements of the ideal speech situation (Habermas, 1984).

As an ecological system engaged in continual reconstruction, CPI exemplifies Vygotsky's (1978) notion of learning as a process whereby what happens *between* us is internalised so that it happens *within* each one of us. For example, if someone argues through offering an example, or analysing an example for its relevance, venturing a hypothesis, identifying an unstated assumption or seeking clarification of someone else's statement, these communicative moves are transformed through the 'internal reconstruction of an external operation' into moves within the universe of my personal thinking. In my internal dialogue, I begin to think of examples, entertain hypotheses, seek my own assumptions, etc. And in returning to CPI, I bring that growing armamorium of critical skills back to the group, where it contributes to the 'external operation' of the conversation. The group leader's role is to facilitate that process.

THE CONCEPTUAL WORK

Philosophical inquiry is an inquiry into *concepts*. As pedagogues, whose primary interest is in philosophy as a communal, collaborative praxis rather than as a form of contemplation or *apodeixis*, we are satisfied with an operational notion of concept as an idea or assemblage of ideas that both influence and are influenced by our interactions with our world(s). Concepts, on this account, emerge and develop as a result of both experience and reflection, and both transform and are transformed by experience. My concept of friendship, for example, emerges quite early in life, undergoes all the experiential vicissitudes that follow, and influences them as well. Concepts are always to some extent cultural and historical artefacts, and, as already suggested, they are found in relational networks, or dynamic structures. Deleuze and Guattari (1994) speak of 'zones of neighbourhood' and 'thresholds of indiscernability' with other concepts, of 'internal consistency' and 'exoconsistency', and of a constant process of 'deterritorialisation' and 'reterritorialisation'. Concepts may be said to have conscious and pre or subconscious elements. To that extent, they can harbour unexamined or even unrecognised assumptions.

Concepts are shaped by beliefs (whose relation to concepts, of which they could very well be instances, we will not attempt to determine here)—beliefs about how self and world work—and for concepts that are ethical or that have ethical implications, about how self and world *should* work. As such, concepts have a potential opening or 'crack' in them, whether between the naïve and the scientific, the descriptive and the normative, or the individual and the universal. This crack in the concept is where contradiction is encountered, problematisation begins, and where its propositional content breaks open into a question, or series of questions. The concept of friendship, for example, cracks open on the normative question of whether I am or could or should be a friend of all humankind, or whether there is such a thing as friendship across species. It could be argued that this crack, and the questions that emerge from it, is the focal point for our historical potential as a species, for it is here that cognitive, and by implication psychological, social and political reconstruction become possible, and the actual encounters the utopian.

The concepts 'alive', or 'friendship', or 'time', or 'truth', or 'body', or 'play', or 'mind', or 'measurement', or 'infinity', or 'number', or 'order', can be distinguished from other concepts—for example 'vehicle' or 'eating' or 'sleep'—in that they are common, central, and contestable (Splitter and Sharp, 1995); although it could be argued that the latter can be moved into the realm of the contestable by pushing their semantic boundaries, or 'zones of neighbourhood'. They are common because, for example, we all—even the most individualistic loner—have a concept of friendship; central because how we construct them is important to how we think about and how we perform our lives; and contestable first, because there are as many versions of them as there are people, and second, because they are—or, we believe, ought to be—under continuous reconstruction as a result of ongoing experience and reflection.

The process of problematisation and reconstruction tends to begin when we encounter some stimulus—whether artefact, event, or intuitive realisation—that makes us see or feel the crack in a concept. Usually common, central, and contestable concepts are already problematised in our own inner lives anyway through the contradictions that emerge through everyday experience, and as such, we are existentially primed for this moment. Another major impetus for problematisation may be our common interest in resolving the tension between our multiple versions of the same concept through entering dialogue, where we can take advantage of the shared underlying structures of our concepts, which are linguistic and logical, in order to find points of convergence of meaning, and where we realise that, although they are marked by difference, concepts are neither infinite nor without constraints.

In keeping with the notion that a concept is approached initially as a set of propositions which, when deconstructed, turn into questions, probably the most widely known school curriculum in CPI—the Philosophy for Children novels and manuals—is comprised entirely of questions clustered around the concepts it offers for interrogation. This curriculum favours the story over the textbook as stimulus, because the latter tends to understand itself as a book of answers, and the former a provoker of questions. The textbook assumes that the question has already been asked, and thus suppresses it. Any question it might pose is a rhetorical one—a question to which the answer is already known. The philosophical novel, because it is a narrative as opposed to an expository text—makes it possible to represent the multivocal, dialogical and non-linear, contextually situated practice of group deliberation. It can portray the inquiry process through character, plot and dialogue, 'the way we think when we inquire', as Lipman (2003, p. 85) puts it. The narrative[3] can be so constructed that it assumes nothing, or at least seeks to identify and question its own assumptions. It can dramatize the emergence of questions, and the dialogue that those questions trigger. And the Lipmanian manuals that accompany the novels are, at base, simply lists of questions about the concepts that are highlighted in the novels, aimed at triggering and enhancing critical dialogue.

In contradistinction to the approach of Socrates, and perhaps influenced by the fact that this particular formulation of CPI methodology has its origins in a programme for children, the Lipmanian discussion plan tends to approach concept-work through analogical reasoning and categorical play. It seeks to render the concept 'fuzzy'—to push it beyond the boundaries of its conventional use through a sort of poetics of instantiation: the concept is applied beyond its familiar denotation through playing with its extensional possibilities, which sets up a dialectical relation between the 'literal' and the metaphorical. For example, a discussion plan on thinking in the manual for a novel for young children (Lipman and Gazzard, 1987, p. 21) presents a list of things and asks if they 'think'—cats, beetles, trees, houses, automobiles, computers, a piano player's fingers, and so on. The imposed limitations on the applications of the concept within ordinary speech are challenged,[4] on the wager that through exploration of the fuzzy regions of the concept, in the transitional space of CPI, it returns to the space of everyday life richer, more complex, more positively ambiguous, more reflexive, more flexible.

The process of reconstruction involves conflict, but it is a conflict of ideas, and it is conflict in the service of building on each other's ideas rather than negating or polarising them. It requires a certain level of tolerance of suspense, because the concept in fact is never completely reconstructed, or if so, only as a provisional construct, or 'warranted conclusion' that assumes the warrants are always open to revision. As such, it represents a qualitative shift in epistemological outlook. This new relationship to certainty, and this willingness and capacity to suspend judgment indefinitely is in fact one key epistemological characteristic of critical thinking (Dewey, 1898) and the reconstruction of subjectivity in an age of globalisation.[5]

In community of philosophical inquiry the concept comes apart through interrogating it, and the group begins rebuilding it, session by session. It might be thought of as a communal house building project, except that the building will only be finished 'in the long run', and in our actual experience we are continually moving, replacing, altering or reshaping the pieces, or even tearing down what we have and redesigning it. Each time we leave a session we take a slightly revised notion of the concept—and of how concepts work in general—with us, which we tend to reflect on in terms of our own individual experience. And as we explore one concept we encounter their connections with others—concepts that seem logically prior to or even part of the one we are working on reconstructing.

We might find that in working on the concept of justice for example, we find that we have to define 'person', which might lead us to ask whether justice can be applied to 'animals'. This might lead us to reflect on the similarities and differences between animals and humans, which might— if the question of whether animals 'think' arises—prompt us to deliberate on what we mean by thinking, then on how language works—and so on. In other words, a CPI curriculum is inherently emergent and rhizomatic (Deleuze and Guattari, 1980), with interlinking and recursive multiple strands. We would hesitate, however, to characterise it as a rhizomatic system *per se*. Rather, observation leads us to describe the phenomenon as a dialectical struggle between two impulses—crudely put, the vertical and the lateral—in spontaneous group argumentation, and affective and political (that is, power) organisation as well (Kennedy, 1997). The vertical, 'arborescent' impulse seeks unification through establishing classes and categories, and identifying criteria through which the relationships between all things are illuminated and clarified. In vertical organisation, above is distinguishable from below, and everything finds its proper place. The lateral impulse, which the philosopher Emmanuel Levinas (1969), in opposition to totality or sameness, calls infinity, and which here is called the rhizome, is the impulse of difference, multiplicity, the plural. It makes distinctions that are not assimilable by a unity that includes them both; rather, it holds those distinctions in loose and provisional—to use Deleuze's and Guattari's term—'assemblages'. Rather than arrange an idea above or below another, or in a relationship of exclusion or inclusion, the horizontal or rhizomatic impulse typically offers the counterexample that negates the all-statement status of the generalisation, moves sideways or into another semantic field altogether, and sets up asymmetrical but related connections with the concept from which it broke away. This appears to be directly contradictory to the metaphor of building a house together, because a building requires things that hold each other up, and which rest on a foundation. The rhizomatic metaphor has no obvious centre or ground, no one fulcrum of support or main root.

Even if we console ourselves with Wittgenstein's (1969) suggestion that 'the foundation walls are carried by the whole house', the conflict between the two principles of organisation appears irreconcilable. One is based on criteria that include other criteria, all of them superseded by yet another, higher criterion of 'reasonableness' or 'likelihood'. The other is based on the principle of the rhizome. One aspires to order, control and clear boundaries through the imposition of a binary logic of hierarchical, nesting classes, with clear lines of inclusion and exclusion; the other insists on unpredictable, emergent 'assemblages' and a 'non-hierarchical, a-centred field of knowledge', on the principle of multiplicity as opposed to the principle of unity, and for open-ended creation of concepts as opposed to the reproduction or repetition of established patterns as essential to insight.

However, in the actual functioning of CPI, both principles can be seen to be operating, playing together, sometimes like a cat chasing its tail, and sometimes in a dialectical struggle. For example, the argument quite often proceeds by someone making a proposition or generalisation, an 'all statement' direct or implied, which—in the spontaneous emergence of dialogical argumentation—triggers a counterexample, which moves the group (or the personified 'Argument') to work to reconstruct the concept so that it can assimilate the counterexample. This results in a new generalisation, and this movement from general to specific and back to general again contributes to a condition of Deleuze's and Guattari's 'connection and heterogeneity', in which the concept divides but its elements remain connected, thus creating a new structure.

CPI ACROSS THE DISCIPLINES

We now wish to move, in a rhizomatic fashion, to a brief discussion of the uses of CPI as a model for curriculum development in pre-collegiate education, and to reflect on the implications of the introduction of this form of 'community of interpretation' into the 'natural community' of the school. The emergent and rhizomatic character of the developmental movement of CPI has, we would suggest, broad implications for curriculum reconstruction—both in deconstructing the artificial divisions between self-contained units that now characterise school curriculum, and in extending philosophical inquiry across all the content areas. The activity of CPI promises to open a dimension in curriculum in general, in which the common, central, and contestable concepts of each discipline—their 'big ideas'—assume a certain epistemological priority. To include, as part of a history class, for example, regular interrogation of concepts such as fact, truth, objectivity, perspective, power, conflict, progress, civilisation, causation, period (epoch), agency, narrative, cause, and so on, is to confront that discipline with its own philosophical assumptions, and reveal the extent to which it is a cultural and historical construction—in short, to render it critical and self-reflective.

The majority of common, central, and contestable concepts are present, not just in philosophy class, but also all the way across the content areas. Some, like 'measurement', or 'equality', or 'fact', obviously appear in more than one place, and others will emerge in the specific context of the discipline. In fact it should be no surprise that the collective assemblages of concepts that express and articulate our belief systems underlie the school curriculum. They and their relationships influence how we approach anthropology, history, language, mathematics, art, economics and so on. In this sense, philosophy—or at least philosophy understood as the ongoing reconstruction of concepts—is implicit and potentially present in every class we teach. What is necessary for it to emerge as a discourse in a discipline is to identify the set of concepts that inform the discipline and to develop sets of questions for inquiry, or texts designed to trigger questions, or both. It is even possible to use the standard textbook as a framework. We could take, for example, a set of concepts in science—organism, life, measurement, fact, experiment, nature, environment, matter, energy, cause, hypothesis, theory and so on—assign them to those chapters of the textbook in which they figure most obviously, and take them as a guide to practicing CPI once a week in science class. In this way we add a philosophy of science component to the science curriculum itself. Once students become adept at spotting common, central, and contestable concepts, which typically happens extremely quickly, they themselves can identify them in the textbook, thus approaching the latter critically—as a narrative rather than an exposition of the 'truth'.

THE CASE OF MATHEMATICS

By way of illustration of this process of 'philosophising' school curriculum, we would like to reflect briefly on the case of mathematics. In maths education the term 'community of inquiry' usually refers to a classroom that engages the learning community in doing mathematics collaboratively. Most documented research in this area portrays community of mathematical inquiry as collective work, with or without a facilitator, on well-defined mathematical problems, where students are in a position to ask practically oriented or procedural questions aimed at solving specific mathematical problems.

This certainly promotes more flexible thinking and greater procedural fluency in problem solving, in its attempt to replace exclusive concern for the right answer with a care to explore different possible ways of answering the question, and in many cases, to investigate different possible representations of the situation that might lead to different methods of solving the problem. But from an epistemological point of view, this sort of conceptual understanding and procedural fluency in mathematics is still not enough to evoke higher-order thinking in students, unless this thinking is connected with their knowledge in other epistemological domains, and with authentic mathematical experience—that is, with the experience of using and reflecting on the use of mathematics in the world. Philosophical inquiry allows for and encourages a search for meaning in mathematical concepts beyond procedural fluency and conceptual under-standing within the system, by offering students the possibility of questioning mathematics as a system *per se*—its nature, uses, its power and its limitations, and its existential value. CPI, with its dialectical process of knowledge construction, invites children to pose questions of their own about mathematics, both in its internal relations and its relation to the world—and, by implication, across the disciplines.

One major avenue for such inquiry is, as we have argued above, through the problematisation of the common, central, and contestable concepts that are common to mathematics, science, history, and other school curricula—like measurement, fact, objectivity, certainty, change, chance, equality, structure, and so on. Each of these concepts is an assemblage of different meaning-aspects derived from each disciplinary landscape it populates. For example, measuring an object's height in mathematics or physics is different from measuring learning, or anxiety, or the difference between two poems. In a sense, every new conceptual aspect brought to light may produce a new synthesis of the problematised concept. And since every concept is related to other concepts, it is impossible to approach a thorough grasp of a concept without tracing these connections, and not only those already given, but those created in the process of synthesising it, or in Deleuze and Guattari's (1994) words, in 'bringing [it] forth'.

For example, in problematising the concept 'algorithm', which might be defined as 'a finite sequence of well-defined instructions for completing a task', we may examine the differences between the use of the concept in our everyday lives and how it is used in mathematics. One may inquire, for example, whether 'algorithm' is recognisable in psychological and socio-logical contexts—for example, do we think algorithmically in our everyday activities? Are there subconscious or unconscious algorithms that guide or underlie events like arguments, or shopping expeditions? Is an unconscious algorithm an algorithm at all, or something else? Is there a difference between algorithms in assembling a device of some kind and algorithms in mathematics? Is a mathematical formula an algorithm? Does the use of any algorithm require mathematical reasoning, and if so, what kind of reasoning? These questions interrogate the relation between this concept and other related concepts, such as automatisation, and even thinking in general.

Our expectation is that, after exporting the concept into other contexts and examining it there, our understanding is enhanced when it is re-imported into the universe of mathematics, with all of its newly acquired dimensions, acquired from its traversal of other disciplines. Similarly, spaces for the problematisation of more strictly mathematical concepts may be located in the discrepancies between different students' definitions, interpretations, and understandings of a given concept, in the exploration of the relations between various internal aspects of a concept, or the relationships between it and other related concepts. We understand this as a kind of conceptual boundary work, which acts not only to reveal and explore any ambiguity, vagueness, and misunderstanding in our understanding of the concept and its use, but also to reconstruct our conceptual schemata through a process of deterritorialisation and reterritorialisation. This in fact is the most common approach taken by the multitude of discussion plans in the Philosophy for Children 'manuals', the great majority of which encourage exploration of a concept with questions that push it beyond its 'normal' semantic boundaries, and into the realm of the 'fuzzy'.[6]

By way of example, questions like the following lead to the process of de- and reconstruction of our understanding of the ontology of number: What is number? Do numbers exist in nature? Is mathematics a language? If so what role do numbers play in it? How are numbers and letters the same or different? What can or cannot be expressed in numbers? In an ideal situation, a discussion plan like this one is compiled from students' questions, then added to by the facilitator to deepen or refine it.

Philosophical mathematical inquiry with children often oscillates, in our experience, between two major overarching themes: a) the issue of the presence and the role of mathematics in the world—whether the focus on world be physical, psychological social, economic, epistemological, ontological, or some other; and b) the nature of mathematics as a universe or a language, and how we know and understand it. Students usually start with questions that concern the first theme, which is a testimony to the implicit, culturally inherited idea of the power and importance of mathematics. The following is a set of fifth grade students' questions regarding the first theme, collected in the course of a CPI session conducted by the authors in a fifth grade in a US school.[7]

A World Without Numbers

- What would the world look like without numbers?
- Could we survive without numbers?

- Could we track anything without numbers?
- Could you measure without numbers?
- Would there be a calendar without numbers?
- Would time be felt differently without numbers?
- Would there be time without numbers?
- Would we age if we did not know numbers?
- Would money exist without numbers?
- Would maths be possible without numbers? If so, what kind of maths would it be?
- Would maths be possible without numerals?
- Would the calculation of numbers be possible without numerals?
- Is another maths without numbers possible?

And the following plans, also developed by fifth grade students and added to by a facilitator, explore the second theme:

Knowing Numbers

- Where do numbers come from?
- Are numbers real?
- Were numbers invented or discovered?
- If number were invented, why?
- Do plants and animals understand numbers? If so, what is the difference between the human and the animal understanding of number?
- Can the body count?
- Can we know numbers without symbols?
- Do things come with a specific number?
- Why is that the rules for addition, subtraction, multiplication, and division of numbers always work?

The goal of such questions about number is a marriage of mathematical and philosophical inquiry, which encourages students to build an active conceptual nexus, where a mathematical concept is not just an isolated idea or confined to localised practice, but has rich connections with other concepts, personal experience, informal knowledge, and other disciplines. Philosophical inquiry integrated into maths classes offers an interrogative space that is not artificially divided by subject walls, and promises the development of a dispositional set oriented towards critical inquiry that may be carried with them when students leave school.

PHILOSOPHICAL DIALOGUE ACROSS CURRICULUM AND SCHOOL

Finally, we wish to sketch in broad strokes a curriculum that would integrate communal philosophical inquiry into some or all of the traditional school content areas. At the very least, three models for organising inquiry into the common, central and contestable concepts within the disciplines are possible—a single-discipline, an inter-disciplinary, and a whole-curriculum approach. Each of these corresponds to a more general organisational model for curriculum planning—that is, within a single classroom, between classrooms, and across the whole school. Each can function more or less emergently—meaning that the concepts are not pre-planned, but arise in the course of the inquiry—and more or less democratically, meaning that the concepts and the questions are generated by the students themselves, with the teacher as co-participants.

The first model has already been discussed: a single-discipline approach will identify a group of contestable concepts in, say, science, and through a process of shared questioning and their own deliberative dialogue, teachers and students will develop a series of exercises, discussion plans and activities. Those concepts may be keyed to a textbook currently in use, such that the concept 'organism', for example, is explored through communal philosophical inquiry in the chapter in which it is produced and defined. This is in fact an invaluable strategy for demythologising official texts and encouraging students and teachers to enter into dialogue with their epistemological assumptions, rather than accept them as given. As an expository text, the textbook presents its assumptions as final and authoritative—that is, it denies they are assumptions, and states them as necessary axioms for learning. It assumes, in a linear and hierarchical fashion, that grasping the 'basics'—in this case a previously determined understanding of the concept—is necessary to constructing further knowledge. To understand the concept as contestable introduces an element of de- and reconstruction into the learning situation, and promises the development of new meanings. When a window for problematisation of concepts through philosophical dialogue is opened, the textbook loses its status as bearer of hegemonic, officially sanctioned knowledge, and takes on a narrative status—that is, it is understood as a voice, a speaker, an interlocutor, as conditioned by ideology, historical placement, and material conditions as any text—with which one can enter into dialogue. Because it keeps the axioms of the discipline in open view, staying aware of their historical and contextual character, this form of reading is fundamental to the development of critical literacy.

The second model extends the identification of concepts across disciplines, and thus connects the elements of the curriculum as a whole through a network of contestable concepts. The concept 'measurement', for example, can be problematised in multiple school subjects—whether science, mathematics, history, psychology, anthropology, economics, art, or music—and in fact allows the extension of student inquiry into the ruling and guiding assumptions of the process of schooling—based as it so often claims to be, on measurement—itself. This model would entail teachers and students keying the concept to the texts in the various disciplines, and thus creating an interweaving network of inquiry, which would encourage teachers to understand the school curriculum as a whole, and to collaborate in the organisation of their material, as well as in identifying readings and assigning writings that connect disciplines, and even sharing classroom time and space.

A third model would open the generation of common, central and contestable concepts to the whole school. The use of a 'central subject', either grade-wide or school wide, is one precursor of this, but the generation of emergent philosophical themes that become the deliberative objects of the entire community—concepts like justice change, technology, violence or nature—goes beyond this in scope and participation. A concept like justice can be woven through different content areas in the classroom, become the subject of whole or part-school meetings and dialogue groups, and culminate in school-wide action groups—whether concerned, for example, with justice within the school community, within the larger community in which the school is set, or somewhere else on the planet. In this stage of collaborative inquiry, philosophy returns to its own disciplinary boundaries in the sense that it is no longer bound by one content area or another, but it also responds to actual, immediate instances where the concept is in play, and has the potential of resulting in real democratic action.

In fact it is not just in collaborative deliberation that common, central, and contestable philosophical concepts undergo reconstruction, but in lived experience and the politics of relation, and the school is the embryonic society in which habits, not just of deliberation, but of neighbourhood, community and global activism are forged. In this school-wide model, philosophy, after dispersing itself among the disciplines, returns to the *agora*—the public space—which is its rightful place in an authentic democratic community, and deliberative communal dialogue functions as the emergent compass, the tutor, and the normative horizon of that adult-child collective called 'school'. As such, the utopian possibilities that CPI offers for the reconstruction of childhood education are significant, but that is matter for another article.

NOTES

1. We would argue that even groups with no appointed leaders contain emergent ones, in keeping with the inherent *telos* of the group toward distributed facilitation (for which see below).
2. We would argue further that in fact these moves are not merely linguistic products but originate in the lived world of perception, and are linked with the operations of what Piaget (1952) described as 'sensori-motor intelligence', but this is too bold and complicated a claim for this article to attempt to justify. Nor is there space or occasion to explore the status of these moves in the context of speech act theory, but this would also be of interest.
3. Although 'narrative' here refers to the novel, any stimulus can become one in the sense given here—whether a work of art, natural artefact, or even an expository text, if that text is approached in a critical manner.
4. And even scientific speech that has become normalised and left behind by science—the concept 'alive', for example, which has grown past the seven characteristics cited in every biology textbook.

5. The historical and political implications of this epistemological shift towards the 'critical' subject was a major theme of 20th century psychology and social theory, and can be identified in multiple versions—whether Fromm (1941), Adorno *et al.* (1950), Kelly (1963), Dewey (1922), or many others. While these thinkers generated multiple descriptive categories, both positive and negative, of psychological and sociological types, we can draw at least a crude distinction between the monological and the multilogical thinker. The critical, multilogical thinker both recognises the importance of a given common, central, and contestable concept (of justice, for example) in living the 'good life', and thus the importance of reflecting on it, of reconstructing it—and recognises the limitation of the concept as well. The monological thinker tends to totalise and reify concepts, and attempts to locate them outside history, culture and context. In so doing, he avoids or refuses the possibility of their problematisation—an evolutionary habit which is increasingly dangerous in a multilogical word, in which multiple perspectives confront each other in a global common space. The capacity for entertaining multiple perspectives, and the skills and dispositions for collaborative, dialogical deliberation, are adaptive habits that have become necessities in the emergent human evolutionary environment.

6. As such, we avoid a head on confrontation with the question whether a large degree of 'internal' understanding of a discipline is necessary before one can problematise the contestable concepts that inform it, given that our method consists of a deliberate transgression of domain boundaries, and the practice of a kind of poetics of transfer. This question of domain specificity was a main subject of debate in critical thinking circles in the late 1980s, and centred around issues of epistemological subject specificity, interfield commonalities, transfer, and the feasibility of general thinking skills (Ennis, 1989; McPeck, 1981, 1990; Perkins and Salomon, 1989). Nor are the issues raised by that debate resolved.

7. The discussion plans that follow were developed in a fifth-grade classroom in a public school in Montclair, NJ, as part of a curriculum pilot project currently being conducted by the authors, using as text a philosophical novel focusing on mathematics, designed for upper elementary students.

REFERENCES

Adorno, T. W., Frenkel-Brunswik, E., Levinson, D. J. and Sanford, R. N. (1950) *The Authoritarian Personality* (New York, Harper and Row).

Bohm, D. [1996] (2004) *On Dialogue*, L. Nichol, ed. (London, Routledge).

Corrington, R. (1992) *Nature and Spirit: An Essay in Ecstatic Naturalism* (New York, Fordham University Press).

Davydov, V. V. (1988) Problems of Developmental Teaching, *Soviet Education*, 30.8, pp. 15–97; 30.9, pp. 3–83; 30.10, pp. 3–77.

Davydov, V. V. (1990) *Types of Generalization in Instruction: Logical and Psychological Problems in the Structuring of School Curricula* (Reston, VA, National Council of Teachers of Mathematics).

Davydov, V. V. (1993) Three Perspectives on Activity Theory, *Multidisciplinary Newsletter for Activity Theory*, 13.14, pp. 50–53.

Deleuze, G. and Guattari, F. (1980) *A Thousand Plateaus: Capitalism and Schizophrenia*, B. Masumi, trans (Minneapolis, MN, University of Minnesota Press).

Deleuze, G. and Guattari, F. (1994) *What is Philosophy?* (New York, Columbia University Press).

Dewey, J. (1898) *How We Think* (Boston, MA, Houghton Mifflin).

Dewey, J. (1916) *Democracy and Education* (New York, Macmillan).

Dewey, J. (1922) *Human Nature and Conduct* (Carbondale, IL, Southern Illinois University Press).

Dewey, J. (1938) *Logic: The Theory of Inquiry* (New York, Henry Holt).

Ennis, R. H. (1989) Critical Thinking and Subject Specificity: Clarification and Needed Research, *Educational Researcher*, 18.3, pp. 4–10.

Fromm, E. (1941) *Escape from Freedom* (New York, Rinehart and Co.).

Habermas, J. (1984) *The Theory of Communicative Action* (Boston, MA, Beacon Press).

Kelly, G. A. (1963) *A Theory Of Personality* (New York, W.W. Norton).

Kennedy, D. (1997) The Five Communities, *Inquiry: Critical Thinking Across the Disicplines*, 16.4, pp. 66–86.

Kennedy, D. (1999a) Thinking For Oneself and With Others, *Analytic Teaching*, 20.1, pp. 40–45.

Kennedy, D. (1999b) Philosophy for Children and the Reconstruction of Philosophy, *Metaphilosophy*, 30.4, pp. 338–359.

Kennedy, D. (2004a) The Role of a Facilitator in a Community of Philosophical Inquiry, *Metaphilosophy*, 35.5, pp. 744–765.

Kennedy, D. (2004b) Communal Philosophical Dialogue and the Intersubject, *International Journal of Applied Philosophy*, 18.2, pp. 203–218.

Kennedy, N. S. (2005) *The Role of Paradox in Argumentation and Concept Transformation in a Community of Mathematical Inquiry: A Dialectical Analysis*. UMI Dissertation Publishing, UMI ID: 921046091.

Kennedy, N. S. and Kennedy, D. (2010) Between Chaos and Entropy: Community of Inquiry from a Systems Perspective, *Complicity: An International Journal of Complexity and Education*, 7.2. http://ejournals.library.ualberta.ca/index.php/complicity/index.

Lave, J. and Wenger, E. (1991) *Situated Learning: Legitimate Peripheral Participation* (Cambridge, Cambridge University Press).

Leontiev, A. (1978) *Activity, Consciousness and Personality* (Englewood Cliffs, NJ, Prentice-Hall).

Levinas, E. (1969) *Totality and Infinity*, A. Lingis, trans. (Pittsburgh, PA, Duquesne University Press).

Lipman, M. (2003) *Thinking in Education*, 2nd edn. (Cambridge, Cambridge University Press).

Lipman, M., Sharp, A. M. and Oscanyon, F. S. (1980) *Philosophy in the Classroom*, 2nd edn. (Philadelphia, PA, Temple University Press).

Lipman, M., Sharp, A. M. and Oscanyon, F. S. (1984) *Philosophical Inquiry: An Instructional Manual to Accompany Harry Stottlemeier's Discovery*, 2nd edn. (Lanham, MD, University Press of America).

Lipman, M. and Gazzard, A. (1987) *Getting Our Thoughts Together: Instructional Manual to Accompany Elfie* (Montclair, NJ, Institute for the Advancement of Philosophy for Children).

Lushyn, P. (2002) The Paradoxical Nature of Facilitation in Community of Inquiry, *Analytic Teaching*, 24.2, pp. 110–115.

Lushyn, P. and Kennedy, D. (2000) The Psychodynamics of Community of Inquiry and Educational Reform: A Cross-Cultural Perspective, *Thinking: The Journal of Philosophy for Children*, 15.3, pp. 9–16.

Lushyn, P. and Kennedy, D. (2003) Power, Manipulation, and Control in a Community of Inquiry, *Analytic Teaching*, 23.2, pp. 103–110.

McPeck, J. E. (1981) *Critical Thinking and Education* (New York, St. Martin's Press).

McPeck, J. E. (1990) Critical Thinking and Subject Specificity: A Reply to Ennis, *Educational Researcher*, 19.4, pp. 10–12.

Mead, G. H. (1934) *Mind, Self, and Society* (Chicago, IL, University of Chicago Press).

Mercer, N. (1994) Neo-Vygotskian Theory and Classroom Education, in: B. Stierer and J. Maybin (eds) *Language, Literacy, and Learning in Educational Practice* (pp. 92–110. London, Open University).

Perkins, D. N. and Salomon, G. (1989) Are Cognitive Skills Context-Bound?, *Educational Researcher*, 18.1, pp. 16–25.

Peirce, C. S. (1966) The Fixation of Belief, in: P. Weiner (ed.) *Selected Writings* (New York, Dover).

Piaget, J. (1952) *The Origins of Intelligence in Children*, M. Cook, trans. (New York, International Universities Press).

Piaget, J. (1970) *Structuralism*, C. Maschler, trans. (New York, Harper and Row).

Rogoff, B. (1990) *Apprenticeship in Thinking* (New York, Oxford University Press).

Splitter, L. and Sharp, A. M. (1995) *Teaching for Better Thinking: The Classroom Community of Inquiry* (Melbourne, ACER).

Vygotsky, L. (1978) *Mind in Society: The Development of Higher Psychological Processes* (Cambridge, MA, Harvard University Press).

Wertsch, J. V. (1991) *Voices of the Mind: A Sociocultural Approach to Mediated Action* (Cambridge, MA, Harvard University Press).

Wittgenstein, L. (1969) *On Certainty*, D. Paul and G. E. M Anscombe, trans. (New York, Harper and Row).

7

The Provocation of an Epistemological Shift in Teacher Education through Philosophy with Children

JOANNA HAYNES AND KARIN MURRIS

POSITIVE CHALLENGES

Philosophy has not been part of the school curriculum in most countries. Over the last three decades interest in Philosophy with Children (P4C/ PwC)[1] has grown. It has stimulated rich debate about the nature of philosophy, philosophy with children and philosophy in school curricula. The practice has been dismissed by some as faddish, therapeutic navel-gazing, and a distraction from serious content knowledge (Ecclestone and Hayes, 2009). Other critics have questioned the philosophical integrity of the practice or the instrumentalism of its aims (Biesta, 2009; Gledhill, 2008; Long, 2005; Vansieleghem, 2005). Some have argued that 'real' philosophy is too difficult for children (Kitchener, 1990; White, 1992; Wilson, 1992). In educational circles, PwC has caused valuable disturbance, and we wholeheartedly welcome serious exploration of the ground opened up through the introduction of philosophy with children, an educational approach which is in its infancy. This article argues that the bringing together of philosophy and child calls for creative and fresh discussion of teacher education and professional development and that the community of enquiry characteristic of PwC offers a critical framework for such a project.

The new territory creates uncertainty for a number of reasons. Very few philosophy graduates are employed as primary or secondary school teachers. Teachers lack familiarity with both content and methods of philosophy. Even for someone with a background in philosophy, PwC offers significant positive challenges with its demands for radically open listening. The pedagogy of PwC assumes an epistemological shift in the

Philosophy for Children in Transition: Problems and Prospects, First Edition. Nancy Vansieleghem and David Kennedy. Chapters © 2012 The Authors. Editorial organization © 2012 Philosophy of Education Society of Great Britain. Published 2012 by Blackwell Publishing Ltd.

role of the educator and an open countenance towards philosophy. It implies a changed balance of power between educator and learner. We aim to practice PwC as a critical pedagogy[2] that challenges predominant constructs of both 'child' and 'philosophy' and enables transformative experiences of thinking and dialogue for both children and educators who take part in it (see Haynes and Murris, in press). PwC usually takes place within the arguably undemocratic space of compulsory schooling. It is undemocratic in the sense that children have no choice but to be there, little say in the content and direction of their learning, and minimal influence in wider aspects of school life. The curriculum in many countries is highly prescribed; teaching is led by assessment and the customary emphasis on fast paced teaching and exam results may appear at odds with the 'slow-burn' pedagogy of PwC. It is 'slow-burn' in that it relies on the teacher placing considerable trust in participatory ways of working that, little by little, enable learners to think for themselves, in collaboration with others in their group. It takes practice for learners to share responsibility for making good judgments in respect of each enquiry. Teachers may hesitate to adopt deeper approaches that take time to establish, such as PwC, in spite of considerable evidence to demonstrate their positive impact on learning and achievement (e.g. SAPERE, 2006; Trickey and Topping, 2004, 2007).

TEACHING THROUGH DEMOCRACY

When approached as a critical pedagogy, PwC cannot be a matter simply of introducing a once-a-week lesson where children are allowed to ask questions and influence the direction of enquiry. It involves learners' participation in democratic life itself as 'communicative democrats' (Enslin, Pendlebury and Tjiattas, 2001, p. 129), which needs to be reflected in the internal organisation of a school as non-hierarchical and non-authoritarian (Biesta, 2006, p. 125). Critical pedagogues seek to sustain and extend the democratic process through making power more accountable. School is a site of struggle and social change and critical pedagogues value freedom of expression for students and seek an active role for learners in the social production of meaning in the classroom. A participatory democracy implies that people rule—not through representation, but through participation. As a political concept, participatory democracy is understood to include moral principles such as freedom and equality of opportunity (see in particular Kelly, 1995), and it is assumed that schools make space for children to participate as citizens in contexts that are meaningful to them. From a pedagogical perspective, the participatory nature of a democracy suggests a non-authoritarian approach that emphasises self-regulation and reasonableness, which requires schools to make room for young children to strengthen their reasoning skills and to participate through deliberation in democratic processes. To advocate academic freedom and to make room for the voices of learners is to take a moral and a political stance. A participatory democracy presupposes non-dualist epistemologies and implies that all voices in the classroom, including those of teachers, are viewed as partial and as needing to be questioned as part and parcel of the open discourse (see Haynes, 2007). To realise such values in the course of everyday life in classrooms makes particular demands on PwC practitioners—to reflect on their exercise of authority, to listen attentively to students, to negotiate the curriculum, to create opportunities for student decision-making.

PwC has to take account of the inequality and injustice that constrain children and young people's participation in classroom dialogue—it has to recognise its own limitations, to be considered as a democratic pedagogy. This has implications for the education of PwC practitioners. Critical pedagogues understand that institutional authority does not just disappear when teachers opt for alternative teaching and learning methods (Lensmire, 1998). There certainly is the risk that the 'success' of Western dialogical pedagogies is idealised, as, for example, by South African teacher educator Jonathan Jansen when he argues that, especially in authoritarian societies (as opposed to Western educational practice),

> [w]hen students initiate a question, the familiar impulse of the educator is to anticipate and correct, respond and direct an answer toward the goals of the lesson. This representation of the teacher as the authority who knows all and who controls the classroom is routinely presumed in texts and manuals on classroom management and student discipline. It is especially the case that when controversial questions or difficult subjects emerge, the teacher is even more attentive to 'managing' the classroom situation lest things get out of control (Jansen, 2009, p. 263).

What our selection of critical episodes aims to show is how PwC positively disrupts or interrupts the implicit epistemological frameworks that inform educators (in)formal practices of teaching through telling, demonstrating authority, and imparting knowledge. Supporters of critical pedagogy cannot assume that their approaches will redress the imbalance of power and create a qualitative change in relationships. Lensmire (1998) suggests that in practice teachers' encouragement of students' participation and agency is sometimes not so far from coercion in the classroom. Innovations soon become routines. In the attempt to make classroom practice more democratic there is always a fine and complex balance. Any critical approach has to acknowledge the partiality of teachers and the risks of idealising teaching as dialogue. The disruptiveness of philosophical teaching by the PwC facilitator often throws up ethical problems and choices for educators, it reveals contradictions and moral dilemmas, as we will illustrate with a selection of critical episodes in this article.

A deeply responsive framework for practice, underpinned by a thoroughly explored and well-articulated epistemological perspective, is needed for the complex judgments required in teaching PwC. This can begin to provide teachers with the confidence and understanding to adopt more philosophically informed approaches in their wider practice.

A PHILOSOPHICAL FRAMEWORK FOR PRACTICE—SOME OBSTACLES

Our critical episodes show how one major obstacle to a *philosophical* approach to PwC is the prevalent *psychological* paradigm in education. To illustrate, Jansen suggests that the success of a new post-authoritarian pedagogy in South Africa, for example, is attributable to there being highly skilled teachers who are confident in their subject matter and comfortable with diverse students who can manage difficult thematic knowledge (Jansen, 2009, p. 263). He emphasises the importance of 'active' and 'attentive' listening, but his conceptual framework is psychological (p. 264), in that the teacher listens 'for the pain that lies behind a claim', and is alert to 'the distress that is concealed in an angry outburst' or 'the sense of loss that is protested in a strident posture'. Moreover, it is individualistic and undemocratic in that the teacher is firmly in charge of all the important decision-making. Significantly, the teacher is the person who asks the questions and manages the classroom exchanges psychologically. Examples of such questions are: 'What are you afraid of?', 'Why do you feel so strongly about that?', 'Has this happened to you before? Tell me about it'. Although 'emotional attunement' (p. 264) is indeed essential for thoughtful educational practice, we argue in this article for a *philosophical* response to the emotions involved, as will be exemplified in the critical incidents below, which necessitates in this context a 'listening out' for opportunities to explore the implicit epistemological beliefs that teachers bring to their practice—for example, what counts as progress in enquiry, what truth is, which questions are valuable for knowledge acquisition and what the relationship is between question and answer. What the critical incidents show is the constructive role of PwC in opening up a space in teacher education to problematise the apparently straightforward meaning of key educational concepts (e.g. knowledge, truth) and significantly different terms (e.g. between knowledge and understanding, meaning and truth). Without such pedagogical awareness and facilitation skills, the non-relational, dualist epistemological assumptions of the transmission view of knowledge assumed in authoritarian education will remain firmly embedded in teachers' way of life.[3]

Another obstacle to more philosophically informed approaches to PwC practice is that much current evaluation of PwC tends to focus on students' 'performance'—the instrumentalism mentioned in the introduction. What is 'measured' is the impact of PwC on other aspects of educational attainment, level of intelligence, self esteem or test results. In order to get a foot in the classroom, PwC practitioners often justify the inclusion of

PwC in the curriculum by arguing that it will produce more 'skilled' thinkers, readers, writers, team-players, selves or citizens. Whilst recognising the pragmatic need for such initiatives and assessments when operating within mainstream education, we believe that such overtly instrumental pre-occupations can detract from the ways in which philosophical thinking can enrich and strengthen all education. Targets hinder authentic, open-ended philosophical exploration.

The contested nature of education, philosophy and child means that politically and philosophically sensitive forms of evaluation of PwC are required, taking into account social conditions and pushing at the boundaries of current theory and practice in education. A deeper approach to evaluation is needed, that not only measures impact on children's learning, but also genuinely informs teacher education and professional development. We understand this project as a form of ongoing practitioner action research, framed as 'thoughtful practice'. Our article illustrates our framework for ongoing refinement of philosophical practice with children, via the investigation of salient events and anecdotes (Haynes, 2007, 2009; Tripp, 1993; Van Manen, 1997) and through analysis of recurring moments of disequilibrium (Murris, 2009b) in the context of our experience in the field over the last two decades. We will return to our motivation for such a research methodology at the end of this article.

THE EDUCATOR IN PHILOSOPHICAL PRACTICE

Facilitation of philosophical enquiries involves many intuitive decisions, and reaches far beyond the mechanical application of a philosophical toolbox. It requires complex, practical judgments balancing critical, creative, caring and collaborative thinking as well as exercising social intellectual virtues, such as courage, modesty, honesty, respect, patience, awareness and constructiveness in giving and receiving critical challenge (Quinn, 1997). Burbules also acknowledges the importance of moral virtues in what it means to be a reasonable person. His subtle account of reason includes sensitivity to cultural difference and diversity, modesty about claims to universality, situatedness in human relations and moral reflection, and groundedness in the practical, social activities of speaking, listening and reflection (Burbules, 1995, pp. 87, 88). Matthew Lipman, compares progress in a classroom community of enquiry with the movement of a boat tacking into the wind (Lipman, 1991, pp. 15, 16). The teacher as facilitator supports the sailors of the boat in their effort to construct new knowledge by building (and helping others to build) on each other's ideas. Without grounded, situated interventions from the facilitator the boat will float like driftwood, especially in the beginning. Lipman and others insist that knowledge of academic philosophy, and especially logic, is crucial for progress to be made (Lipman *et al*., 1977). To what extent immersion in the discipline of philosophy is a necessary source of significant moves by the philosophical facilitator is not the focus of this article (see e.g. Murris, 1999, 2000). One challenge is to consider how best to support teachers who are seeking such knowledge. Academic philosophy does not necessarily provide the skills or the courage to engage and support others in philosophical conversations.[4] Our project over the last twenty years has been to find an embedded way of working collaboratively with teachers to develop philosophical facilitation, starting from their direct experiences.

It is our experience that the rigour of philosophically building on ideas causes anxiety to some PwC educators with little philosophy in their educational background. The democratic practice and respect for child that the theory presupposes often generates discomfort and disturbance with *all* educators, including many philosophically trained PwC educators. In other words, knowledge of the history of philosophical ideas is not the only matter to be explored in relation to the role of the teacher in PwC. There is something else going on that has much wider relevance to adult/child relations in the context of education.

The implementation of a pedagogy that profoundly questions the power balance in schools, the status of knowledge and the existing prejudice against children's ability to think abstractly from a much earlier age than suggested by, for example, developmental psychologists, is much harder to achieve in an educational culture that divorces theory from practice. One's answers to the philosophical questions 'Who has authority to speak?' or 'What is "child"?' alter what counts as valuable in education. Naturally, teachers bring their epistemological and metaphysical assumptions to their practice, and the pedagogy of PwC gives rise to 'critical moments' of uncertainty, and therefore insecurity, in the facilitation role (Haynes, 2005, 2008; Haynes and Murris, 2009; Murris, 2009b), which provokes a positive re-thinking of one's role as educator in teaching and learning.

These critical moments regularly emerge in our own practice as teacher educators and expose educators' struggle with the changed teacher-learner relationships that are possible in PwC. The uncertainty and insecurity is also a product of teachers' public role and accountability in the current climate, one that is often fearful about childhood. The examples of such moments that follow offer rich opportunities to engage in dialogue with teachers about the 'rough ground'[5] of practice. They have made us pause and reflect on our own role as teacher educators.

In our professional work with teachers we have noted moments of experience that seem to be particularly troublesome and disturbing for (student) teachers and identified certain recurring themes. These are what we term 'recurring moments of disequilibrium', and we believe these to be particularly instructive.

We have grouped some of these moments into a non-exhaustive list of recurring themes, and each is discussed briefly in the section that follows. The examples illustrate clearly the educative and philosophical value of disruption and disequilibrium. It is learning how to make use of this rough material that can help shape PwC practice and offer pointers in enabling teachers to take up their philosophical role.

RECURRING THEMES IN THE PRACTICE OF PWC EDUCATORS
Preparing for the Unexpected

Even in the West, teachers are used to a culture of schooling that prioritises 'transmission' of knowledge. Teaching in PwC contrasts strongly with teaching through a lesson plan with clear direction and outcomes. In PwC, learners are invited to raise questions in response to material (initially) chosen by the teacher, such as texts and/or images. Learners are collectively responsible for choosing which questions to pursue. The 'answering' of these questions, through critical reasoning, forms the content of subsequent lessons. The questions raised are not known in advance of the lesson and teachers cannot plan in the same way as usual. Our experience is that teachers often embrace wholeheartedly the searching questions. However, the open space can be alarming as teachers feel pulled between the educational promise of the questions and the constraints of time, immediately measurable results, what can and cannot be talked about, and wider accountability. There may be a temptation to fall back on prescribed 'thinking skills' resources or exercises that do not deliver the same quality and depth of engagement and participation. Similarly, teacher educators can often be persuaded that PwC knowledge can be standardised and transmitted through ready-made packages. Such programmes with their suggestions of 'ground that needs to be covered' can stifle dialogical and philosophical responses.

Implications for Teacher Education   The disequilibrium here is prompted by the difficulty in articulating the educational value of PwC within the dominant epistemological framework of knowledge 'delivery' as well as justifying the time spent. What PwC reveals is the pressing need for an epistemological project in education offering opportunities to explore the contested meanings of key concepts, such as 'understanding', 'skill', 'knowledge', 'meaning' and 'truth'. By the same token it also provides the means to open up such a professional dialogue through the community of enquiry methodology. Teacher education should engage (student) teachers with tentative talk and with preparing for the unexpected in classrooms. The challenge is how to create conditions for responsive teaching in the face of teachers' lack of confidence and habits of 'delivering' lessons.

Non-linear Progression

A second significant recurring theme identified is the frustration educators experience when a dialogue fails to progress in a linear direction. We often hear remarks such as 'They are going round in circles', or 'They keep going off on a tangent'. Apart from the earlier mentioned 'boat-tacking-into-the-wind' metaphor, Lipman uses another helpful analogy for progression in enquiry. He compares the progress a classroom community makes with walking. When you walk, you constantly shift your weight from your left foot to your right and so on (Lipman, 1991, p. 229), and the balance between forces is simultaneously restored in the movement. What initially appears to be linear 'progress' is in fact part of a larger spiral, or just another 'string of spaghetti' without beginning or end (Murris and Haynes, 2002, 2010; Murris, 2011; see also endnote 3). The 'products' of such spiralling enquiries are 'reasonable judgments' and as such are never set in stone, but are understood as 'temporary resting places' (Lipman, 1991, pp. 17, 65). Influenced by various metaphors (e.g. the metaphor of knowledge-as-a-tree) people tend to believe that arguments should have a goal, a beginning, and should proceed in a linear fashion (Murris, 1997). Metaphor-saturated everyday language shapes educators' expectations of what constitutes educational progress and what counts as the content of a lesson. It also explains why practitioners often emphasise the need to frequently return to the original question.

Implications for Teacher Education The issue of 'progress' in PwC is a matter of practical judgment, made by the self-critical classroom community of enquiry. The practical judgments involved in the philosophical work are regulated democratically through 'artful'[6] facilitation initially by the teacher.[7] For example, on some occasions, participants may decide to abandon or reformulate their original starting question for enquiry. On other occasions, they may prefer to stick with it. PwC questions not only the idea that progress in conceptual enquiry can be made in individual lesson 'units', it also places the participants at the heart of the decision-making about whether progress has been made. Such open-endedness is at odds with the current norm of lesson management.

   The disequilibrium in PwC draws attention to the need to reconsider progress and the nature of content in dialogue. Content is constructed by the enquiring community. Much of the philosophical work involved is linguistic. It focuses in particular on the conceptual nature of our thinking as opposed to transmission of content knowledge. PwC challenges common assumptions in education about the teaching of subject knowledge, e.g. geography, science or history, and the possibility of *describing* the world-as-it-is, unmediated by human ideas and language. PwC proposes to engage communities of enquiry in the kind of thinking that, for example, geographers, scientists or historians routinely are involved in, and it offers opportunities to problematise the concepts inherent within those disciplines.

The Difficulty of Asking Philosophical Questions

The problem around 'progress' is closely related to many educators' difficulty in making sufficiently clear distinctions between psychological and philosophical questions. One reason for this is the association commonly made between the abstract or symbolic and the philosophical. An example from an in-service course illustrates the complexity involved in formulating philosophical questions.

The traditional English nursery rhyme *Humpty Dumpty*[8] was used to show teachers how they could organise and facilitate a PwC session in their classrooms. Teachers new to PwC had selected the question: 'Once broken, can we be fixed?' to begin their enquiry. The challenges here for teacher education are profound. Firstly, *symbolic* readings of texts are often equated with *philosophical* readings of texts. Educators are quick to learn to identify abstract philosophical concepts and to generate philosophical questions with a 'what is . . . ?' structure. Abstract concepts with a social or personal theme are particularly popular: e.g. 'What is friendship?', 'What is happiness?' By contrast, questions about time or infinity are unlikely to be followed up—even when students raise them. However, this new-found knowledge can easily become a technique, giving educators what looks like a foolproof tool to help tell the difference between 'good' and 'bad' philosophical questions. In the *Humpty Dumpty* example, the follow-up philosophical questions became 'What is "fixed"?' and 'What is "broken"'?

Such moves in a philosophical enquiry are often born of the belief that experiences and objects *have* inherent properties that can be 'captured' by definitions. This implicit objectivist epistemology helps to explain the struggle to distinguish between abstract discussions and philosophical investigations. For us, philosophy with children is concerned with the *interactional properties* of a concept—that is, how people *use* the concept in a variety of situated contexts. Progress is made in an enquiry when the meanings of central concepts are illuminated and new understandings constructed collaboratively by locating a concept, an activity or a story in a framework which is connected to something in our own experience (Splitter and Sharp, 1995, p. 71).

Wittgenstein warned against using abstract concepts without the contextualisation of everyday language and a form of life (Wittgenstein, 1958). After all, embedding abstract philosophical questions in concrete experiences or narratives cannot be reduced to a *technique*; it requires practical wisdom and knowledge of the history of philosophical ideas. On the whole, educators struggle with the difference between psychological and philosophical responses to abstract questions (see e.g. Gardner, 1995). What counts as an explanation in science, history or mathematics is different in philosophy, as the answers to philosophical questions remain contestable. In the *Humpty Dumpty* example, a philosophical way forward would be to question the validity of the assumption in the question: Is it indeed true that we can be 'broken'? What does it mean for a self to be 'broken'? Does a self need to be 'whole' before it can be 'broken'? Where or what is this 'self'? Even when a procedure has been agreed upon by the enquiring community, to answer these questions (e.g. conceptual analysis), a necessary meta-move is to question the procedure itself on its sufficiency or validity.[9]

Implications for Teacher Education Philosophical teaching can be frustrating. (Student) teachers sometimes resist the struggle involved in conceptual labour and the formulation of good philosophical questions that such labour presupposes. Philosophical practice with children challenges teachers to examine why psychological responses are more usual and validated in everyday educational practice. It opens up opportunities to explore with (student) teachers what constitutes the 'right' question when facilitating learning, and who 'owns' them, which is another recurring theme to which we now turn.

Students' Ownership of Questions

We often notice the desire to avoid conflict in philosophical enquiry. Teachers work on the basis that they generally *know* what might upset children or teachers and therefore try and avoid certain topics. This practice influences who is asking the questions and which questions are encouraged and avoided. In PwC, children's interests and questions shape the content and direction of an enquiry, and the children are also co-responsible for its procedures, its rules and its identity. We have frequently noticed that taboo or sensitive topics, such as death, sex or religion—even when children have chosen to talk about them—can trigger censorious reactions in teachers as well as PwC educators (Haynes and Murris, 2009, in press). More or less subtle choices of facilitation strategies (e.g. by using a procedure called 'blind voting'[10]) can substantially change the course of an enquiry, sometimes motivated by a concern on the part of the teachers to protect others, and possibly also themselves.

The epistemological significance here is that the extent to which philosophical enquiries are meaningful depends on the connections and links made by the community between abstract concepts or ideas, and the interests and experiences of its members. When, for example, using the picturebook *Angry Arthur* (Oram and Kitamura, 1993), young children have asked unexpected questions such as 'Why is only his bed left?', or 'Is he going to die now?'—these can startle teachers. This humorous, gloriously illustrated picturebook features Arthur, who is so angry after his Mum has refused his request to stay up later and watch television that he causes first a storm cloud, then a hurricane, then a typhoon and finally a universequake. After all this destruction, we see him sitting on his bed stuck to a broken-off piece of planet Mars floating in space. He comments that he cannot remember why he was so angry in the first place. Teachers' motivation to use this book is around the topic of anger: how it manifests itself, how it can get out of hand and how unreasonable it can be. Prepared with a list of ready-made questions, the story can be used to give a clear moral lesson: some thinking time in your bedroom can calm you down, bring you to your senses and restore equilibrium. Educators have expressed their interest in using *Angry Arthur* as a useful tool for children to learn to control and manage their emotions.[11]

Used philosophically this picturebook can raise some fascinating questions—questions to which adults also have no certain answers. Are we always angry *because of* something? Alternatively, can a seemingly obvious cause—for example, not being allowed to watch a television programme—hide a deeper reason or cause (for example, being neglected or unfairly treated)? Following Aristotle, one reading might be that Arthur holds the cognitive belief (not just the feeling or emotion) that his mother has slighted him. She is responsible for him not watching television and he perceives it as morally unjustified (Kristjánsson, 2005, pp. 673, 4). Could it, for example, be the case that usually he *is* allowed to stay up and watch television, but for some reason (visitors?) he is not now? Or, perhaps she is just inconsistent in her parenting: sometimes he is, and sometimes he is not allowed, and this is never properly communicated or negotiated? The story could also easily provoke questions about mothers and involve an exploration of our moral expectations of mothers and their constructed identities.

Implications for Teacher Education Educators can be anxious about not knowing the questions in advance, and can be reluctant to regard children as experts in respect of their experiences. A willingness to experiment and play with new ideas, such as the significance of the object 'bed' in a human life, demands philosophical steps from the known to the unknown in which the educator needs to resist the urge to 'translate' what is being said into the more familiar terms normally embodied in the curriculum.[12] If not, children will simply conform to teachers' efforts to control.

The disequilibrium is associated with feeling perplexed or at a loss. What PwC offers here is the experience of how the Socratic facilitator is like a stingray that numbs not only others but also itself. If a teacher allows herself to be as perplexed as the learner, a space is opened up in which the role of the teacher is that of a co-enquirer and co-researcher (Murris, 2009b).

Epistemological and Moral Relativism

Our final theme in this article is the popular view—found even in PwC teacher education[13]—that philosophy has no *right or wrong answers*. Such a reassurance can indeed be liberating for teachers and students new to PwC and may have psychological benefits, but it fails to communicate the rigour required to make PwC philosophical. PwC does aim to give equal opportunities for participants to speak, where every participant is a potential source of insight and worthy of being listened to responsively. But it is not the case that 'anything goes' or is accepted uncritically: some contributions can still be treated as invalid, incorrect or irrelevant by the community of enquiry. To support and guide the building of ideas, grounding in philosophical thinking (e.g. informal logic) can be helpful.

It could be the case that such explicit permission to others to express opinions freely, without insisting on philosophical rigour, significantly reduces a teacher's *own* anxiety about a lack of knowledge in the area in question. Also, there is a significant political and moral dimension to this recurring theme. In teacher education, even gentle, open disagreement and challenge are sometimes rejected as 'rude' or 'impolite' and avoided because they cause discomfort. Our experience is that emotional disturbance tends to be avoided in teacher education and professional development, even when it offers rich opportunities for the community of enquiry to explore its values and procedures at meta-level, and to strengthen its practice. Race and racism often crop up as problematic 'no-go' areas. When, for example, during a PwC course a teacher objected to a teacher educator's use of Edward de Bono's 'black hat'[14] (because of its apparent racist connotations), most members of this enquiry struggled with a subsequent attempt to explore the meta-question asked by the facilitator: 'What are the words, phrases and questions we should and should not use?' The teacher who had raised the issue originally was firmly committed to a particular answer from the outset (that the particular strategy was indeed racist), and the others seemed determined to restoration of the peace. We know that the dialogical process can press some painful buttons and do not avoid but seek the 'upheaval of thought'[15] it may provoke. We value the rich openings philosophical teaching creates for everyone involved to play freely with new ideas. The aim of education should not be a mere focusing on the acquisition of knowledge, or a process of socialisation into an existing order, but to speak with one's own voice and to bring something new into the world (see, for example, Biesta, 2010). The pedagogy thrives on dissensus and disagreement as it enables opinions to be put to the test and subjected to critical scrutiny, guided by experienced facilitators who need to be able to have the courage to be moved and changed by what happens in a community with others who are different from them.

The disequilibrium PwC provokes is the encounter with difference and diversity at a religious, political, cultural and social level. Tolerance is often wrongly confused with the implicit belief that opinions cannot and should not be challenged—even in respectful dialogue. Although various individuals or cultures may disagree about the moral correctness of certain ideas or practices, it does not follow that therefore some of them are not morally wrong. Just because someone holds a belief, it does not follow that this belief is right, as, for example, is implicit in the often heard expression in SA, 'In my culture we believe that . . . ', and what is implied is that therefore you are not in a position to disagree with a practice if you do not belong to that culture (see, for example, Rachels, 2009).[16] This relativist position amounts to confusing the *cultural* with the *moral*, which has profound implications for social justice. PwC makes it possible to enquire into the validity of moral relativism and notions such as knowledge and truth in teacher education.

THE VALUE OF ONGOING PRACTITIONER ACTION RESEARCH

The motivation for our particular methodology arises from the desire to strengthen freedom of expression, in order to encourage criticality and self-criticality, and to increase democratic participation in education. To guard against the pitfalls of pure instrumentalism and to reflect the methods through which our professional work in education has evolved, we have adopted a stance of ongoing philosophical enquiry, mirroring the critically reflective methodology of PwC. We refer to this as *philosophical* practitioner action research.

Our ongoing enquiry sets out to tap our experiences as teachers of children, students, student teachers, teachers and teacher educators in PwC. We put these experiences to work to achieve further pedagogic refinement through practical judgment.[17] For Joseph Dunne, practical judgment is not the *application* of theories to particular cases (Dunne, 1997, p. 157), and the implications for teaching are that 'teacher's capacity for reasoning cannot first be taught 'in theory' and then applied "in practice"' (Kristjánsson, 2007, p. 166). In his characterisation of the 'life of practice' Dunne adopts Wittgenstein's metaphor of 'rough ground' to express the need for flexibility, responsiveness and improvisation on the one hand and the need for 'rooted-ness', on the other. Such rootedness is available through a practitioner's history of participation in the community of practice itself, through 'grounding' in its dispositions and the subtleties of its culture. Dunne cautions that this particular notion of a 'field of practice' is questionable in a technique and target orientated world of education (Dunne, 1997, p. 378). To work in the contemporary world of education is often to experience a kind of schizophrenia, to hear competing voices clamouring for attention.

We argue that it is possible to create an authentic and humane space in the university or school classroom and to hold on to the sense that practice, of both research and teaching, has an 'open texture' (Dunne, 1997, p. 379). Rather than PwC being an approach to teaching that we seek to apply or *do* to others, then evaluating their performance within it, its dialogical enquiry methodology is one that we internalise, a practical everyday philosophy, extending beyond our PwC 'lessons'. Morwenna Griffiths argues that practical philosophy is 'with and for' rather than 'about or applied to' (Griffiths, 2003, p. 21), and it acknowledges its origins in the concrete communities in which it operates and then seeks to speak 'to something more universal, to something inclusive of, for instance, classroom teachers as well as academics, and young people as well as teachers' (Griffiths and Cotton, 2005).

The significance of personal experience, of 'rootedness' (Dunne, 1997) and of 'situational understanding' (Elliott, 2006) are also expressed in feminist approaches to enquiry, which Maxine Greene and Griffiths characterise as 'less a theory—or a set of theories—and more a perspective, a lens, a handle on the world and its ideas, a way of acting and speaking' (Greene and Griffiths, 2003, p. 77). For Greene and Griffiths, this perspective is held together by certain preoccupations, not necessarily exclusive to feminism, and 'each philosopher marked by feminism makes her own trajectory' (2003, p. 75). Our article offers an account of our 'situated philosophy'—a view from *somewhere* that has taken its bearings from the guideposts of our lived experience, just as Greene and Griffiths argue 'we cannot be the unmoved movers, or take the view from nowhere' (2003, p. 77).

The integration of wider political and professional concerns and the situated outlook of this article are rooted in an orientation towards social justice (Griffiths, 1998; Sikes, Nixon and Carr, 2003) as well as in feminist perspectives in philosophy (Benhabib, 1992; Greene and Griffiths, 2003). This integration expresses connections between passion, imagination and reason, and between private and public domains, shaping our understanding particularly of what it means to listen and what it means for children and (student) teachers to participate in philosophical dialogues. These ethics are articulated through the exploration of significant moments and through their narrative representation. Seyla Benhabib (1992) suggests that female experience tends historically to be attuned to the narrative structure of action and the standpoint of the concrete 'other', or what she terms the art of the particular. The concrete and particular events presented here as critical episodes, emerge from many enquiries with children in different settings, as well as several years of training sessions with students and teachers, mainly in the UK and in South Africa, working with what is salient or troublesome.

Much large scale and funded evaluation in education is determined and framed by government policies and can be self-affirming. By contrast, grounded enquiry and research begin from what catches our attention or what is troublesome, and it can be structured via a practitioner action research approach. In this field of professional development a number of accounts are offered of events that trigger enquiry and alert us to a something that must be questioned. Jean McNiff refers to moments when practitioners identify a concern through a felt gap, or contradiction, between values and action (McNiff, 1993, p. 33). John Mason refers to these moments as 'noticing' and has distinguished 'forms of noticing' (Mason, 2002, p. 33) as well as practical processes for using these in a disciplined way to inform professional practical judgment. David Tripp (1993) suggests that incidents in practice become significant when they strikingly appear as examples of a wider social category or perspective (as is the case with our 'recurring themes' in PwC practice) or dramatically contrast with previous experience. These events stand out and can become turning points in professional life. The moment of surprise, awareness or noting the distinctive character of such events is a first step, but for the episode to become critical it has to be interpreted and interrogated (Tripp, 1993, p. 25). The salience of events in practice may not become conscious at the time of their happening.

An incident becomes critical when it leads to increased sensitivity to values and to a re-examination of implicit beliefs and ideas. Tripp writes:

> . . . critical incidents are not 'things' which exist independently of an observer and are awaiting discovery like gold nuggets or desert islands, but like all data, critical incidents are created. Incidents happen, but critical incidents are produced by the way we look at a situation: a critical incident is an interpretation of the significance of an event (p. 8).

Tripp argues that certain kinds of critical incident are more strongly directed towards biographical or to political understanding (p. 97). These are often emotionally charged and lead to searches into the origin of values expressed in a particular response to a situation. Such critical episodes help to describe the relationship between practitioners, students and their socio-political contexts and epistemological frameworks. A series of such incidents taken together made it possible to identify recurring themes, as we have shown in this article. This is the framework we have adopted in furthering our own practice and in our in-service and pre-service work. We have argued that such themes help to illuminate the ground that needs urgently to be explored.

Philosophical practitioners can play a crucial role in opening up new spaces for self-critical enquiry. The discovery of this role, and the epistemological shift it provokes, is the hub of the project of bringing philosophy into schools and universities. On the basis of our noticing of critical episodes in our practice, we have identified a number of recurring themes: meeting the unexpected; the nature of educational progress; the 'right' (philosophical) questions; the avoidance of conflict or the unknown; no right and wrong answers (relativism); tolerance versus challenging with reasons. These themes begin to form the epistemological project the practice of PwC opens up for teacher educators. The dialogical space opened up by PwC's community of enquiry pedagogy challenges educators to reflect on their own role in teaching and learning, and provokes questions about their implicit epistemological values and priorities. Teacher education needs to provide a much stronger foundation in philosophical methods that can inform professional practical judgments, by embedding them in the ongoing investigation of classroom practice and the lives of teachers and students in educational communities. Philosophy *in* education gives urgency to the philosophy *of* education.

NOTES

1. Some fifty years ago, and inspired by the philosophies of Plato and John Dewey, philosophy professor Matthew Lipman pioneered the teaching of philosophy to children as a response to his concerns that children do not think as well as they are capable of, or as is necessary for a well functioning truly democratic society. He speculated that early intervention through a logically, rather than empirically, sequenced specially-written curriculum would tap into children's original curiosity, sense of wonder and enthusiasm for intellectual enquiry, and strengthen their philosophical thinking. In collaboration with colleagues at the Institute for the Advancement of Philosophy for Children (IAPC) at Montclair State University (USA), he developed the Philosophy for Children (P4C) Program. Globally, it is the most widely used resource, and has also inspired others to create a variety of alternative resources and approaches to support teachers in their innovative work, either for practical reasons (e.g. shorter, cheaper), or for philosophical and pedagogical reasons. When Murris developed her own approach to P4C using picturebooks, Lipman requested for the sake of clarity in 1992 that she did not use 'Philosophy for Children' or 'P4C'. Since then she has used the phrase Philosophy with Children (PwC), which has also been taken up by others as it expresses the democratic and collaborative nature of the practice: philosophy adults do *with*, not *for* children. PwC practitioners differ in their choice of educational resource material, but on the whole there is consensus about the 'community of enquiry' as the PwC pedagogy. American pragmatist Charles Sanders Peirce (1839–1914) was the first to fuse together the terms 'community' and 'enquiry' in the domain of scientific inquiry, but it was Lipman who introduced the phrase to describe the pedagogy for teaching philosophy in schools. It is now used in all subject areas, with all age groups and also includes informal education
2. Critical pedagogy is concerned with critiquing educational institutions and transforming both education and society (See Freire, 1972; Giroux, 1988; Morrow and Torres, 2002). It aims for a better world. A critical pedagogy is one that seeks to redress social inequalities and challenge the prevailing social order and forms of discourse. It assumes that dominant groups in society tend to determine the dominant meanings attached to culture and that these are the meanings most commonly expressed through the official curriculum of schools.
3. In another paper (Murris, 2011), it is explained in more detail how certain constructions of knowledge and the use of metaphors shape our pedagogical practices. In contrast to the tree metaphor of knowledge (with a root, trunk and branches), conceptualizing knowledge differently, e.g. as an endless tangle of cooked spaghetti, makes it possible to conceptualise knowledge as non-hierarchical, shooting in all directions without beginnings or endings, and always *in between*. This profoundly challenges habits of thought about development, progression and the organisation and planning of lessons.
4. The matter of preparing teachers to facilitate PwC is the subject of ongoing debate in PwC communities and something that the authors of this paper are currently working on developing.
5. The motivation for this metaphor will be explained below.
6. Although 'artful' is often associated with 'devious', we still prefer this description to the more obvious choice of 'skilful' as philosophical facilitation is a practice involving tact, knowledge, insight and a myriad of highly complex ethical, political and aesthetic judgments. We resist a 'toolkit' or skills-based approach to PwC as mentioned at the beginning of this paper and further explained and argued for in many of our publications, including Haynes and Murris (in press).
7. Over time participants start to internalise the thinking moves that are regularly and authentically modelled by the educator.
8. The nursery rhyme goes as follows:

   Humpty Dumpty sat on a wall.
   Humpty Dumpty had a great fall.
   All the King's horses and all the King's men.
   Couldn't put Humpty together again.

9. In philosophy there are no set methods of asking or answering philosophical questions. Philosophy as a critical practice involves reflection on the adequateness or appropriateness of

established philosophical methods, as, for example, the method of conceptual analysis: a logical mapping of the territory. It presupposes that individuals can distance themselves from this logical geography and establish the objective rules of a concept's use. The empirical and inductive approach of analytical philosophers (how as a matter of fact do people use concept x or y?) can become the object of study in PwC teacher training. It could be argued, for example, that concept analysis prevents an imaginative and creative use of concepts and does not take into account the alternative point of view: that understanding a concept involves a situated knowing of how a concept shapes the lives of people who use it, and that therefore such enquiries are always relational and not the result of an atomistic, individualistic philosophical analysis (see, e.g., for an interesting discussion, Laverty, 2010).

10. With 'blind voting' all participants of an enquiry have their eyes closed during the voting process. The idea is that students will feel less inhibited and constrained by peer pressure and will make more genuine choices. However, it also makes it possible for the teacher to change the final result of the voting process as in theory there are no witnesses to who voted for which question or topic.

11. For an exploration of a philosophical approach to emotions in PwC, see Murris, 2009a

12. Interpreting transcripts of enquiries with children is profoundly complex. This needs to be explicitly thought through by researchers as the implicit criterion is often what is familiar and not the unexpected (see, in particular, Haynes and Murris, 2009).

13. See, for example, the DVD *Thinking Allowed* (2007) which features an interview with a teacher reflecting on her experiences with PwC in Gallions Primary School in the London Borough of Newham. A learner also comments that there are no right or wrong answers in philosophy.

14. This thinking strategy, originally devised by Edward de Bono, involves the following role play. By putting on a hat of a particular colour, a person has to adopt a particular thinking perspective: neutral (white hat), emotional (red hat), positive (yellow hat), creative (green hat), calm (blue hat) and critical, negative (black hat).

15. 'Upheavals of Thought' is the title of a book by Martha Nussbaum (2001). After Proust, she refers to emotions as 'upheavals of thought', that is, like geological upheavals, they are part of the same landscape of cognition, and as 'thoughts about value and importance they make the 'mind project outward like a mountain range' (Nussbaum, 2001, pp. 1, 3). Emotions are not just 'props' or 'supports' for intelligence but are essential elements of human intelligence. We suggest that the multi-layered, complex mix of emotions involved in PwC philosophically informs, rather than detracts or distorts, insights gained in the pursuit of meaning and truth in communities of enquiry.

16. For an excellent literary review of student relativism and how to respond to it philosophically, see Erion, 2005.

17. Although the philosophers of education mentioned here refer explicitly to the highly influential but complex notion of *phronesis* from Aristotle's *Nichomachean Ethics*, we decided to use 'practical judgment' instead to highlight the action research character of our philosophical reflection on practice. It is beyond the scope of this paper to do justice to the current differences of opinion in the field about the relationship between practice and theory in *phronesis*, the specific role of the emotions, and the kind of virtues and character required for *phronesis*. For example, building on Dunne's interpretation of *phronesis*, and critiquing subsequent interpretations and popular applications in academic literature, philosopher of education Kristján Kristjánsson exposes some of the pitfalls in interpreting Aristotle's core concepts and insights. He argues that Dunne's influential book *Back to the Rough Ground* (1997) calls for a return to the 'rooted roughness' of practical school life with its flexibility and open texture, away from the 'misguided smoothness of theory' (Kristjánsson, 2007, p.173). Instead, Kristjánsson urges educators to take the 'smooth with the rough' for the reasons he sets out in his scholarly book *Aristotle, Emotions and Education*. A significant contribution to the thinking in the philosophy of education field is offered by his analysis of the relationship in Aristotle's writings between *phronesis*, *praxis*, *poiesis* and *techne*. Kristjan Kristjánsson is highly critical of what he calls 'PPP', i.e. the *phronesis-praxis* perspective, currently so popular especially in Scandinavia and

the UK. He states: 'one could, in fact, speak of an all-you-can-eat *phronesis-praxis* buffet currently underway in educational circles, with reverberations reaching other work-related subjects such as medicine and nursing' (Kristjánsson, 2007, p. 157). The motivation behind PPP, Kristjánsson Kristjánsson continues, is the desire 'to resolve one of the most intractable historical problems of education—the uneasy relationship between educational *theory* and *practice*—by reconfiguring (eliminating or transcending) the very dichotomy underlying it, through a retrieval of certain Aristotelian insights' (p. 158).

REFERENCES

Benhabib, S. (1992) *Situating the Self: Gender, Community and Postmodernism in Contemporary Ethics* (Cambridge, Polity Press).

Biesta, G. (2006) *Beyond Learning* (Boulder, CO, Paradigm Publishers).

Biesta, G. (2009) Philosophy, Exposure—and Children: How to Resist the Instrumentalisation of Philosophy in Education. Paper presented at the Annual Conference of the British Educational Research Association, Manchester, 2–5th September.

Biesta, G. (2010) *Good Education in an Age of Measurement: Ethics, Politics, Democracy* (Boulder, CO, Paradigm Publishers).

Burbules, N. C. (1995) Reasonable Doubt: Towards a Postmodern Defense of Reason as an Educational Aim, in: W. Kohli (ed.) *Critical Conversations in Philosophy of Education* (London, Routledge), pp. 82–102.

Dunne, J. (1997) *Back to the Rough Ground: Practical Judgment and the Lure of Technique* (Notre Dame, IN, University of Notre Dame Press).

Ecclestone, K. and Hayes, D. (2009) *The Dangerous Rise of Therapeutic Education* (London, Routledge).

Elliott, J. (2006) Educational Research as a Form of Democratic Rationality, *Journal of Philosophy of Education*, 40.2, pp. 169–185.

Enslin, P., Pendlebury, S. and Tjiattas, M. (2001) Deliberative Democracy, Diversity and the Challenges of Citizenship Education, *The Journal of Philosophy of Education*, 35.1, pp. 115–130.

Erion, G. J. (2005) Engaging Student Relativism, *Discourse*, 5.1, pp. 120–134.

Freire, P. (1972) *Pedagogy of the Oppressed* (Harmondsworth, Penguin).

Gardner, S. T. (1995) Inquiry is no Mere Conversation (or Discussion or Dialogue): Facilitation is Hard Work!, *Creative and Critical Thinking*, 3.2, pp. 38–49.

Giroux, H. (1988) *Schooling and the Struggle for Public Life: Critical Pedagogy in the Modern Age* (Minneapolis, MN, University of Minnesota Press).

Gledhill, J. (2008) Can Philosophy Change Your Life?, *Culture Wars*. Available at: http://www.culturewars.org.uk/index.php/site/article/can_philosophy_changeyour_life/

Greene, M. and Griffiths, M. (2003) Feminism, Philosophy and Education: Imagining Public Spaces, in: N. Blake, P. Smeyers, R. Smith and P. Standish (eds) *The Blackwell Guide to the Philosophy of Education* (Oxford, Blackwell), pp. 73–92.

Griffiths, M. (1998) *Educational Research for Social Justice: Getting off the Fence* (Buckingham, Open University Press).

Griffiths, M. (ed.) (2003) *Action for Social Justice in Education: Fairly Different* (Maidenhead, Open University Press).

Griffiths, M. and Cotton, T. (2005) Action Research, Stories and Practical Philosophy. Paper presented at conference of Collaborative Action Research Network/Practitioner Action Research *Quality of Practitioner Research/Action Research: What's It About, What's It For and What Next?* Utrecht, The Netherlands, 4–6th November.

Haynes, J. (2005) The Costs of Thinking, *Teaching Thinking and Creativity*, 17, pp. 32–37.

Haynes, J. (2007) Listening as a Critical Practice: Learning Through Philosophy with Children. PhD Thesis, University of Exeter).

Haynes, J. (2008) *Children as Philosophers. Learning through Enquiry and Dialogue in the Primary School*, 2nd edn. (London, RoutledgeFalmer).

Haynes, J. (2009) Dialogue as a Playful and Subversive Space, *Journal of Critical and Reflective Practice in Education,* 1:1. Available at: http://www.marjon.ac.uk/research/criticalandreflecti-vepracticeineducation/volume1issue1/

Haynes, J. and Murris, K. (2009) The Wrong Message: Risk, Censorship and the Struggle for Democracy in the Primary School, *Thinking: The Journal of Philosophy for Children,* 19.1, pp. 2–11.

Haynes, J. and Murris, K. (in press) *Picturebooks, Pedagogy and Philosophy* (New York, Routledge Research in Education Series).

Jansen, J. (2009) *Knowledge in the Blood: Confronting Race and the Apartheid Past* (Stanford, CA, Stanford University Press).

Kelly, A. V. (1995) *Education and Democracy* (London, Paul Chapman).

Kitchener, R. (1990) Do Children Think Philosophically?, *Metaphilosophy,* 21.4, pp. 427–438.

Kristjánsson, K. (2005) Can We Teach Justified Anger?, *Journal of Philosophy of Education,* 39.4, pp. 671–689.

Kristjánsson, K. (2007) *Aristotle, Emotions, and Education* (Aldershot, Ashgate).

Laverty, M. (2010) Learning our Concepts, *Journal of Philosophy of Education,* 43.Suppl. 1, pp. 27–41.

Lensmire, T. J. (1998) Rewriting Student Voice, *Journal of Curriculum Studies,* 30.3, pp. 261–291.

Lipman, M. (1991) *Thinking in Education* (Cambridge, Cambridge University Press).

Lipman, M., Sharp, A. M. and Oscanyan, F. S. (1977) *Philosophy in the Classroom* (Philadelphia, PA, Temple University Press).

Long, F. (2005) Thomas Reid and Philosophy with Children, *Journal of Philosophy of Education,* 39.4, pp. 599–615.

McNiff, J. (1993) *Teaching as Learning: An Action Research Approach* (London, Routledge).

Mason, J. (2002) *Researching your own Classroom Practice: From Noticing to Reflection* (London, RoutledgeFalmer).

Morrow, R. A. and Torres, C. A. (2002) *Reading Freire and Habermas: Critical Pedagogy and Transformative Social Change* (New York, Teachers College Press).

Murris, K. (1997) Metaphors of the Child's Mind: Teaching Philosophy to Young Children. Unpublished PhD Thesis, University of Hull.

Murris, K. (1999) Philosophy with Preliterate Children, *Thinking: The Journal of Philosophy for Children,* 14.4, pp. 23–34.

Murris, K. (2000) The Role of the Facilitator in Philosophical Enquiry, *Thinking: The Journal of Philosophy for Children,* 15.2, pp. 40–47.

Murris, K. (2009a) A Philosophical Approach to Emotions: Understanding *Love's Knowledge* through a *Frog in Love*', *Childhood and Philosophy*: *The Official Journal of the International Council of Philosophical Inquiry with Children* (ICPIC), 5. 9, pp. 5–30. Available at: http://www.periodicos.proped.pro.br/index.php?journal=childhoodandpage=index

Murris, K. (2009b) Philosophy with Children, the Stingray and the Educative Value of Disequilibrium, in: R. Cigman and A. Davis (eds) *New Philosophies of Learning* (Oxford, Wiley-Blackwell), pp. 293–311.

Murris, K. (2011) Epistemological Orphans and Childlike Play with Spaghetti: Philosophical Conditions for Transformation, *Critical and Reflective Practice in Education,* 3, pp. 1–16.

Murris, K. and Haynes, J. (2002) *Storywise: Thinking through Stories* (Newport, Dialogueworks).

Murris, K. and Haynes, J. (2010) *Storywise: Thinking through Stories; Revised International E-book* (Johannesburg, Infonet Publications).

Nussbaum, M. (2001) *Upheavals of Thought: The Intelligence of Emotions* (Cambridge, Cambridge University Press).

Oram, H. and Kitamura, S. (1993) *Angry Arthur* (London, Random House).

Quinn, V. (1997) *Critical Thinking in Young Minds* (London, David Fulton).

Rachels, J. (2009) *The Elements of Moral Philosophy,* 6th edn. (London, McGraw-Hill).

Sikes, P., Nixon, J. and Carr, W. (eds) (2003) *The Moral Foundations of Educational Research: Knowledge, Inquiry and Values* (Maidenhead, Open University Press).

Splitter, L. and Sharp, A. M. (1995) *Teaching for Better Thinking; The Classroom Community of Enquiry* (Melbourne, Acer).

Thinking Allowed (2007) DVD; published by Gallions Primary School, London. Available from: orders@gallions.newham.sch.uk.

SAPERE (2006) *P4C Report: For the Innovations Unit January 2006* (Oxford, Westminster Institute of Education-Oxford Brookes University, SAPERE).

Trickey, S. and Topping, K. J. (2004) Philosophy for Children: A Systematic Review, *Research Papers in Education*, 19.3, pp. 363–278.

Trickey, S. and Topping, K. J. (2007) Collaborative Enquiry for School Children: Cognitive Gains at 2 Year Follow Up, *British Journal of Education Psychology*, 77.4, pp. 787–796.

Tripp, D. (1993) *Critical Incidents in Teaching: Developing Professional Judgment* (London, Routledge).

Van Manen, M. (1997) *Researching Lived Experience: Human Science for an Action Sensitive Pedagogy*, 2nd edn. (London, ONT, University of Western Ontario, Althouse Press).

Vansieleghem, N. (2005) Philosophy for Children as the Wind of Thinking, *Journal of Philosophy of Education*, 39.1, pp. 19–37.

White, J. (1992) The Roots of Philosophy, in: A. P. Griffiths (ed.) *The Impulses to Philosophise* (Cambridge, Cambridge University Press), pp. 73–78.

Wilson, J. (1992) Philosophy for Children: A Note of Warning, *Thinking*, X.1, pp. 17, 18.

Wittgenstein, L. (1958) *Philosophische Untersuchungen* (Frankfurt am Main, Suhrkamp Verlag).

8

Philosophy, Exposure, and Children: How to Resist the Instrumentalisation of Philosophy in Education

GERT BIESTA

'Harmlessness breeds harmlessness, but danger generates thinking.'
(Sloterdijk, 1996, p. 121; my translation)

WHAT MIGHT PHILOSOPHY ACHIEVE?

I fear that this article boils down to two questions: 'What is philosophy?' and 'What might it achieve?' The reason for using the word 'fear' is that both questions are in a sense impossible to answer—and perhaps, therefore, even impossible to ask. The question as to what philosophy *is* has been one of the perennial questions in the writings of those who call themselves philosophers. The answers that have been generated are extremely diverse, ranging from claims for some kind of 'essence' of philosophy to views which emphasise the arbitrariness of what counts as philosophy, such as Richard Rorty's idea of philosophy as 'a kind of writing' (Rorty, 1978) or Peter Sloterdijk's characterisation of the philosophical tradition as a community of letter writing friends (Sloterdijk, 2009). Discussions about the definition of philosophy are often also attempts to police the borders of the field—a 'good' example being the opposition from a number of philosophers to the proposal to award Jacques Derrida an honorary doctorate at the University of Cambridge (see Derrida, 1995). The question as to what counts as philosophy is virtually impossible to answer, therefore, because it belongs to the very nature of the genre to reflect upon the identity and the borders of the field, and to do so without the ambition or hope of a final settlement. The question as to what philosophy might achieve is similarly difficult to

Philosophy for Children in Transition: Problems and Prospects, First Edition. Nancy Vansieleghem and David Kennedy. Chapters © 2012 The Authors. Editorial organization © 2012 Philosophy of Education Society of Great Britain. Published 2012 by Blackwell Publishing Ltd.

answer because philosophy in its many forms and guises may achieve many things—both things that lie within and things that lie beyond our control and imagination. Nonetheless, questions of definition and effect are important when philosophy is being mobilised to do something, and they are perhaps even more important when philosophy is being mobilised to do something *educational,* such as in the case of philosophy for children. In this regard, then, the two questions are at the very same time impossible and inevitable.

The use of philosophy in educational programmes and practices under such names as philosophy for children, philosophy with children, or the community of philosophical enquiry, has become well established in many countries around the world. This is first of all due to the efforts of Matthew Lipman and colleagues, but also the result of the work of numerous others who have followed in his footsteps or have taken inspiration from his and others' work. The main attraction of the educational use of philosophy— which I will use as the phrase to cover a range of approaches—seems to lie in the claim that it can help children and young people to develop skills for thinking critically, reflectively and reasonably. By locating the acquisition of such skills within communities of enquiry, the further claim is that engagement with philosophy can foster the development of moral reflection and sensitivity and of social and democratic skills more generally. Claims like these provide a set of arguments for the inclusion of philosophy in the school curriculum that goes well beyond philosophy as just another curricular subject or body of knowledge. Here is, for example, how the website of SAPERE, the UK Society for Advancing Philosophical Enquiry and Reflection in Education, lists the wider benefits of philosophy for children ('P4C').

> Independent research during 2003–4 in 100 English schools showed that P4C raises achievement, IQ and test scores, and improves self-esteem and motivation across the ability range. Controlled tests in America in the 1980's showed that not only could children's reasoning powers be enhanced through philosophical enquiry, but so could their reading and mathematical skills. Reading and comprehension improvements were also shown by UK studies in Derby and South Wales in the 1990's. Teachers have found that the Community of Enquiry approach suits a holistic concern for their students: self-esteem rises with children's ability to communicate in a personally meaningful way with their peers. There was support for this in the late 1990's, in very positive OFSTED [the English School Inspection Organisation; GB] reports on two schools with philosophical enquiry in their curriculum.[1]

Although I do not wish to doubt that engagement with certain forms of philosophy can have these kinds of effects—albeit that there is the question what the exact 'cause', the exact 'effect', and the exact relationship between the two is (see also Biesta, 2007, 2010c)—and although I can see the attraction of this particular way of making a case for the inclusion of philosophy in the curriculum, the case for philosophy that is presented along these lines is not without problems. The ambition of this article is to raise some questions about the conception of education that appears to inform the discussion about the educational use of philosophy. My aim is to suggest an *additional* rather than an alternative view about the educational use of philosophy. This means that I do not have the ambition to suggest a new 'programme' for philosophy in education but rather wish to suggest a perspective that can act as a reminder of a different way in which one can 'engage' with philosophy—which in a sense can also be read as a reminder about how philosophy might 'engage' with us. The philosophical distinction in terms of which my argument is phrased is that between 'humanism' and 'post-humanism'—and I wish to make clear from the outset that 'post-humanism' does not stand for an approach which tries to do away with the humanity of the human being, but rather articulates an approach which, in the words of Emmanuel Levinas, denounces huma*nism* 'because it is not sufficiently human' (Levinas, 1981, p. 128). The guiding concept in this additional view is that of 'exposure' (and the 'absent-present' in my argument—already in brackets—is the child).

PHILOSOPHICAL ENQUIRY OR SCIENTIFIC ENQUIRY?

Given the sheer diversity of schools, views and positions within the field of philosophy, one of the important questions in relation to the educational use of philosophy concerns the particular selection(s) made from the field. One thing that is remarkable in relation to this is the strong orientation towards knowledge and truth. Hannam and Echeverria (2009), for example, argue that in the community of philosophical enquiry 'the purpose is to construct knowledge together' and the aim is 'to promote cooperation in illuminating a path to come closer to the truth of things' (Hannam and Echeverria, 2009, p. 8). Although this is not the whole of what happens or may happen in the community of philosophical enquiry, and although there is also a strong emphasis on the provisional character of all claims to truth (see ibid., passim), this, and the wider 'pedagogy' of the community of philosophical enquiry, gives the impression that at least to a certain extent the approach is less about a community of *philosophical* enquiry and more about a community of *scientific* enquiry, one based, moreover, on a particular 'rational-epistemological' view of what scientific knowledge is and how it is brought about. Here is, for example, how the website of SAPERE summarises the pedagogy of 'P4C.'

Key principles of P4C

- the key practice that starts and drives the whole thinking process is enquiry (interpreted as going beyond information to seek under-standing)

- the key practice that results in significant changes of thought and action is reflection These aims and processes can be made more explicit if the teacher asks appropriate questions. These can range from a general invitation (such as: Can anyone respond to that?) to more specific calls that require a considered response. There are ten key elements the teacher can introduce to elicit a considered response.

1. *Questions* (What don't we understand here? What questions do we have about this?)
2. *Hypotheses* (Does anyone have any alternative suggestions or explanations?)
3. *Reasons* (What reasons are there for doing that? What evidence is there for believing this?)
4. *Examples* (Can anyone think of an example of this? Can someone think of a counter-example?)
5. *Distinctions* (Can we make a distinction here? Can anyone give a definition?)
6. *Connections* (Is anyone able to build on that idea? or Can someone link that with another idea?)
7. *Implications* (What assumptions lie behind this? What consequences does it lead to?)
8. *Intentions* (Is that what was really meant? Is that what we're really saying?)
9. *Criteria* (What makes that an example of X? What are the things that really count here?)
10. *Consistency* (Does that conclusion follow? Are these principles/beliefs consistent?)[2]

That the educational engagement with philosophy tends to model itself on a rational-epistemological interpretation of the community of scientific enquiry is also visible in its focus on the development of thinking skills, and particularly higher order thinking skills (see ibid.). Hannam and Echeverria argue, for example, that the development of thinking skills takes place through the interaction between four 'key elements' which are listed as critical thinking, creative thinking, collaborative thinking and caring thinking (2009, p. 13) and four 'categories of skill', namely good reasoning skills, investigatory skills, conceptual skills, and translation skills (see pp. 91, 159). Particularly the first three of the latter set give the strong impression that the community of philosophical enquiry is more like a community of scientific enquiry which proceeds towards the truth though the employment of reasoning, investigation and conceptual development, while the skills listed under the category of 'translation' are not that far away from the four norms of scientific practice as articulated by Robert K. Merton (1942): communalism, universalism, disinterestedness and organised scepticism. This again shows that at least part of what occurs within the community of philosophical enquiry is modelled upon a particular conception of scientific enquiry.

While this does raise the question about the *justification* for this particular selection from the philosophical tradition—to which I turn below—the other thing to bear in mind at this point is that the conception of scientific enquiry informing the practice of the community of philosophical enquiry is in itself a very specific reconstruction of the way in which science is thought to proceed. It represents the practice of science predominantly in epistemological and procedural terms and, in this regard, can be characterised as *ideological* not in the least because there are radically different accounts of how we should understand the 'practice and culture' of science, including ones that say that epistemology and rational procedure are the least helpful in making sense of science (see, for example, Latour, 1988; Bloor, 1991; Pickering, 1992).

Lipman (2003) tries to address this point by arguing that the idea of the community of enquiry should not be understood as 'an attempt to substitute reasoning for science' but rather as an effort 'to *complement* scientific inquiry' (Lipman, 2003, p. 111; emphasis added). Nonetheless his focus for what the community of enquiry is about is based on an acceptance of the epistemological understanding of science—and perhaps we could even say that it is based on an uncritical acceptance of this view—and sees reasoning exclusively as having to do with knowledge. As he explains:

The information derived from science—its theories, data and procedures—are not in dispute. What reasoning helps do is (a) *extend* knowledge through logical inference; (b) *defend* knowledge through reasons and arguments; and (c) *coordinate* knowledge through critical analysis (Lipman, 2003, p. 111).

A PERFORMATIVE CONTRADICTION

Yet even where the community of philosophical enquiry is focused less on knowledge and truth and more on meaning and understanding, it still articulates a particular selection from the philosophical tradition. This, in itself, should not be seen as a problem as the philosophical tradition—including all the work that occurs on and, according to some, even beyond its borders—is too vast and too diverse to be represented in full. At the same time, however, there is something uncomfortable about a too self-assured presentation of a particular selection of the tradition as representing all of 'philosophy'. While there is a strong emphasis in the literature on the provisional and always revisable character of *knowledge*, this is less so with regard to philosophy itself. This, of course, brings us back to the 'impossible' question I started this article with. Rather than to get into this discussion, I simply wish to log the question about the representation of philosophy *within* philosophy for and with children and *within* the community of philosophical enquiry as an issue for further discussion.

There is, however, another 'level' at which the question of the particular conception of philosophy can be asked. This is not about how philosophy is explicitly *represented*—which is the question of selection—but about the way in which philosophy is *deployed* in and through the educational use of philosophy. This, in a sense, brings us to the question of what philosophy might achieve.

What is noticeable in the educational use of philosophy within philosophy for/with children and the community of philosophical enquiry is an *instrumental* use—and also an instrumental 'positioning'—of philosophy (see also, for example, Long, 2005; Murris, 2008). Philosophy is deployed as an instrument that is supposed to work upon individuals so that they can develop and/or acquire certain qualities, capacities and skills. While this tendency might be characterised as a psychologisation of philosophy, I prefer to use the more general term of instrumentalisation—philosophy as an instrument for 'producing' something—albeit that within the literature there is indeed a strong emphasis on the ways in which individuals, through engagement with philosophy in the community of philosophical enquiry, are supposed to develop a range of skills, including cognitive and thinking skills, moral and social skills, and democratic skills.

Hannam and Echeverria (2009), who focus their discussion on philosophy with teenagers, add an extensive discussion on identity development during adolescence to the 'mix' of possible outcomes of the engagement with philosophy In addition they emphasise the potential impact of the community of philosophical enquiry on emotional development and emotional well-being and 'healthy perceptions of others' (see ibid., p. 43), on the 'growth in cognitive competencies which in turn facilitate the development of understanding and tolerance of different points of view' (p. 44), on the development of the 'personal qualities of self-governance [and] self-control' (p. 65), and on the development of literacy skills (see p. 84). SAPERE, as I have shown above, lists such potential effects as an increase in achievement, IQ and test scores, the improvement of self-esteem and motivation, and the enhancement of reasoning powers and reading and mathematical skills.

These claims may all be true and they may all be considered important. My aim here is not to contest these potential effects in themselves—although I do wish to repeat my concern about the extent to which it is possible to identify causes, effects and their interrelationships. I rather wish to highlight the underlying conception of the human being as a kind of 'developing organism' or, in the words of Usher and Edwards (1994, p. 24), as 'a certain kind of subject who has the inherent potential to become self-motivated and self-directing'—a conception which seems to inform the pedagogy of the community of philosophical enquiry conceived as a process aiming at facilitating the development of a range of qualities, competencies and skills. When we look at the educational use of philosophy from this angle it becomes clear that the whole 'project'—in its intentions, its effects, and its pedagogy—is not only based on a particular *conception* of the human being but also and, from a philosophical point perhaps more problematically, on a particular *truth* about the human being.

My concern here is not with the particular conception of the human being that seems to inform the work, but with the implications of the fact that the educational use of philosophy appears to be based on a particular truth about the human being. It is the latter which situates the educational use of philosophy more explicitly within what philosophers such as Heidegger, Levinas and Sloterdijk have characterised as 'humanism', understood as the idea that it is possible to know and articulate the essence or nature of the human being—an idea which is often accompanied by the assumption that it is possible to use this knowledge as the foundation for subsequent action in such domains as education, politics or ethics. Levinas characterises such a form of humanism as entailing 'the recognition of an invariable essence named "Man", the affirmation of his central place in the economy of the Real and of his value which [engenders] all values' (Levinas, 1990, p. 277).

One way to identify a potential problem—or at least raise a point for discussion—in relation to this, is to point at the possible contradiction between an ethos of reflection and questioning at the level of the *practice* of the community of philosophical enquiry and an unreflective and unreflected foundation of this practice enacted through a particular pedagogy and a wider justification of this practice which sees (engagement with) philosophy as an instrument to 'produce' a particular kind of human subjectivity. The contradiction here is a performative one, as it is not that questions about the human being and about being human are not or cannot be on the agenda of the community of philosophical enquiry. The contradiction rather arises from the tension between what the community of philosophical enquiry is committed to and the assumptions that appear to inform its justification and pedagogy.

This is also the point made by Nancy Vansieleghem (2005) in her critique of instrumentalist tendencies within philosophy for children, particularly with regard to the ambition to contribute to the formation of the democratic person. The question Vansieleghem raises in this context is whether we should think of education as the production of a pre-defined identity or whether education, if it has an interest in the human subject and its freedom, should always remain open to something else, something new. Vansieleghem argues that philosophy for children, 'with its emphasis on critical thinking and autonomy is actually 'nothing more than the reproduction of an existing discourse', which is why 'the autonomy the child gains through Philosophy for Children by critical thinking and dialogue is nothing more than the freedom to occupy a pre-constituted place in that discourse' (Vansieleghem, 2005, p. 25).

The issues for discussion, then, are [1] how and why this contradiction is a problem, and [2] how we might be able to overcome it. A partial and 'quick' answer to the first question is that it *does* matter to find dogmatic elements within any philosophical endeavour—which is not to say that it is always easy to overcome such elements (on this see also Biesta and Stams, 2001; Biesta 2009). But in order to explore the wider implications and articulate the outlines of a different pedagogy, some more detail is needed.

THE TROUBLE WITH HUMANISM, PARTICULARLY IN EDUCATION

In 20th century philosophy humanism has basically been challenged for two reasons. On the one hand questions have been raised about the *possibility* of humanism, that is, about the possibility for human beings to define their own essence and origin. Foucault and Derrida have both shown the impossibility of trying to capture our own essence and origin—an impossibility which has become known as the 'end of man' or the 'death of the subject' (see Foucault, 1970; Derrida, 1982). On the other hand questions have been raised about the *desirability* of humanism. This line has particularly been developed by Heidegger and Levinas (see Biesta, 2006 for more detail; see also Derrida, 1982, pp. 109–136). For Levinas the 'crisis of humanism in our society' began with the 'inhuman events of recent history' (Levinas, 1990, p. 279). Yet for Levinas the crisis of humanism is not simply located in these inhumanities as such, but first and foremost in humanism's inability to effectively counter such inhumanities and also in the fact that many of the inhumanities of the 20th century—Levinas mentions 'the 1914 War, the Russian Revolution refuting itself in Stalinism, fascism, Hitlerism, the 1939–45 War, atomic bombings, genocide and uninterrupted war' (ibid.)—were actually based upon and motivated by particular definitions of what it means to be human. This is why Levinas concludes—with a phrase reminiscent of Heidegger—that 'humanism has to be denounced [. . .] because it is not *sufficiently* human' (Levinas, 1981, p. 128; emphasis added).

The problem with humanism is that it posits a *norm* of what it means to be human and in doing so excludes those who do not live up to or are unable to live up to this norm. This point is not simply a general and philosophical one; it also has important educational ramifications. From an educational point of view the problem with humanism is that it specifies a norm of what it means to be human *before* the actual manifestation of 'instances' of humanity. It specifies what the child, student or newcomer must become before giving them an opportunity to show who they are and who they will be (see also Vansieleghem, 2005). This form of humanism thus seems to be unable to be open to the possibility that newcomers might radically alter our understandings of what it means to be human. The upshot of this, to put it briefly, is that education becomes focused on the 'production' of a particular kind of subjectivity.

A POST-HUMANIST THEORY OF EDUCATION: ACTION, UNIQUENESS AND EXPOSURE

The challenge to overcome humanism is, therefore, a double challenge, as there is not only the question how this might be done *philosophically*, but also the question how it might be achieved *educationally*—and the two questions are partly separate as I do not wish to see educational theory as simply the application of philosophy. In my own work I have responded to this challenge through a combination of two sets of ideas—captured in the notions of 'coming into the world' and 'uniqueness'—which, together, constitute what might be characterised as a post-humanist theory of education (see particularly Biesta, 2006; 2010a). On the one hand I have suggested that instead of understanding education as having to do with the production or promotion of a particular kind of subjectivity, we should think of education as being interested in how new beginnings and new beginners come into the world. The idea of 'coming into world' thus aims to articulate an educational interest into human subjectivity but does so without a template, that is, without a pre-defined idea about what it means to be and exist as a human being. It thus tries to overcome a humanistic determination of human subjectivity.

A focus on how individuals come into the world bears resemblance to forms of child-centred and student-centred education. But whereas extreme forms of child- and student-centred education would simply accept anything and anyone that announces itself (on this see Oelkers, 1996), I have emphasised that there is always a need for *judgment* about what and who comes into the world. My only point is that such judgment should occur *after* the event of coming into the world, not before. 'Coming into the world' should not be understood as a 'one-off' event but has to do with the ongoing 'stream' of initiatives, which means that the question of judgement is one that poses itself continuously as well (see below). There is, of course, a risk entailed in this, but the question here is not whether we should try to do away with this risk. The question is whether in order to prevent a new Hitler or a new Pol Pot from coming into the world we should forfeit the possibility of a new Mother Theresa, a new Martin Luther King or a new Nelson Mandela from coming into the world as well. It is as simple—and of course also as complicated—as that. The other notion I have used in order to respond to the challenge outlined above is the idea of *uniqueness*, where uniqueness is precisely about the way in which each individual is not a specimen of a more general definition of what it means to be human.

Coming into the World

The idea of 'coming into the world' draws inspiration from the writings of Hannah Arendt, particularly her ideas on *action*. For Arendt to act first of all means to take initiative, that is, to begin something new. Arendt characterises the human being as an *initium*: a 'begin*ning* and a begin*ner*' (Arendt, 1977, p. 170; emphasis added). Arendt compares action to the fact of birth, since with each birth something 'uniquely new' comes into the world (see Arendt, 1958, p. 178). But it is not only at the moment of birth that something new comes into the world. We *continuously* bring new beginnings into the world through our words and deeds. Arendt connects action to freedom but emphasises that freedom should not be understood as a phenomenon of the will, that is, as the freedom to do whatever we choose to do, but that we should instead conceive of it as the freedom 'to call something into being which did not exist before' (Arendt, 1977, p. 151). The subtle difference between freedom as sovereignty and freedom as beginning has far-reaching consequences. The main implication is that freedom is not an 'inner feeling' or a private experience but by necessity a public and hence a political phenomenon. 'The *raison d'être* of politics is freedom', Arendt writes, 'and its field of experience is action' (p. 146). Arendt stresses again and again that freedom needs a 'public realm' to make its appearance (p. 149) Moreover, freedom only exists *in action*, which means that human beings *are* free—as distinguished from their 'possessing the gift of freedom'—as long as they act, 'neither before nor after' (p. 153). The question this raises is how freedom can appear.

To answer this question it is crucial to see that 'beginning' is only half of what action is about. Although it is true that we reveal our 'distinct uniqueness' through what we say and do, everything depends on how others will take up our initiatives. This is why Arendt writes that the agent is not an author or a producer, but a subject in the twofold sense of the word, namely one who began an action and the one who suffers from and is subjected to its consequences (see Arendt, 1958, p. 184). The upshot of this is that our 'capacity' for action—and hence our freedom—crucially depends on the ways in which others take up our beginnings, which immediately means that the 'capacity' for action is not a capacity that can ever be in our possession or under our control (and in this way the 'capacity' for action is not a skill or disposition). The 'problem', after all, is that others respond to our initiatives in ways that are unpredictable and beyond our control. Although this frustrates our beginnings, Arendt emphasises again and again that the 'impossibility to remain unique masters of what [we] do' is at the very same time the condition—and the *only* condition—under which our beginnings can come into the world (p. 244). We can of course try to control the ways in which others respond to our beginnings. But if we were to do so, we would deprive others of their opportunities to begin. We would deprive them of their opportunities to act, and hence we would deprive them of their freedom. Action is therefore never possible in isolation. Arendt even goes as far as to argue that 'to be isolated is to be deprived of the capacity to act' (p. 188). This also implies that action in the Arendtian sense of the word is never possible without plurality—or to be more precise: action in the Arendtian sense is never possible without the exposure to otherness and difference. As soon as we erase plurality—as soon as we erase the otherness of others by attempting to control how they respond to our initiatives—we deprive others of their actions and their freedom, and as a result deprive *ourselves* of the possibility to act, and hence of our freedom. All this is captured in Arendt's statement that '(p)lurality is the condition of human action' (p. 8). This should, however, not be read as an empirical statement but rather as the normative 'core' of Arendt's philosophy, a philosophy committed to a world in which everyone has the opportunity to act, appear and 'achieve' freedom.

Uniqueness

The notion of 'uniqueness' plays an important role in the ideas I have taken from Arendt, particularly her claim that we disclose our 'distinct uniqueness' through action—which, as I have shown, implies that we can only disclose this uniqueness if we are willing to run the risk that our beginnings are taken up in ways that are different from what we intended. What is important about Arendt's views is that they can help to approach the question of uniqueness in relational, political and existential terms, as she links the idea of 'uniqueness' to the particular ways in which we *exist* with others (on the political significance of such a 'existential' view see Biesta, 2010b). But the idea of disclosing one's distinct uniqueness through action runs the risk of conceiving of uniqueness in terms of characteristics or qualities of the subject—and would thus conceive of uniqueness in terms of what we *have* or *posses*. It would, to put it differently, turn the question of uniqueness into a question of identity.

There are several problems with this way of understanding uniqueness. One is that if we think of uniqueness in terms of the characteristics we have, we must assume that there is some underlying 'substratum' which can be the carrier of such characteristics. This brings us close, again, to the idea of an underlying human essence, and thus would bring humanism in through the backdoor. There is, however, a second problem which in my view is the more important one. This has to do with the fact that if we would only relate to others in order to make clear how we are different from them, there would, in a sense, be nothing 'at stake' in our relationships with others. Or, to put it differently, we would only 'need' others in order to find out and make clear how we are different from them—how my identity is unique—but once this has become clear we wouldn't need others any more. Our relationship with others would therefore remain instrumental.

The philosopher who has helped me most to think through these issues and articulate an alternative way of approaching the idea of uniqueness is

Emmanuel Levinas. What is most significant about Levinas's work is *not* that he has generated a new theory about the uniqueness of the human being—and I would argue that he actually has not develop any theory at all—but that he instead has introduced a different *question* about uniqueness. Instead of asking what *makes* each of us unique—which is the question of characteristics and possessions—Levinas has approached the question of uniqueness by asking when it *matters* that I am unique, that I am I and no one else. Levinas's answer to this question, to put it briefly, is that my uniqueness matters in those situations in which I cannot be replaced by someone else, that is, in those situations where it matters that *I* am there and not just anyone. I have referred to this as 'uniqueness as irreplaceability' as distinct from 'uniqueness as difference' (see Biesta, 2010a, ch. 4).

Exposure

The situations Levinas has in mind are those in which I find myself in a position of responsibility for a concrete other; that is, in a situation in which someone calls me, singles me out so to speak, and where it is up to me to respond. It is, therefore, in situations where I am *exposed* to the other—or to be more precise: where I am exposed to an 'imperative' (see Lingis, 1994, p. 111)—that my uniqueness matters, as it is in those situations that it is for *me* to respond not just for anyone. It is important to mention that for Levinas this responsibility is not issued from our will or our decision to become responsible, nor from a judgement that we should take up our responsibility. For Levinas responsibility comes *before* subjectivity which is why he has argued that responsibility is 'the essential, primary and fundamental structure of subjectivity' (Levinas, 1985, p. 95). Uniqueness, then, ceases to be an ontological notion—it is not about what we possess or are in terms of identity—but becomes an *existential* notion that has to do with the ways in which we are exposed to others, are singled out by them.

One important implication of these ideas is that they do not lead to some kind of educational programme that can generate action and produce uniqueness. Action and uniqueness are phenomena that are structurally *beyond* our control—which means that as soon as we try to control then, as soon as we try to bring them into our grasp, they actually disappear. Although action and uniqueness cannot be produced—and in this sense are beyond the reach of any educational programme—it is possible to create situations in which it becomes very unlikely that action and uniqueness will appear. This is the case when we block any exposure to otherness and difference. It is the situation in which we are 'immune' from any interruption from the outside, from any intervention of the other (on immunisation see Masschelein, 1996; Masschelein and Simons, 2004). The choice, therefore, is between education that contributes to immunisation and education that keeps the possibility for interruption and intervention open—with no guarantee, of course, that anything may emerge from this. (For a thoughtful discussion of some of the tensions in the ideas of exposure and interruption in education see Bonnett, 2009.)

A DIFFERENT PHILOSOPHY FOR DIFFERENT CHILDREN

In this article I have focused on the assumptions underlying the pedagogy of the educational use of philosophy. I have characterised this pedagogy as an *instrumental* pedagogy in that it focuses on the way in which engagement with philosophy can produce an individual with certain qualities and skills. I have brought the wider set of assumptions informing this pedagogy in relation with humanist thinking in education. I have suggested that the educational use of philosophy appears to be based on a particular idea—and perhaps we can say a particular truth—about what the human subject is and how the human subject can become 'better', for example as a more critical, reflective and reasonable thinker. This at least partly seems to be connected with a tendency to see the community of philosophical enquiry first and foremost as a community of *scientific* enquiry. This, as I have argued, is not only problematic because it enacts a rather narrow representation of what philosophy can be about, but also raises problems because the particular depiction of science as a disinterested search for truth is itself ideological.

In order to overcome the instrumentalist tendencies in the educational use of philosophy I have suggested that we not just need a different pedagogy, but also actually need to shift the assumptions informing our pedagogy. This led me to the wider discussion about the humanist foundations of modern education and to some suggestions for a post-humanist understanding of education, one that is not based on a particular truth about the nature and destiny of the human subject but rather wants to see education as a concern for the ways in which individuals-in-their-uniqueness might come into the world. The central educational concept emerging from these ideas is that of *exposure*. Exposure is not an educational technique to produce unique individuals. Exposure rather denotes a 'quality' of human interaction and engagement that may make the event of the incoming of uniqueness possible. Exposure is the moment when I am singled out, so to speak; it is the moment where I am exposed in my singularity. Exposure is therefore not about the revelation of a unique, pre-existing identity; it is about the constitution of me as being irreplaceable in the face of an appeal, in the face of a call. Exposure does not produce; exposure only interrupts.

A pedagogy focusing on exposure and interruption is therefore no longer a pedagogy that aims to produce a particular kind of subject or particular qualities of the subject or that aims to equip the subject with a range of 'useful' skills. A pedagogy focusing on exposure and interruption is a pedagogy that may bring about hesitation, an experience of not knowing, an experience that makes us stop rather than that it rushes us into the pseudo-security of questions, hypothesis, reasons, examples, distinctions, connections, implications, intentions, criteria, and consistency. There are parts of the philosophical tradition that have the potential to make us hesitate, to put us on the spot, to put our normal ways of being and doing into question. This, however, has to do with a quality of philosophy that is rather far away from the model of scientific enquiry, as it is not focused on knowing and the improvement of knowledge, but has an orientation towards *not*-knowing. One could even say that when engagement with philosophy leads to interruption and hesitation, it puts us, in a sense, in the position of the child as the one whose seeing, thinking and doing is not yet 'filled' with the knowledge, categories and ways of speaking of others. I am not referring here to a kind of romantic unmediated wholeness-with-the-world, but to a situation in which we can not rely on existing knowledge, patterns, structures and traditions so that it is up to us to invent a unique response and thus to invent ourselves uniquely in and through this response. This child-like position of not-knowing that can follow from exposure may well suggest an entirely different set of possibilities for the educational engagement with philosophy and may well give the phrase 'philosophy for children' an entirely new meaning.[3]

NOTES

1. Available online at: http://www.sapere.org.uk/content/index.aspx?id=46. Accessed 22 July 2010.
2. Available online at: http://www.sapere.org.uk/content/index.aspx?id=45. Accessed 22 July 2010; emphases in original.
3. I would like to thank Nancy Vansieleghem and David Kennedy for their invitation to contribute to this issue and I would like to thank them and the reviewers for their helpful comments on an earlier version of this article. I would also like to thank Patricia Hannam for inspiring discussions about philosophy, education and children.

REFERENCES

Arendt, H. (1958) *The Human Condition* (Chicago, IL, The University of Chicago Press).
Arendt, H. (1977) What is Freedom?, in H. Arendt, *Between Past and Future: Eight Exercises in Political Thought* (Harmondsworth, Penguin), pp. 143–171.
Biesta, G. J. J. (2006) *Beyond Learning. Democratic Education for a Human Future* (Boulder, CO, Paradigm Publishers).
Biesta, G. J. J. (2007) Why 'What Works' Won't Work. Evidence-Based Practice and the Democratic Deficit of Educational Research, *Educational Theory*, 57.1, pp. 1–22.
Biesta, G. J. J. (2009) Witnessing Deconstruction in Education. Why Quasi-Transcendentalism Matters, *Journal of Philosophy of Education*, 43.3, pp. 391–404.
Biesta, G. J. J. (2010a) *Good Education in an Age of Measurement: Ethics—Politics—Democracy* (Boulder, CO, Paradigm Publishers).
Biesta, G. J. J. (2010b) How to Exist Politically and Learn from It: Hannah Arendt and the Problem of Democratic Education, *Teachers College Record*, 112.2, pp. 558–577.

Biesta, G. J. J. (2010c) Why 'What Works' still Won't Work: From Evidence-Based Education to Value-Based Education, *Studies in Philosophy and Education*, 29.5, pp. 491–503.

Biesta, G. J. J. and Stams, G. J. J. M. (2001) Critical Thinking and the Question of Critique. Some Lessons from Deconstruction, *Studies in Philosophy and Education*, 20.1, pp. 57–74.

Bloor, D. (1991) *Knowledge and Social Imagery*, 2nd edn. (Chicago, IL, The University of Chicago Press).

Bonnett, M. (2009) Education and Selfhood: A Phenomenological Investigation, *Journal of Philosophy of Education*, 43.3, pp. 357–370.

Derrida, J. (1982) *Margins of Philosophy* (Chicago, IL, The University of Chicago Press).

Derrida, J. (1995) *Honoris Causa*: This is Also Extremely Funny, in: E. Weber (ed.) *Points. . . Interviews, 1974–1994* (Stanford, CA, Stanford University Press), pp. 399–421.

Foucault, M. (1970) *The Order of Things. An Archeology of the Human Sciences* (New York, Random House).

Hannam, P. and Echeverria, E. (2009) *Philosophy with Teenagers* (London/New York, Continuum).

Latour, B. (1988) *Science in Action* (Cambridge, MA, Harvard University Press).

Levinas, E. (1981) *Otherwise than Being or Beyond Essence* (The Hague, Martinus Nijhoff).

Levinas, E. (1985) *Ethics and Infinity* (Pittsburgh, PA, Duquesne University Press).

Levinas, E. (1990) *Difficult Freedom. Essays on Judaism* (Baltimore, MD, The Johns Hopkins University Press).

Lingis, A. (1994) *The Community of Those Who have Nothing in Common* (Bloomington, IN, Indiana University Press).

Lipman, M. (2003) *Thinking in Education*, 2nd rev. edn. (Cambridge, Cambridge University Press).

Long, F. (2005) Thomas Reid and Philosophy with Children, *Journal of Philosophy of Education*, 39.4, pp. 599–615.

Masschelein, J. (1996) Individualization, Singularization and E-ducation (between Indifference and Responsibility), *Studies in Philosophy and Education*, 15.1–2, pp. 97–105.

Masschelein, J. and Simons, M. (2004) *Globale Immuniteit* (Leuven, Acco).

Merton, R. K. (1942) *The Sociology of Science: Theoretical and Empirical Investigations* (Chicago, IL, The University of Chicago Press).

Murris, K. S. (2008) Philosophy with Children, the Stingray and the Educative Value of Disequilibrium, *Journal of Philosophy of Education*, 42.3–4, pp. 667–685.

Oelkers, J. (1996) *Reformpädagogik. Eine kritische Dogmengeschichte* (M ü nchen, Juventa).

Pickering, A. (ed) (1992) *Science as Practice and Culture* (Chicago, IL, The University of Chicago Press).

Rorty, R. (1978) Philosophy as a Kind of Writing: An Essay on Derrida, *New Literary History*, 10.1, pp. 141–160.

Sloterdijk, P. (2009) Rules for the Human Zoo: A Response to the 'Letter on Humanism', *Environment and Planning D: Society and Space*, 27.1, pp. 12–28.

Sloterdijk, P. (1996) *Selbstversuch. Ein Gespräch mit Carlos Oliveira* (München, Hanser).

Usher, R. and Edwards, R. (1994) *Postmodernism and Education* (London/New York, Routledge).

Vansieleghem, N. (2005) Philosophy for Children as the Wind of Thinking, *Journal of Philosophy of Education*, 39.1, pp. 19–37.

9

Philosophy with Children as an Exercise in *Parrhesia*: An Account of a Philosophical Experiment with Children in Cambodia

NANCY VANSIELEGHEM

INTRODUCTION

The last few decades have seen a steady growth of interest in doing philosophy with children and young people in educational settings. Philosophy with children is increasingly offered as a solution to the problems associated with what is seen by many as a disoriented, cynical, indifferent and individualistic society. It represents for its practitioners a powerful vehicle that teaches children and young people 'how' to think about particular problems in society through the use of interpretive practices and procedures especially designed for this purpose. It typically conceives of the work of truth-telling as the work of dialogical reasoning, which is understood as leading to an increasingly conscious use of deductive and inductive mental and methodological procedures. In one way or another, this is identified as the appropriate way to think for oneself: one should express one's (real) opinion through a process of questioning one's own beliefs and values. Thus, its truth-telling practice assumes a kind of consciousness as a fundamental means of getting access to the truth.

My intention to write an article on philosophy with children starts, however, from another point of view and reflects another kind of interest. What I want to do here is not related primarily to the question of *how* to think for oneself and with others in an appropriate way. Rather, I am trying to phrase a different way of thinking philosophy with

Philosophy for Children in Transition: Problems and Prospects, First Edition. Nancy Vansieleghem and David Kennedy. Chapters © 2012 The Authors. Editorial organization © 2012 Philosophy of Education Society of Great Britain. Published 2012 by Blackwell Publishing Ltd.

children. I want to articulate an understanding of the process not as matter of becoming conscious of oneself in order to gain access to the truth but rather, and following Michel Foucault, as a practice oriented by the care of the self—in the interest of a transformation of the self by the self (cf. Peters, 2003; Franĕk, 2006; Masschelein, 2006; Luxon, 2008). Care of the self as I understand it here does not refer to a *technē* through which one compensates for one's deficiencies, but as an affirmation of one's existence. From this angle, philosophy with children is not to be understood as something that orients us towards the making of valid knowledge claims, but as an act of becoming *present in the present*.

I shall explore this conception of philosophy with children by way of a description of a concrete philosophical experiment with children that I carried out in Cambodia a few years ago. This experiment allowed me to suspend the common idea of philosophy with children as a programme that teaches us how to think, and offered me an occasion to open up a mode of thinking about philosophy with children that is not dependent on knowledge. Rather, it gave both the children and me the opportunity to speak outside the terms of abstract signification and the discourses of knowledge production. Moreover, the experiment opened the possibility of thinking about philosophy with children not as a practice that requires knowledge or competencies in order to speak, but rather in terms of *ascetic* exercises that expose oneself to oneself and to the procedures by which learns.

In order to elaborate this tentative idea, I draw generally upon the work of Foucault, but more specifically on his analysis of three major ways in which one relates oneself to the truth. This analysis offers me the chance to articulate the experiment in terms of an exercise in *parrhesia* (roughly translated, 'frank speaking') and to compare it with rhetoric and flattery as other ways of approaching the truth. I shall argue that *parrhesia* implies a form of thinking in which the self is not seen as an object of knowledge, but rather as an object of care. In a final section, I shall suggest some implications concerning the consequences of thinking of philosophy with children as a practice that constitutes the caring subject in terms of the kinds of exercises it requires. These exercises will be conceived of as both an open-ended and a highly focused preparation of the individual for *the events of life*. I shall begin with the philosophical experiment that I carried out in Cambodia.

A PHILOSOPHICAL EXPERIMENT WITH CHILDREN IN CAMBODIA: THE INTRODUCTION OF A TRUTH-TELLING PRACTICE BEYOND DIALOGICAL PROCEDURES AND STRATEGIES

In 2006 I was invited by the VVOB[1] to organise a workshop on philosophy with children at a teacher training college in Siem Reap.

The general aim of the VVOB is, in keeping with its overarching commitment to the improvement of the quality of education in developing countries, to create teaching methods the focal point of which is the development of pupils' talents and capacities. In relation to this goal, philosophy with children has been identified as a relevant approach, especially insofar as it provides challenging environments that stimulate students' self-reflective and dialogical competence. As I had written a PhD dissertation on philosophy for children (cf. Vansieleghem, 2006), I was considered to be an expert in this matter. It was at this moment that it struck me that philosophising with children may perhaps not be best conceived as a method, with its dedicated strategies and procedures, that teaches us how to think about particular problems in the world, but that it should rather be understood in terms of the care for the self and of *exposition*.[2] Indeed it was particularly the prospect of philosophising with children whose language, culture and background I did not know that gave me cause to think—not in the sense that I realised that I might not have enough (meta-)dialogical competence or expertise, but in the sense that, in the face of the strangeness of the situation, I was faced with a question that required a response from me not as an expert but *as a person*.

At the time when I was appointed to this role, I was reading an article by Jan Masschelein (2006) in which he elaborates the idea of critical research as a way of *walking* or traveling on foot towards an answer that the researcher does not know in advance: that is, she does not know where she will arrive or how she will get there. Referring to Walter Benjamin, Masschelein writes about the difference between walking along a road and flying over it by aeroplane in terms of different ways of relating oneself to the world and to the present. Inspired by that article, I decided to invite the children of Cambodia to go walking. And indeed, this is what we did—we walked. Walking and nothing but walking, in the hot and dusty terrain of Siem Reap. Left foot, right foot, left foot, right foot . . .

. . . step by step and without any direction. We were just walking and talking—talking in the language that we shared, which is the language that is spoken, you might say, between the tourist and the street vendor. 'Do you know Angkor Watt?'; 'Do you want to buy a postcard?'; 'Do you want bracelets?' . . . —such were the questions the children asked me. I was the tourist, they the sellers.

We were walking next to each other in a sort of desert—a strip of land dividing their homes from the tourist attractions (the Temples of Angkor Watt). It was a place that had no function, which only existed as space between their homes and the temples. You might say it was a no-man's land, a place of abandonment. It was a place of garbage and dust, where there was, apparently, nothing to experience or to see.

We wandered for hours in this open place—or non-place—with no specific route or plan. There were only the tourist attractions in the distance, reminding us only that we were *not there*.

It was also a place of exhaustion. If walking was the first element, exhaustion was the second.

The heat and the walking made the mind and the body empty, and the relationships between us gradually changed. Less and less attention was paid to maintaining the usual forms of politeness, to keeping up appearances. The growing exhaustion made everyone more honest, more direct and more quiet. 'What am I doing here?'; 'There is nothing to see!'; 'There is nothing to experience!'— questions such as these ran though the mind.

The children had been invited to go for a walk, but this walk could not be classified under any of the categories of traditional education. It was something that could be made to fit into the school curriculum. It was a walk that directed us, step by step,

towards a kind of exposure and to what there is to see before our eyes. It directed us toward and attached us to what did not have a meaning (at least to anything that could be thematised in the familiar terms of educational thought, with its obsession with knowledge or competencies)—to what did not have a meaning but that existed nevertheless.

The walk and the exhaustion broke the rhythm of the systematic and the cliché. They prepared the rupture necessary to expose our thinking to what was actually happening, and to move past our own reflections in order to see anew.

The tourist language that we spoke gradually disappeared, and the stranger that I was stopped being a tourist. But perhaps I, the foreigner, now became a real stranger, an intruder, someone who had penetrated their gaze: someone who was not easy to receive, nor perhaps even to conceive of—someone who just was *there*. This stranger became someone who walked with them, who brought them into a position in which they no longer recognised or knew themselves as learners, but at the same time someone who no longer recognised herself as an expert. Both expert and learners became strangers to themselves. A gradual slippage was separating selves from themselves, and both expert and student emerged from this adventure in a position of being lost. For a moment, roles or positions (with their familiar signifiers) no longer had a meaning, just as, in a very real sense, these were no longer our own roles, or our own positions. In a single moment, we were withdrawn as if to an infinite distance, and we subsided into an intimacy more profound than any interiority of reflection: we became *present in the present* and exposed— exposed to the situation and to each other. Gradually we registered what we were doing and not doing, and this became more important than who we were and what might happen. With this the walk appeared as an invitation to act and to speak: to begin again and this time no longer as a part of a predetermined discourse. We moved step-by-step and side-by-side, to the heartbeat of the mechanical movement of walking, and the temples, the school, the expert no longer functioned as arbiters of truth but gradually became vestigial remnants of what we had believed about truth. We—pupils and expert—were confronted with the realisation that there is a world or a language possible other than the one of the vendor and the tourist, the expert and the learner, a world or a language that does not have an interior or a limit that has to be discovered and yet that does not have to be defended by any truth or convention, but that simply asks how to carry on.

And at a certain moment the children wanted to stop. I was waiting at a distance, nervous and attentive to each sign and gesture. The children decided to return to school, and I followed. The discourse of the expert was no longer needed: a reversal of relationships was taking place.

When we reached the school, I asked the children to draw a self-portrait. No more explanation was given. The drawing assignment was not an attempt to reinstall the traditional curriculum; rather, it was an invitation to remember oneself as a subject of action and to articulate other ways of thinking and acting. Drawing a self-portrait was part of an exercise that had the advantage of two simultaneous, possible uses. After this moment of exposure, the invitation to draw was intended to enable the child to look again—at themselves, at their thoughts, at their actions—thereby incorporating the sensitivity that they had experienced during the exercise. Drawing was meant, then, to conserve this sensitivity, to keep it available and thus to make the experience an object of conversation, between them and within themselves. In this way a kind of *ethos* or habit for the body was established that created an attentiveness to what was happening. What this provided was not so much a matter of *information*—say, about their inner thoughts, feelings, needs or purposes—but rather the possibility of articulating and expressing opening. Thus, the self-portrait was meant also to encourage attentiveness to others, involving new ways of thinking, acting and behaving. Through this articulation and expression, thoughts were reactivated, inviting others to *do* the same.

The children painted for another two hours, not to satisfy the requirements of a specified task, nor simply to get the job done, but in such a way as to bring about a change in their relations—to themselves, to others and to the world. Drawing, painting or speaking then came to involve 'placing' themselves 'in' the activity. The experience the children then had was such that it seemed that it was not *they* that painted, expressing themselves, so much as the painting that expressed them. To paint a self-portrait did not mean to paint one's true self or to represent one's deepest emotions. It meant something more like being attentive to what needs to be said and thought, to what needs to be drawn: it was *in* the portrait that this became clear. This became visible not only in the way that the children painted, but also to the extent that they tried to paint what had to be painted. What was said through the portrait was embodied by the painter. No norm of this embodiment could be specified: it expressed itself primarily in what they did.

What the painting presented was something true. For the children painting was not just a task they had to carry out. Although the children were exhausted, and although the official school day was already over, they continued to work, care and attention manifest in their paintings. This was particularly evident in the work of one girl. I praised her work, but what I said did not stop her from working again at the colour of the lips, changing them from red to pink, which in the end was the detail that particularly caught the eye. This correction of the colour made the image plainer and more sober, more vulnerable. For the child, this was nothing to do with vanity, and neither was she interested in gaining the approval of the teacher: she was doing what she had to do, seeking only to produce effects of truth and feeling.

To say as much is undoubtedly to interpret, and it may well be the case that this interpretation is no different from any other. But it does, perhaps, provide the occasion to take a look again at philosophy with children, and to see this not primarily as a means (say, a method or technique) of gaining access to the truth of the subject or the world, but as an exercise that in fact suspends this presumption. Let me clarify what I mean here. The workshop was an occasion and an experiment. Nevertheless it disclosed a truth about philosophy with children in the sense that it opened the possibility of thinking about philosophy with children not only in terms of acquiring access to the truth, but in terms of *exposition*, of becoming present in the present, and thus not detached from the present, but fully present in the present. In the light of Foucault's *The Hermeneutics of the Subject* (2005), this experience of becoming present in the present might be understood as an aspect of *parrhesia*, where, in being exposed, one experiences the capacity to speak. Philosophising here is not a matter of putting something to the test of logical argument, nor a set of interpretative practices through which we decide whether it is real or not. It does not have to do with an activity that leads to a definition of the self by the self, but with an opening of the self to oneself (Luxon, 2008, p. 390). It is, in other words, about a matter of a certain sensitivity and attentiveness to things as they truly appear, here and now, and not as we wish them to appear, here and now. Philosophy with children then comes to seem an attempt to articulate the figures that are constituted through dominant discourses and making them objects of attention.

To clarify this difference further I want to refer to the ancient Greek distinction, recalled by Foucault (2005), between three ways of relating oneself to the truth, and the technical procedures, or forms of *technē*, that this requires: *flattery*, *rhetoric* and, as identified above, *parrhesia*. I shall try to show how the first two forms are based on the principle of knowing oneself, while the last refers to a care for the self (see Masschelein and Simons, 2008). Against this background I shall argue that the dominant mode of thinking about philosophy with children is conceived in terms of a method that *produces* a knowing subject. This is a figure for which truth-telling is based on knowledge (achieved through particular strategies and methods) that one has to acquire in order to speak the truth. In contrast to this figure, I am concerned with the figure for which knowledge does not exist; at least, it does not exist in relation to the truth behind something. For this figure, the only possible preparation is doing exercises in the form of *askesis* and experiment.

THREE FORMS OF THE PRACTICE OF TRUTH-TELLING

In *The Hermeneutics of the Subject* Foucault identifies the practice of truth-telling as a relationship between the subject and the truth, and in terms of the way the subject has access to the truth, or constitutes herself as a subject of truth-telling. The central image of this practice—or more precisely the central image of the way truth-telling was understood by the ancient Greeks and recalled by Foucault—is connected with *parrhesia*. What is basically at stake in *parrhesia* is 'the frankness, freedom, and openness that leads one to say what one has to say, as one wishes to say it, when one wishes to say it, and in the form one thinks one is necessary saying it' (Foucault, 2005, p. 372). The practice of *parrhesia*, as it was understood in Greek antiquity, is thus explicitly related to freedom, and expressed in terms of free speaking, or, in French, *franc-parler*. In order to understand this practice on the part of the person who speaks—and the *ethos* or moral attitude it embodies—Foucault compares the *parrhesiast* with two other discursive forms. First, there is *flattery*, the moral adversary against which *parrhesia* must struggle. The second, *rhetoric*, is also its adversary but its technical partner as well. So, according to Foucault, there must be opposition and struggle against *flattery*, while in relation to *rhetoric* there must be a setting free. Let me explain these oppositions further.[3]

Flattery occupies a position that is inferior in principle, since it is a way for the inferior to win over the greater power of the superior through gaining the latter's favour. The flatterer is someone who, when speaking, works to enhance the superior's sense of power in order to get what he wants from him. In making use of the superior's superiority in this way, he also reinforces it. 'He reinforces it since the flatterer', says Foucault, 'is the person who gets what he wants from the superior by making him think that he is the most handsome, the wealthiest, the most powerful, etc.' (p. 375). Consequently, Foucault continues, 'the flatterer may succeed in diverting the superior's power by addressing himself to the superior in a mendacious discourse in which the superior will see himself with more qualities, strength, and power than he possesses' (p. 276). In this way the flatterer is the person who renders the flattered blind and impotent, since he accedes to a discourse that is based on a lie. As a result, the superior finds himself in a dependent and weakened position, since he needs the flatterer's discourse in order to understand himself as superior. And in view of the fact that this discourse is a lying discourse, it can be said that this way of speaking is a trap. It silences the one to whom the flattery is directed, and it renders him dependent on the duplicity of the flatterer's discourse.

The second adversary, *rhetoric*, is first of all characterized as a technique whose methods do not in any obvious way aim at establishing a truth: 'rhetoric is defined as an art of persuading those to whom one is speaking, whether one wishes to convince them of a truth or a lie: a non-truth' (p. 381). It is about convincing someone of something, and necessarily covering up one's own beliefs in the process (cf. also Peters, 2003, p. 212). It is not the content and the question of truth that matters here, but the art of persuading the listener. As such, it can be said that rhetoric refers to the truth as *technē*, but only as what is known through the person speaking, not in terms of the truth contained in what that person says. Hence, rhetoric as *technē* is directly linked to a truth—the truth known, possessed and controlled by the person speaking—but not to the truth of what is said and so not from the point of view of the person being spoken to (Foucault, 2005, p. 382).

Notwithstanding their differences, both rhetoric and flattery imply a mode of thinking and speaking that is based on a specific type of relation to one's interlocutor—that is, both notions refer to a mode of thinking (a logic) in which one needs the other's discourse in order to speak. In the case of the flatterer, this means that one speaks not the discourse of the superior, but a discourse that boosts the superior's power: a discourse, therefore, that uses 'tricks of rhetoric'. In the case of rhetoric, things are slightly different, in the sense that this is an art that is defined, codified and taught, and this not 'by a personal or individual relationship,' Foucault suggests, 'but ... by the "tactical situation" of the person speaking face to face with the person he is addressing' (p. 383). Rhetoric is a way of speaking that takes into account possible assumptions, positions and counterarguments, and that employs its particular skills in order to convince the other (and the self) of a particular line of thought or idea. It could be said, therefore, that its utterances always assume the necessity of knowledge or skills in order to convince the listener. The person who uses rhetoric is one for whom truth-telling is based on the particular strategies and methods one has to acquire in order to speak in such a way as to persuade the listener.

Parrhesia is something totally different. It is not an art, and nor is it something that can be taught, or that has to be acquired in order to speak. It has no rules and no knowledge—no meta-discourse. It does not rely on the questioning, reasoning, defining, speculating, testing and summarising skills that are required to turn our thinking into science, and to codify and to reproduce the insights we have gained. Neither does it require particular competencies or feelings, such as empathy, self-esteem, self-awareness, etc., that imply an aesthetic turn inwards. *Parrhesia* does not refer to the truthfulness of the subject matter of what someone is saying or defending, measured by certain abstract principles or ideals, and evaluated as true or not according to those principles or ideals. True or veridical speech as described by Foucault is not given—on the contrary, it relates to 'the naked transmission' by the one who speaks, 'as it were, of truth itself' (p. 382). It relates to the person's exposure to what is the case at that particular moment, and to one's presence in the present. Being present in the present then involves not so much *discussing* particular subject matter as *practising*—say, being genuinely engaged in—the subject matter we are speaking about. '*Parrhesia* as it appears in the field of philosophical activity in Greco-Roman culture is not primarily a concept or a theme, but a practice that tries to shape the specific relations individuals have to themselves' (Foucault, 2001, p. 106).

What is required of the *parrhesiast* then is not a grand gesture of transgression or liberation, but a certain modest philosophical and pragmatic work upon the self; one could say a moral attitude or *ethos* (cf. also Franěk, 2006). In this sense, *parrhesia* concerns an activity that refers to the transformation of the subject's being, and this implies work upon the self. Here, speaking is not undertaken with a view to convincing the other, as is the case with rhetoric. The aim of *parrhesia* is not 'to pursue the unspeakable, nor to reveal the hidden, nor to say the unsaid, but on the contrary to capture the already-said, to collect what one has managed to hear or read' (Foucault, 1997, p. 211, in Luxon, 2008, p. 381). As such, the *parrhesiast* is someone who, in particular, looks and watches carefully, records what is said and thought, and questions how to relate herself to this. This means that what is at stake in *parrhesia* is not the gaining of knowledge about a subject matter, but the transformation of the self into a subject of care. Adapting to the other's discourse is not important, but work upon the self is, and this work demands that the subject remains open to forms of problematisation—in particular, to the power relations it represents—and attentive to the discursive elements that make up the present and that constitute the subject in that present (Rabinow and Rose, 2003).

Hence, *parrhesia* does not oppose itself to rhetoric, but rather suspends or frees the self from rhetoric. It might be said, therefore, that the *parrhesiast* is 'a sort of figure among rhetorical figures, but with this characteristic: that it is without any figure since it is completely natural' (Foucault, 2001, p. 21). *Parrhesia* requires that one removes oneself from the current discourse in order to say what one has to say, taking into account 'what the Greeks called the *kairos*, or "the critical moment"' (Foucault, 2001, p. 111). This involves an activity in which one's existence is at stake—in which the question arises whether there is a harmonic relation between the rational discourse one uses and the way that one lives one's life. This is not, however, a transitional activity leading to becoming someone or becoming something else—it is not the discovery of a 'deep' self, the 'true' self—but a form of speaking in which the person produces a break within the self, or a de-subjectivation of the self. It is a putting of oneself at stake by being open to such questions as 'Who are we today?' and 'How should we look at ourselves, the other and the world here and now'? (Foucault, 1984). It is the exposition of what is thought and said, and it implies, therefore, one's presence in it, which in turn necessitates full awareness of and attentiveness to the words one speaks, in the presence of the self, the other and the world. *Parrhesia* means that one must disclose who one *is*—in terms not of one's relationship to future events, but of one's present relation to the truth (p. 103). What is at stake for the *parrhesiast*, then, is a matter not of knowing what one does, but rather of thinking about what one does and says: to converse with oneself, and to interrogate one's own words and thoughts in the context of the game of forces that constitute existence (cf. Peters, 2003).

The criterion for truth-telling is not the extent to which knowledge of a particular subject matter has been achieved. The 'truthfulness' in question situates itself rather at the level of a person's actions. She is recognised as a *parrhesiast* when there is not the slightest discrepancy between what she says and what she does (Foucault, 2001, p. 100). The recognition of truth-telling in this tradition is thus related not to the internal and external conditions of rhetoric, understood as a means of gaining access to truth, but to ethical-existential conditions. It is not what one says that is at stake, but rather the one who speaks—as in the case of Socrates. In the *Apology*, Socrates tells his interlocutors that he has to be executed because he is a *parrhesiast*. This does not mean that he is a great rhetorician—after all, as Socrates says, he knows only that he does not know. What his truth-telling guarantees is first of all his philosophical attitude: the fact that he is taking care of his soul instead of calculating his chances of surviving in court. Free speech requires, in other words, a transforming care of the self, a stylising of existence: it requires care for the soul. And the soul is the name of the subject of veridiction.

PARRHESIA VERSUS DIALOGICAL PROCEDURES AND STRATEGIES AS TRUTH-TELLING PRACTICE

Perhaps at first sight *parrhesia* does not fundamentally differ from what philosophy with children generally tries to achieve. After all, Socrates' appeal to us to wake up—to refuse what we previously accepted, or sometimes to accept what we previously refused—is also of crucial importance within the current debate on philosophy with children. Karin Murris, for example, writes that philosophy with children as the practice of Socratic questioning 'begins to shake the habitual certainty with which people take for granted the meaning of everyday abstract concepts, such as "respect" and "space"' (Murris, 2008, p. 670). And along the same lines, Oscar Brenifier argues that '[t]he thoughts we entertain necessarily stop us from having other thoughts, especially if those thoughts are the kind of general principles that determine what is acceptable and what is not.' Thus, 'we have to become a stranger to ourselves in order to think, we have to alienate ourselves in order to be' (Brenifier, 2006, p. 3). 'De-subjectivise yourself!' says Brenifier to the children with whom he is philosophising (De Haas, 2007). Accordingly, within the actual discourse of philosophy with children, the general aim is to make the other conscious of herself,

> First, by asking her to be conscious of her own question: through analysis, conceptualization, explanation, and other forms of deepening the signification and implications of it. Second, through inviting this person to observe carefully her own thought and behaviors and pass judgment on herself. Third, by periodically asking her to take the counterposition of her ideas, and to dwell in depth on that perspective. Fourth, to accept and enjoy the 'unthinkable' that she has necessarily produced in the process, which most likely deals in a profound fashion with her own problem or question (Brenifier, 2006, pp. 4–5).

As an example of the practice of philosophy with children, and notwithstanding the fact that it represents a strong critique of a form of speaking that is based on flattery, Brenifier's account differs from Greek *parrhesia*. In contrast to the latter, philosophy with children, thus construed, does not invite the child to take up the word, to look at and to think about what presents itself; rather, it shows the way to a deep truth, to what lies behind the things we see and think. It is concerned with the task of progress in one's understanding through an examination of relevant evidence, thereby recalling the attitude of a search for a better world. Here, the truth-teller is not someone who knows that he does not know, but someone who organises a scene in which the child is confronted with the shortcomings and *aporias* in his thinking and acting. It is the attitude of a teacher who does not invite the child to speak, but above all demands that she discover and recognise her shortcomings in relation to a tribunal (a kingdom of truth). Or as Jacques Rancière (1987) defines it, it is the attitude of the teacher who commands the movements, the actions and the reactions of his student. As for himself, the teacher has the certainty of knowing how to handle the process—it is all at his disposal. Step by step, he leads the mind of the pupil towards the ends of the enquiry. The pupil, in turn, is amazed at arriving at such ends and in consequence admires the teacher. This puts him at the same time in an inescapable position of inferiority and dependence: the pupil experiences himself as not able to speak without a training of his mind by an expert.

What we see more generally within philosophy with children, however, cannot be conceived simply as a domination of children by the teacher, with her effective knowledge and techniques, but as a kind of technologisation of philosophy and the child. By this I mean that, within the current discourse on philosophy with children, both the teacher and the child are addressed as individuals who need to reflect on new strategies and techniques in order to promote and to stimulate better, more effective, critical, creative and caring ways of thinking, with the aid of dialogical strategies and techniques dedicated to the purpose. Strategies of this kind do not, however, function as a norm. Rather, they function as a kind of powerful steering mechanism in today's permanently changing environment (cf. Bröckling, 2006). As such, they may be understood as the correlate to an attitude of flattery. Or, to put it otherwise, when it is assumed that thinking for oneself is guaranteed by using particular dialogical strategies and techniques, then *not* to use these strategies would seem to risk losing, if not actually to block, the possibility of thinking and speaking for oneself. Such a practice of philosophy with children could be described as a method in which care for the self is replaced by dialogical procedures and technologies—in short, by a method. And method, as Foucault writes, 'is a form of reflexivity that makes it possible to fix the certainty that will serve as criterion for all possible truth and which, starting from this fixed point, will advance from truth to truth up to the organization and systematization of an objective knowledge' (Foucault, 2005, p. 460 in Geerinck *et al.*, 2010, pp. 8–9). However such dialogical procedures and strategies may change, their advocates persist in the assumption that the world is divided into people who have knowledge and people who do not. Although philosophy with children ostensibly criticises this assumption, it continues to imagine a form of life to which efficient dialogical practice might be sufficient. Why, it might be said, would anyone be against this? The question is not, however, whether we are for or against this: the question is whether we are able to refuse it. This implies not only that the need for dialogical programmes and technologies not only constitutes its own starting assumption but also that this need is also constantly and automatically stripped of any reinteriorisation: that is, it is without *critique*, and thus without *responsibility*.

Hence, the difference between philosophy with children so described and the practice of *parrhesia* concerns the difference between a form of truth-telling that takes self-actualisation as its point of departure, and a form of speaking that suspends this idea. In contrast to philosophy with children, for the *parrhesiast* it is not self-actualisation that is at stake, but the affirmation that one *can* speak, think and see. The *parrhesiast* does not understand speaking, thinking or seeing as skills one has to acquire—say, through 'learning by doing'—but as a work upon the self, with the experience of being able to say something more, while realising and affirming what one is used to saying and thinking. In this sense the *parrhesiast* does not coordinate a discursive scene or focus an argument. The work upon the self that he performs is not regulated by knowledge, by competence or by (humanistic) ideals, but by willingness to put the limits of one's own experience to the test of one's own thinking. This does not reveal underlying regularities or a stable foundation for thought. The result of the work upon the self that Foucault speaks of is never an indication of particular problems and possible solutions for these problems (cf. Rabinow and Rose, 2003). It does not offer a better, truer or more complete view, a view that allows us to transgress the limits of individual perspectives. It is not a guide to how to think and act. On the contrary, what the work of the *parrhesiast* undertakes is not an analysis and decipherment of the self, but an exposition—a work of concentrated exertion, of being there. This means that the *parrhesiast* is not someone who takes an external or meta-position. Rather, exposition establishes direct contact. It enables, and in a certain sense necessitates, the experience of con-frontation, face-to-face with what happens or, more precisely, with whoever we are with in our actual present. It leads the listener into giving an account (*didonai logon*) of oneself, 'of the manner in which one now spends one's days, and of the kind of life one has lived hitherto' (Foucault, 2001, p. 96). This requirement, then, does not refer to the quest for a confession of the listener's faults or sins. To give an account of one's life is not to give a narrative of the historical events that have taken place in that life. Instead, it is the demonstration of a movement in which one no longer needs the other's discourse. That one no longer needs the other's discourse does not only imply that one is finally relieved of something, but that one experiences the possibility of speaking—which is, in the words of Jean-Luc Nancy, the opening of the mouth, 'because you demanded to hear me' (Nancy, 2006, p. 37).

ASCETIC PRACTICES AS A PREPARATION FOR *PARRHESIA*

The question that arises now is: how does one become able to speak the truth? Can one learn to be a *parrhesiast*? Foucault writes that *parrhesia* is not something one has to acquire through learning; rather it involves exercises in which one 'puts oneself at stake'. These exercises are essentially linked to practices of *askesis*, which lead to the realisation of an *ethos*. They are not, however, to be understood as procedures or methods guaranteeing an objective perspective or meta-position. Neither do they refer to spiritual capacities or competencies one has to acquire in order to be able to 'enter' into a philosophical experience (cf. Cleghorn 2002). The practices I am referring to are, rather, disciplinary exercises of the self upon the self, and these imply a kind of concentration of involvement. *Askesis* does not provide access to the truth, nor is it part of an academic discipline or profession (*askesis* does not proclaim or provide any truth or doctrine). Through ascetic practices one puts oneself at stake and *in* the present. Ascetic practices open one up for what there is to see and to hear—for what strikes the eye. They make exposition possible.

Masschelein (2006) describes concrete practices or exercises such as walking, (re)reading, writing, listening, speaking, copying etc., as forms of *askesis*. What these practices have in common is not their absence of (direct) goal-orientation and methodology, but their rhythmical, repetitive and quasi-mechanical or monotonous character. This relates to the absence of goals and methods and assures a certain endurance, a longevity, that is appropriate for and characteristic of the practice of truth-telling precisely because it enables us to expose things as they are (at that particular moment and time) and not the way we think they are or wish them to be. Ascetic practices, as such, could be called an open preparation of the individual for the events of life and for beginning to speak. They rely on a particular way of disciplining of the body and the mind in order that one become attentive, that one attend to the present, enabling oneself to avoid interpreting, explaining, contextualising or deconstructing the present as a means supposedly to understanding its deeper truth. They open up the opportunity to venture forth the words that need to be heard. That is why these practices are also called 'experimental', because they not only make it clear that what is at stake is not an intellectual enterprise, but that in experiencing truth-telling as truth-telling, one also puts oneself at stake. The experimental character of the exercise resides in the fact that its effects cannot be planned or determined beforehand, as in the case of a programme or procedure. Rather, it calls for a transformation of the subject—which involves extracting the subject from itself and from its reliance on acquired, 'already-there-expertise' as a means to the achievement of a true perspective. Such exercises do not provide the subject with interpretative procedures and strategies, but expose it to what is happening here and now in order that one may become free of oneself—that one may experience oneself as having the possibility of 'always-becoming-something-other-than-itself' (cf. Nancy, 2006, p. 214).

Hence, the educational meaning of *parrhesia* might be said to imply the creation of a singular space; a space that does not demand certain conditions in order to understand what is happening here and now—which is a way of covering up one's own beliefs—but a space that in a certain sense allows one to suspend individual beliefs and perspectives in order to see what needs to be seen.

CONCLUDING THOUGHTS

By way of conclusion, I want to suggest that my Cambodian experiment was an occasion to think philosophy with children as an ascetic practice that granted the experience of a transformation of oneself. Since the experiment did not proclaim or defend any organising principle, but invited a limit experience (hence, the apparent absence of rhetoric), it provided a space not *in* but *ahead of* the present: a space that opened the present or opened truth. It was not a matter of being caught in the flow but rather of being ahead of it. It opened a space situated at the border. But what is it to experience activities at the border? What can this mean? These almost impossible (and uncomfortable) activities, however contrived they may be, are strictly ordered by the conditions of the border itself: by the traces or the images of the things, the activities, the meanings and the languages that are not to be situated *there*. In short, these are activities without a meaning or an end, activities of cadenced regularity, step by step, left, right, left, right, moving from one line to the other as the words 'right' and 'left' indicate, hour after hour, caesura by caesura. Thus, this was not a programmed activity, but a strictly punctual and ordered activity that had the capacity to move those who took part, not to somewhere else, somewhere outside time, but to move them ahead of time—in the face of, in confronting, what 'we' are accustomed to think, say and do. Hence, the border has no real order or meaning. Rather, it constitutes order and meaning, allowing us to think about the ordering of difference, with its organising principles and discourses, its localisations and rhetoric.

This also made the experiment unbearable at times, since it involved an experience of the absence of rhetoric. Rhetoric offers the occasion to think about a problem or an idea *in a particular way*: it offers a comfortable position. The border does not offer comfort but discomfort: it does not offer the possibility of distancing oneself from what is happening, the better to bring to it the ironic gaze and judgment of the philosophical expert. At the border we are exposed to what happens. This means that we no longer experience a discourse (of expertise) that dictates how to think and speak while simultaneously promising freedom at the end. At the border we open our eyes—or, as Nancy writes, 'it opens itself like an eye that looks at us by opening our eyes to it' (Nancy, 2006, p. 203). What we can see then is meaning emptied through the presence of its own presentation. To speak then is, first and foremost, to affirm one's presence in the present. It means that 'I needed to speak in order to speak to you' (see p. 36).

What the experiment revealed was a way of thinking about philosophy with children in terms of a preparation of the self, not in order to get access to another (more real) world (the world of dialogical reasoning, for instance), but in order to gain access to the reality of *this* world. As such, no practice that directs the child to the Promised Land is needed, but a practice that moves the child away from this idea: a practice, in other words, that allows oneself to act as things demand and to hold in suspense dominant regimes of power and thought. What philosophy with children also is about then is the search for border places or practices. This is a search that makes it possible to experience and articulate what is happening here and now.[4]

NOTES

1. The VVOB (Vlaamse Vereniging voor Ontwikkelingssamenwerking en Technische Bijstand) is the Flemish Association for Development Cooperation and Technical Assistance, a non-profit organisation. By order of the Flemish and the Belgian government, the VVOB aims to contribute to the improvement of quality of the education in developing countries. Their core task is to provide technical assistance in projects and programmes and to stimulate sustainable development.
2. The word 'exposition' is intended to carry connotations both of being exposed to others, perhaps in circumstances where one's normal competences and accomplishments are no longer sufficient, and of being out of position, disconnected from one's regular position. And hence it refers to a condition in which one is open to other ways of relating oneself to the self, others and the world.
3. In his lectures at the Collège de France from 1981–1982, entitled *The Hermeneutics of the Subject*, Foucault outlines a genealogical analysis of the meaning of *parrhesia* and its cognates in Greek Antiquity. In particularly he investigates the use of *parrhesia* in specific types of human relationships and the use of procedures and techniques employed in these relationships. In this paper I revisit this analysis. However, I do not do so in order to sketch the changing practices within truth-telling and its relation to education (cf. Peters, 2003). I want simply to point at different forms of truth-telling in order to recall the possibility of *parrhesia* as a form of truth-telling that '"educates" rather than "produces" individuals' (Luxon, 2008, p. 379).
4. I would like to thank Jan Masschelein for his comments on a first version of this paper. Thanks also to David Kennedy and Paul Standish for proofreading the text.

REFERENCES

Brenifier, O. (2006) Nasruddin Hodja, A Master of the Negative Way, *Childhood and Philosophy*, 1.3, pp. 1–14.

Bröckling (2006) Und . . . wie war ich? über feedback, *Mittelweg*, 36.2, pp. 26–43.

Cleghorn, P. (2002) Why Philosophy with Children?, *Education Review*, 15.2, pp. 47–51.

De Haas, L. (2007) De kille dialogen van Oscar Brenifier. De beperkingen van de conceptgerichte benadering in het filosofische gesprek. Available at: http://www.engadin.nl/essays/files/brenifier.pdf. Accessed 13 March 2010.

Foucault, M. (1984) Nietzsche, Genealogy, History, in: P. Rabinow (ed.) *The Foucault Reader* (New York, Pantheon), pp. 76–100.

Foucault, M. (2001) *Fearless Speech* (Los Angeles, CA, Semiotext(e)).

Foucault, M. (2005) The Hermeneutics of the Subject. Lectures at the Collège de France, 1981–1982 (New York, Picador), pp. 76–100.

Franěk, J. (2006) Philosophical *Parrhesia* as Aesthetics of Existence, *Continental Philosophy Review*, 39, pp. 113–134.

Geerinck, I., Masschelein, J. and Simons, M. (2010) Teaching and Knowledge: A Necessary Combination? An Elaboration of Forms of Teachers' Reflexitivity, *Studies in Philosophy of Education*. Published online 23 April 2010.

Luxon, N. (2008) Ethics and Subjectivity: Practices of Self-Governance in the late lectures of Michel Foucault, *Political Theory*, 36, pp. 377–402.

Masschelein, J. (2006) Laat ons gaan, in: J. Masschelein and M. Simons (eds) *Europa Anno 2006. E-ducatieve berichten uit niemandsland* (Leuven, Acco).

Masschelein, J. and Simons, M. (2008) Do Historians (of Education) Need Philosophy? The Enlightening Potential of Philosophical Ethos, *Paedagogica Historica*, 44.2, pp. 647–660.

Murris, K. (2008) Philosophy with Children, the Stingray and the Educative Value of Desequilibrium, *Journal of Philosophy of Education*, 42.3–4, pp. 667–685.

Nancy, J. L. (2006) *Multiple Arts. The Muses II* (Stanford, CA, Stanford University Press).

Peters, M. (2003) Truth-telling as an Educational Practice of the Self: Foucault, *Parrhesia* and the Ethics of Subjectivity, *Oxford Review of Education*, 29.2, pp. 207–223.

Rabinow, P. and Rose, N. (2003) Foucault Today, in: P. Rabinow and N. Rose (eds) *The Essential Foucault: Selections from the Essential Works of Foucault, 1954–1984* (New York, New Press).

Rancière, J. (1987) *Le maître ignorant. Cinq leçons sur l'émancipation intellectuelle* (Paris, Fayard).

Vansieleghem, N. (2006) Gesprek als grenservaring. Een analyse van filosoferen met kinderen als pedagogisch project. Unpublished PhD thesis, Ghent.

10

Childhood, Education and Philosophy: Notes on Deterritorialisation

WALTER OMAR KOHAN

PHILOSOPHY AND CHILDHOOD EDUCATION: THE TRADITIONAL RELATIONSHIP

Childhood has been a privileged object of pedagogical utopias of various sorts throughout the history of Western educational thought, which goes back at least as early as Plato's *Republic* (Plato, 1990). In Book II of that treatise, Socrates suggests that the education of the guardians of the *pólis* is essential in order to guarantee a just community, and that the genesis or cause (*aitía*) of justice or injustice lies in education or its absence (II, 376d). When discussing which stories should replace the traditional Homeric and Hesiodic ones, Socrates affirms (II, 376e–377b) that the first years of life are the most important, because all that comes later will depend on those first steps. This is what makes childhood extraordinarily important, because of the indelible marks that are received in those first moments of the human life cycle (II 378e). For this reason, special attention will be given to those first stages by the designers of the Republic, not so much for what children are but for what they will become.

In the *Republic*, it is someone external—the educator, the philosopher, the legislator of the *pólis*—who will give form to another who in himself has no form, and who is not considered capable of finding it by himself. To give someone a form; to *in*form her: education is understood here *toute simple* as the formation of childhood. In this approach, education is normative, adjusting what is to what ought to be. According to this orientation, children represent adults' opportunity to carry out their ideals, and education is considered an appropriate instrument for such an end.

In this context, not only education but also philosophy itself is understood as in the service of the formation of the young. Certainly,

Philosophy for Children in Transition: Problems and Prospects, First Edition. Nancy Vansieleghem and David Kennedy. Chapters © 2012 The Authors. Editorial organization © 2012 Philosophy of Education Society of Great Britain. Published 2012 by Blackwell Publishing Ltd.

philosophy is not to be taught *to* children because, according to Plato, they are not capable of such a complex form of knowledge. But the knowledge that philosophy entails will inform the best natures, those of the most rigorous character (VI, 503b), those who are capable of becoming the best rulers because they are the best (*aristós*). In this sense, the learning of philosophy as kind of knowledge will facilitate the best formation of those best natures who by rights ought to govern the *pólis*.

Although they may differ significantly in the details of their approach to education, to philosophy, and to childhood, certain contemporary programmes that propose to educate children through philosophy, such as Philosophy for Children, maintain a similar relationship between the three terms, in that the educational potential of philosophy is justified on the basis of its utopian political force. Philosophical education, whether of the child or adult, and whether conducted through instruction or communal inquiry, is defended on the promise of its formative potential for a better world. Whatever the differences in their specific agendas, the fact remains that all these programmes consider philosophy to be an educational vehicle that carries a political component—the Form of the Good in Plato, democracy in Philosophy for Children—that is useful for the optimal formation of the citizens of the *pólis*. Thus, according to Mathew Lipman, the logic of democracy (understood as deliberative inquiry) determines the purposes and meanings of the teaching of philosophy. To bring philosophy to children with its history, its methods and its themes is justified for the social advantages that such a practice will create (Lipman, 1988, p. 198). If a more solid or authentic form of democracy is desired outside schools, democratic practices must be established in them and communicated through them. Children are educated through communities of philosophical inquiry in order that they be shaped into the democratic citizens that society needs. Again, if philosophy is incorporated into childhood education, it is because of the formative benefits of exposing the young to this form of thinking and speaking.

ALTERNATIVE CONCEPTS OF CHILDHOOD

How might education be considered and practised if not under the logic of the formation of childhood? More specifically, how might the purposes of practising philosophy with children be affirmed other than as toward the social and political education of childhood? This complex issue calls for a redefinition not only of philosophy and education, but also of childhood itself. The traditional form of the philosophical education of childhood that I have just described is constructed in keeping with a conception of childhood as a stage of human life. But the history of pedagogical ideas reveals different images of the child, some more positive, some less.

In fact, I would suggest that each conception of childhood presupposes a concept of time. Childhood as stage of life presupposes a chronological concept of time: life is conceived as a sequential and consecutive line of movements. Time is the number of these movements. From this approach, Plato defines *chrónos* as 'the moving image of eternity (*aión*) that moves according to number' (*Timaeus*, 37d). Time understood as *chrónos* is only possible in the imperfect and ever-moving world of birth and death. The perfect world of Ideas is static, ana-chronic, aionic. Some chronological time later, Aristotle defined *chrónos* as 'the number of movement according to the "before and after"' (*Physics*, IV, 220a).[1]

In his fragment 52, Heraclitus (2001) introduces a different relationship between the child and time with the use of the time-word *aión*: 'Time [*aión*] (is) a child childing (playing); its realm is one of a child'. In its more ancient uses, *aión* designates the intensity of time in human life—a destiny, a duration, an un-numbered movement, not successive, but intensive (Liddell and Scott, 1966, p. 45). There is a double relationship between time and childhood in this fragment: time does what a child does (*paízon:* plays) and in time, as *aión*, childhood governs (*basileíe* is a power word, meaning 'realm'). Thus, this fragment can be read as showing that time—life-time—is not only a question of numbered movement (*chrónos*). There is another dimension of living time more akin to a childlike form of being (*aión*), non-numbered. In relation to this kind of time, a child is more powerful than any other being. In aionic life, childhood does not statically exist in one stage of life—the first one—but rather goes through it, powerfully, as an intensity or duration. In this fragment a non-chronological, aionic experience of time emerges and, together with it, a non-chronological concept of childhood. Childhood may here be understood, not only as a period of life but as a specific strength, force or intensity that inhabits a qualitative life at any given chronologic time.

DELEUZE AND BECOMING-CHILD

Many contemporary philosophers have offered us new concepts and vocabularies with which to think non-chronological concepts of child-hood, a few of which I will take up in this paper. My aim is not so much to establish any specific connections between and among them as to sketch a framework that allows space within which alternative ways of relating childhood, philosophy and education might emerge. Gilles Deleuze, for example, proposes an impersonal notion, a non-subjective form to which he gives names like 'becoming-child' or 'block of childhood'. 'Becoming-child' is not a matter of age but of flux, intensity. It is a revolutionary space of transformation. It is not that a given subject becomes a child, transforms himself into a child or lives a childlike life: rather, he occupies a space of transformation. In effect, 'becoming-child' has the form of escape lines—'lines of flight' that cannot be incorporated or co-opted by the system: disrupted movements, changes of rhythm, segments that interrupt the logic of the state of affairs and intersect and divide it, with different roots and targets.

According to Deleuze (1990),[2] becoming opposes history. History gives the set of conditions in order that an event or experience can take place, but in itself, an experience or event is beyond history. An experience becomes, or emerges, it cannot be anticipated or planned in the successive moments of history. On the one hand there is the continuous— history, *chrónos*, contradiction, dialectic, and the majority; on the other, the discontinuous, becoming, experience. Becoming-child is always in the minority, because being majority or minority is not a question of number, but of whether a model is being followed or not. Minorities cannot be numbered or grouped; lacking a model, they are always in process (Deleuze and Guattari, 1980, pp. 585 ff.). The dynamism of minorities resides in their nomadism, which for Deleuze and Guattari (pp. 455 ff.), is a kind of acceleration aimed at escaping control, discipline, and any pretentions of unification; Deleuze characterises this force of resistance as an 'exorcizing [of] shame'.

Besides distinguishing between history and becoming, Deleuze privileges geography over history, in an ontology that is replete with planes, segments, lines, maps, territories, movements. He proposes (Deleuze and Guattari, 1991) a geo-philosophy, a philosophy of the earth. Here, thinking is not a matter of subject and object, but 'the relationship of territory and the earth', which creates the plane of immanence, which is where thinking takes place. In fact, thinking traverses diverse planes of immanence. Human beings also simultaneously traverse different, opposed, parallel, intersecting spaces.[3] On the one hand, there are the spaces of macro-politics, of the state—molar segments, binaries, which are concentric, resonant with each other, and are expressed by the paradigm of the tree, with its principle of dichotomy and axis of concentricity. On the other hand, there are the spaces of micro-politics— molecular segments, the rhizome, where binaries are multiplicities, circles are not concentric, and where becoming-child emerges. In this space, becoming-child is a war machine against the state and adult institutions. As the non-chronological time of becoming, it represents a space of resistance, a source of creativity and of the experience of a different world.

In summary, Plato invented a plane of immanence on which to think childhood as a matter for social transformation through education, and to think education as the formation of childhood. On this plane of immanence, various images of childhood have been drawn, corresponding with diverse political and ideological agendas. As I have suggested, Philosophy for Children in its founding movement was also established on this plane. But new planes can be created in order to think philosophy *between* childhood and education, and Deleuze offers elements of a particularly provocative one.

LYOTARD AND INFANTIA

Jean-François Lyotard offers yet another plane of imminence on which to think childhood, and from a very different perspective. According to Lyotard, childhood represents the difference between what can and what cannot be said—*infantia* (literally 'absence of speech') is for him the unsayable, or as he puts it, 'what is not said' (Lyotard, 1997, p. 13).[4] This childhood has nothing to do with a stage of life either, nor with something that is formed, corrected or overcome over the course of a life. Rather it inhabits, imperceptibly, the sayable as its condition, its shadow, or remainder. Consciousness and discourse attempt to deny, to efface *infantia*, but in this very movement they constitute it as something that is missed. Seen in this way, childhood is understood, not as a stage of language acquisition, but as a latent condition that inhabits every word that is pronounced—not just the words of children, but the words of every human being. To use another image from Lyotard, it could be said that childhood is a survival, an entity that should be dead but is *still* alive (p. 63); childhood passes as infancy, but survives as *infantia*.

Infantia is the state of the soul 'inhabited by something to which a response will never be given' (p. 69) This something is a debt acquired by the fact of birth itself, a debt owed by the newborn to the other, incurred in order that the birth could happen, emerging from non-being, the other of being, what remains forgotten after birth. Childhood keeps alive this forgetfulness of an initial and constitutive debt that each human being carries. The initial non-being out of which every human being is born—this emptiness manifested by the absence of decision or consciousness that marks every act of coming into the world—demands to be remembered in the abulic being that installs itself in the world after each birth. In the words of Lyotard, childhood is 'the event of a possible and radical alteration in the flux that pushes things to repeat the same' (p. 72). Childhood is a faculty that gives a name to something that 'already is' but yet is not 'anything', an abjection, a fright that introduces something that cannot be identified into the world of what is. In yet another Lyotardian metaphor, childhood is the name of a miracle, the interruption of the being of things by the entrance of its other—the other of being.

What the two conceptions of childhood that I have just sketched have in common is that for both of them, childhood is something that inherently constitutes human life, and therefore could never be abandoned, forgotten or overcome. In this way, both refuse to go along with the idea of the transformation of childhood into adulthood as a primary pedagogical project, and introduce the need to think another relation between childhood and education. Beyond the ideal of child-formation, education might be what fosters, nurtures and cares for the experience of childhood itself—what helps us not to forget childhood, but rather to, in Lyotard's words, preserve *infantia* in infancy, or, in Deleuze's, to encounter becoming-child.

I offer these alternative notions of childhood, not because they complement each other, nor to prove the force any given idea of childhood, but on the contrary, in order to avoid the implicit pressure of 'reason' to subscribe to one particular, 'correct' philosophical theory. In a sense it would be simpler—and probably more articulate—to limit myself to one of these conceptions, but I believe that an open interpretive framework offers more hope for clearing the ground for rethinking the relationship between childhood and education, and the place of philosophy between them. Because I prefer to speak, finally, from my own experience, my further remarks will be offered within the context of the actual practice of conducting conversations with children—encounters that I have found, almost universally, to challenge any one theoretical approach.

THINKING THE EXPERIENCE OF PHILOSOPHICAL THINKING IN THE CONTEXT OF BRAZILIAN PUBLIC SCHOOLING

My work in schools and universities in Brazil throughout the past decade and more, during which I and my colleagues have laboured to introduce the experience of philosophical thinking in classroom and other group settings, have led us to question the value of philosophizing within the traditional Platonic ideal of child-formation, or even Lipman's ideal of the formation of the reasonable citizen (Lipman, 1998). Rather, we have sought consciously to promote experiences of philosophical thinking that enable everyone involved in them to *think differently* than the ways we are used to think, and that we are forced or manipulated into thinking by the dominant cultural forces of our time. Our goal has been to establish new relationships within ourselves, with others, to how and what we think, and therefore, to the way we live with ourselves and with the others. We found ourselves driven forward in this search by an experience of cultural dislocation—the outcome of engaging in educational and philosophical work with children and illiterate adults in public schools located in marginalised urban and suburban regions of Rio de Janeiro.[5]

In order to open a space for these new relationships, the three main terms of the concept 'the experience of philosophical thinking' need to be unpacked, for all three are not only philosophical concepts, but contestable ones as well. As our project has both theoretical and practical aspirations, at the same time that we practise the experience of philosophical thinking, we encounter this practice with the theoretical discourses of various contemporary philosophers. We do not belong to any of these philosophers, but befriend them, so to speak, in our efforts to found our practice. And indeed we find that the category of 'experience', for example, has a long history in various philosophical traditions. Michel Foucault's synthesis, for example, identifies experience as an interactive combination of theory and practice. For him, experience is a kind of theoretical practice or practical theory, in which the dominant idea is that of movement, displacement, and transformation. In effect, a thinking experience is a living, dynamic form, through the process of which we never end in the place we began; nor do we think in the same way that we thought when we entered it.

In this same sense, Foucault (1994)[6] opposes experience and truth as two possibilities of writing. One can write a book under the logic of truth, in which case the author's aim is to transmit a truth he possesses to his readers. If the reader is also guided by the model of truth, he reads in order to learn a truth that he does not yet know. On the other hand, a book written under the logic of experience also affirms truths—there is no way not to do so—but the main sense of writing is not to transmit a truth but to put into question the truth in which the writer is already installed. There could also be readers under the logic of experience who do not read a book to learn what they are ignorant of, but to challenge what they already know—to put their relationship to the truths affirmed in the text into question. Of course there is no final, determined relationship between writing and reading, experience and truth. A book written as experience could be read as truth, and vice versa. And according to Foucault, reading as experience is not only about a possible relationship to what is written, but also to the method employed by the writer. When the guiding methodology follows not truth but experience, even the how and the why of the writer's process are put into question. From the point of view of the writer, this means that, at the beginning of the writing experience, he not only does not know what he will write, but also how he will arrive where he finally arrives.

What Foucault suggests about writing could well be considered as a way of thinking about teaching philosophy. A teacher who relates herself to philosophy as truth may expect her students to learn the philosophical truths she will mediate in her classes. On the other hand, there may well be philosophy teachers guided by the logic of experience who will also affirm philosophical truths in their classes, but they do not do so in order that their students learn them, but rather in order to problematise the relationship that both—students and teacher—have to the truths in which they are already installed. The difference, then, is that in the first case, the teacher not only knows exactly what to teach, but she is also concerned that her students learn the pathways, instruments and pedagogical strategies that guide and determine her teaching. In the second case, the teacher not only does not want to anticipate what her students will learn, but her pedagogical method—the method, that is, through which she and her students will arrive at questioning their relationship to what they already know and think—will be constructed through the teaching process itself.

In this sense thinking, guided by the logic of experience, puts itself into question—it thinks itself in such a way that it cannot continue to be thought as it was previously thought. Foucault said it nicely in naming philosophy as a practice (in Greek, *áskesis*). What is philosophy as an activity, as an exercise, if it is not 'the critical work of thinking about itself, if it does not consist in an attempt to think how and to what extent it would be possible to think differently instead of legitimating what we already know'? (Foucault, 1984, pp. 15–16). Therein lies the main significance of promoting philosophical experiences with teachers and students—not to legitimate what we or they know, but to foster difference in their thinking and our thinking as well.

Certainly the question 'What is philosophy?' is also a controversial one, and the expression 'philosophical experience' is not at all clear on its face. The issue is complex enough to resist resolution in a few pages, but a few observations may at least point to the path we are following. One may, for example, distinguish between two dimensions of philosophy, the process and the product—or, we might say, the verb and the noun. The product is constituted in the powerful discursive constructs of iconic texts, well-established institutions, and preferred methods, built up at least since the pre-Socratics into what is called the Western philosophical tradition. The other dimension could be characterised, with Foucault, more by its effects than its activity, as 'a diagnosis of the present' or a 'critical ontology of ourselves' (Foucault, 1994, pp. 665, 575). These latter are the results of philosophical experiences: after them, we are in a better condition to understand our times and our place in them. But experience itself has to do mainly with the verb and the process. Foucault appeals to a parallel conceptual framework when he characterises philosophy as 'the movement through which, not without efforts and obstacles, dreams and illusions, we detach ourselves from what is taken as true, and we look for other rules of the game' (p. 110). That is to say, as experience, philosophy is the movement through which thinking enters a path along which there is no opportunity to return to the point of departure. It entails a kind of radical affectivity, in that our truths and fixed points are disturbed, problematised, questioned. New rules are needed, and a new relation to truth emerges.

Finally, thinking is as controversial a concept as are experience and philosophy. Again, we are faced by another issue with a complex philosophical background. As Foucault was more interested in issues of clear social relevance, like madness, power and sexuality, he did not give specific attention to questions like 'What does it mean to think?' or 'What is the place of thinking in human life?' Here we might call on Deleuze's notion of thinking as encounter, and on his critique of the idea of representation and what he calls the 'dogmatic image' of thinking that has, with few exceptions, pervaded the history of Western philosophy (Deleuze, 1968). His critique is inspiring because of its relevance to contemporary prevalent images of thinking, especially among pedagogical discourses. In the Deleuzian sense, to think is not to produce a representation or to experience a recognition of something, but is an encounter with the external signs that call it to our attention. In order to think, a kind of deconstructive movement is first needed, in order to override the traditional image and to, as much as possible, render us sensitive to what is 'outside' us. Thinking is not opposed to sensitivity; quite the contrary, it is nurtured by it, it originates in it. Even more, thinking is a passion—immanent, spontaneous, self-caused and not the result of some external will.

Thus, in this preliminary sense of the term, we might say that our task consists in promoting the experience of philosophical of thinking with others, in institutions such as schools and universities, but certainly not limited to those places. In so doing, we reclaim and recreate a long tradition of philosophical dialogue. We are not particularly interested in teaching or learning the truths affirmed in the history of philosophy, even though we are readers of that history; rather, we try to do what philosophers of that tradition do. In so doing, we encounter 'lovers of wisdom' (or those with the 'wisdom of lovers', to show the specific form of passion required by practitioners of philosophy)—those looking for something similar to what we are looking for or, to put it differently, those who describe their own philosophical labour in a way close to our own, and who help us clarify and even discover our own. As such, we are engaged in what Pierre Hadot, who strongly influenced Foucault's reading of ancient cultures, called 'spiritual exercises' (Hadot, 1993, p. 19 ff.). As a spiritual exercise, philosophy is a form of living which engages the whole of existence—a life-changing conversion.

The expression 'spiritual exercises' is not free of misunderstanding, as Hadot (1993, p. 20), who highly influenced Foucault's approach to the Greeks, himself acknowledged[7], but its chief virtue here is in its evocation of a culture and a discursive framework in which thinking is not understood as just an intellectual action. Foucault built upon Hadot's concept of philosophy as spiritual exercise to affirm that it is only through what he calls the 'Cartesian moment' that modern philosophy came to be understood as solely a cognitive exercise (Foucault, 2001, pp. 2–39). In spiritual practice, there is no way of building knowledge or reaching truth that does not involve a transformative practice, or *áskesis*, of the self. The notion of self-care is a guiding principle of spiritual practice, and in classical Greek thought is a wide category that includes, among other things, the pursuit of self-knowledge. In modern thought, self-knowledge is understood as no more than a privileged relation to oneself, and thus does not require any transformation of the subject. But in the notion of the experience of philosophical thinking offered here, the entire life is put into question. We are not interested in this or that information or knowledge, in any specific truth; we do not teach techniques in order that students practise intellectual skills, learn how to answer this or that kind of question, or recognise this or that type of fallacy. Rather, we are primarily interested in students and teachers entering a zone of interrogation—in putting themselves, their lives, their passions and beliefs into question through the experience of thinking together.

Within the context of a culture of self-care, some ancient thinkers developed spiritual exercises that are suggestive for the project of the experience of philosophical thinking. Philo of Alexandria left two lists of exercises that include such practices as: thorough investigation (*sképsis*), reading (*anagnósis*), listening (*akróasis*), attention (*prosoché*) and meditation (*melétai*).[8] These are more than exercises in piety; rather, they seek to cultivate a way of seeing and being in the world. As activities, they hardly entail the transmission of pre-determined knowledge from one person to another; nor are they examples of a totalising technique, or a formula which guarantees that the one practising them will thereby achieve epistemological certainty and existential security. Rather the philosophical experience cultivated by these exercises is an individual and at the same time a shared journey of inquiry, discovery and transformation—one that calls upon us to think, not just about living, but about the way we ourselves live.

The experience of philosophical thinking is then, first and most importantly a matter of sensitivity. Rather than a form of knowledge or wisdom, it is a *practical relationship* to knowledge or wisdom. We live in the epoch of the 'knowledge society', in which information is in fact mistaken for knowledge, and every 'citizen' is endlessly encouraged to 'have his own opinion'. Of course it is important that the poor and the dispossessed, those who have been silenced for centuries, embrace their fundamental right to speak and to express themselves. But if we are really interested in their speaking in their own voices, and not in the voices of the ventriloquists of popular culture, the corporate media, the political, academic or therapeutic elites, or, even more directly, in the voices of market or capital, the issue of enabling the voices of the marginalised becomes more complicated. Why would it be so important that everyone express their 'own' opinion if, in the end, very similar opinions are expressed? We can, in fact, make a distinction between 'voice' and 'opinion'. One's own voice emerges, I would suggest, only after a conversion of sorts, which, in the case of the oppressed, involves a recognition and repudiation of the alienating cultural processes to which they have been subjected, and before which they have been rendered epistemologically, politically and pedagogically passive. Otherwise, we risk repeating the dialectic of the oppressor and the oppressed, with the positions slightly shifted to present a media-managed simulacrum of the 'liberation' suggested by having 'a right to one's own opinion.' What is needed is a process of locating and working to deconstruct the deeper structures that disable their own active thinking. What liberation is to be found in any pedagogical practice whose operative metaphor is 'filling', whether from the outside or the inside? What is necessary is to create educational conditions for thinking *with* others in thoughtful and meaningful ways, under the radar of the hugely influential media totality of our time.

Philosophical experience does not 'fill' interlocutors with dogmas, assumptions, and beliefs, nor even with interesting ideas, concepts or questions. Rather, it 'empties' the interlocutors of unexamined ideas, dogmas, beliefs, questions and values. The contemporary Brazilian poet Manoel de Barros expresses this idea succinctly: 'Unlearning eight hours a day teaches the principles [of] ... a didactics of invention' (de Barros, 2000, p. 9). There are so many things to unlearn in order to create conditions for learning differently: unlearn the relationship to thinking fostered by educational institutions; unlearn the way we think about our students. Unlearn, unlearn and unlearn, this is our lemma. Above all, unlearn a way of learning that inhibits experience. If this is true of students who need to recreate conditions in order to think powerfully, it is even more true of teachers whose calling it is to help other to learn to think.

In our practice with teachers and adult students, the project of unlearning is also supported by another spiritual exercise—'becoming a child'. In his book *Exercises on Being a Child* (*Exercícios de ser criança*, 1999) the same Manoel de Barros speaks for what we can learn from practising a childlike way of being in the world. Children, he argues, are less 'full', 'fresher', less prejudiced, more open to putting themselves freely into question. Because of their briefer exposure to oppressive institutions, they are closer to that state in which they can really think for themselves. In our philosophical exercises, teachers learn from their students to 'become a child' by participating in activities such as painting, drawing and formulating questions as a child does them. It is not a matter of imitating a child or of behaving 'childishly', but of facing our own lives as children are used to doing—as if we were doing something for the first time, as if anything were possible. More than once, teachers have told us that through these kinds of experiences, they realise that they have never truly done what they appeared to be doing every day, not only to themselves but also to others. As such, teachers who teach in a childlike way teach as if they have never really taught before, as if they were finding a new beginning for a different practice under the same name.

The prospects for promoting philosophical experience in the great majority of public schools in Brazil are buffeted by contradictory forces. On the one hand, institutional culture and practice seem completely hostile to the experience of philosophical thinking as described above. In effect, they offer disciplinary conditions so adverse that the very possibility of such experiences appears to be a quixotic fantasy. The bureaucratisation of the labour of teaching, the technificisation of human relations within the system, and the outsized social demand for 'productivity' made upon schools in general appear to offer no space for experience. More, the reifying force of culture imprisons everyone in the illusion that everything seems already to have been thought; any kind of problematisation or questioning process seems useless or meaningless, like beating the ocean with a broom. On the other hand, the sensed necessity for transformation—the frustration with a clearly dysfunctional status quo—is equally powerful in those same institutions. And it is in the gaps that sometimes become apparent in this contradictory context that real opportunities for philosophical practice emerge. Wherever we find indications of an open disposition towards and interest in philosophy, we accept the challenge and enter the situation, offering the experience of philosophical thinking to children and teachers in the form of spiritual exercises, in the context of their ordinary practice. We gamble on the force of experience even in adverse contexts, in which there seem to be no conditions for thinking. We play the pedagogical game we are given in a way that suggests changing its rules; we act as if experience and thinking were possible, even if they are not. We do not, as in traditional utopian thinking, move from the real to the possible, but we consider the impossible real, always in expectation of the new—that something interesting might happen.

WHAT IS PHILOSOPHICAL EDUCATION ABOUT? TWO PEDAGOGICAL PARAGONS

I would like now to return to a reflection on the pedagogical assumptions of the practice I am describing in the context of two other philosophers who have provided it with the most inspiration. Again, to call upon a variety of philosophical sources is not intended to affirm any new official heterodoxy, but rather to reinforce a spectrum of theoretical possibility, and to suggest a creative interplay between theory and practice.

Socrates first, of course, but not the Socrates who is usually invoked—the champion, that is, of dialogue, the master of *maiéusis*, who brings to term in students what they are already pregnant with. Rather, I would like to focus on an argument that Socrates offers in the *Apology*. In defending himself against the accusation of corrupting the young, he claims never to have been a teacher of anyone (Plato, *Apology of Socrates,* 33a–c); and yet a little further along, he affirms that if he is killed, his death will be useless because 'those who have learned with me' will continue doing what he does (33a–c; 39c–d). Socrates affirms, then, a sort of pedagogical scandal: the idea of a pedagogical situation in which the student learns without a teacher. What Socrates helps us to think here is that there is no necessary causality, nor even directionality, between teacher and learner, or the acts of teaching and learning. Someone does not teach but others learn with him. Someone learns but does not learn what he learns from someone who teaches it. What Socrates helps us to question is the pedagogical dogma that what a student learns is in the teacher, and is somehow transmitted to, or made to appear, in the learner through a certain behaviour or even a disposition of the teacher.

This Socratic act of deconstruction would appear to emancipate and empower both the learning and teaching processes. But the French contemporary philosopher Jacques Rancière has questioned the political dimension of this position. According to him, Socrates lies: it is not true that he teaches nothing; in fact he does teach, and what he teaches is, specifically, a relationship to knowledge from a position of superiority, which he legitimates through the mythic tale of the Delphic oracle. On this account, he proves his reputation as the wisest man in Athens through searching everywhere for a wiser, and discovering that his superior wisdom consists in the fact that he recognises the small value of his knowledge, whereas no one else does[9]. On the account of Jacques Rancière (1987)—whose philosophical approach has very few elements in common with the Deleuze, Lyotard and Foucault—Socrates is in fact claiming superiority through imposing his view of the 'best' relation to knowledge on others, and thereby teaching what an emancipator would never teach—the distance between the teacher and the student in relation to knowledge. After conversing with Socrates, all his interlocutors know how much further they are than him from the appropriate relationship to knowledge. Even though he does not teach any knowledge content, he does teach that everyone who seeks a proper relationship to knowledge should have a Socratic one. This position cannot but place the learner in an inferior position to the teacher.

Contrary to this position of implicit superiority, Rancière considers that affirming the *opinion* that all intelligences are equal is the single most important condition of intellectual emancipation (Rancière, 1987, p. 77). Rancière opposes opinion to truth. Whereas the latter can be demonstrated, justified, and leads to certainty, the former gives space to *un*certain experiences that will seek to verify it (p. 78). If the pedagogical principle that all intelligences are equal is expressed as an opinion and not a truth, it also means that its value is more political than epistemological. In this view, what differentiates emancipatory from 'obfuscating' pedagogical practices is the relationship to intelligence (and knowledge) and to the will that each establishes. An obfuscating teacher liberates the will of the student, but yokes the intelligence of the learner to the intelligence of the teacher. On the contrary, the emancipatory teacher works upon the will of the student through liberating her intelligence to work by itself—which he can do only under the presupposition that all intelligences are equal. This is why Socrates does not emancipate, since he presupposes an unequal ratio of intelligence between himself and his interlocutors.

Although I am sensitive to this critique, I find both Rancière's *and* Socrates' positions inspiring. In spite of their political disagreement, their emancipatory teachers have something in common. Although we are less sure of how Socrates relates to ignorance than how Rancière does, they both affirm the position of ignorance, and both profess ignorance of what the other learns with them. Both want their students to learn a specific relationship to knowledge, although those relationships are very different. Socrates wants others to know that the most important relation to knowledge is in the realisation of one's ignorance. That is why he deconstructs what others think they know. Rancière wants others to experience the equality of intelligences. As such, we can combine Socrates and Rancière in a pedagogical practice that encounters the other in order to deconstruct her knowledge under the presupposition of the equality of intelligence. We do not need to assume any specific relationship between knowledge and ignorance in order to affirm the value of a pedagogical practice based on deconstruction of what we already know or think. Like Socrates and Rancière, we can operate on the salutary assumption that there is no causal relationship between teaching and learning. We teach without knowing what a student is learning, or even if she is in fact learning anything. We do not know and we do not want to know or anticipate what a student may be learning— whether it be something she already knows, or simply the knowledge of her ignorance. Rather, we work to establish a context for thinking, and a pedagogical relationship in which the student realises that the teacher does not want to transfer, bestow, or engineer the appearance of anything to or in the student, but is confident in the potential of her thinking, and in her capacity to share a thinking process with others.

PHILOSOPHICAL EXPERIENCE AND THE CHILDHOOD OF EDUCATION: SOME FINAL EXAMPLES

At the moment, several valued colleagues and myself are developing experiences in philosophical thinking for a project called 'Em Caxias a filosofia en-caixa?'[10] in two public schools with socio-economically depressed populations in the suburbs of Rio de Janeiro. The project is sponsored by the Centre for Philosophical Studies of Childhood at the State University of Rio de Janeiro. I will finish by offering a few examples of thinking encounters that have already taken place there, in hopes that they may suggest a different form of relationship between childhood, philosophy and education. One of them took place at the University itself. From time to time we bring a class of students there, so that they can become familiar with a territory that is very far both from their lives and from their own imaginary[11]. Once there, we do a philosophical session together, in a classroom that we have furnished with comfortable chairs and pillows, lots of books, games, toys and DVDs.

Last year, something interesting happened on one of these visits. The children—ranging in age from nine to thirteen years old (ages are neither regular nor homogeneous in these classes)—were entering the main building to take the elevators to the 12th floor, where the classroom is located. It was a strange environment for them. The building is huge one, aggressively functional, all grey concrete slabs and pillars, pylons, and exposed utilities, drawing the eye along its sweeping interior vistas. It is a building more or less reserved for adults, and this group of twenty students suggested an odd invasion of the same by difference. When we had entered one of the large elevators, the operator, surprised by the children's sudden appearance there, asked them if they were visiting the University. Nearly at the same moment, a number of them answered loudly, their voices ringing clear and strong, 'No, we are here to do philosophy!' The operator laughed, as did the other adults on the elevator.

This may seem to be a trivial anecdote, but if we imagine substituting these children with a group of philosophy students on their way to the 12th floor to attend their classes in the history of philosophy, and imagine the operator asking the same question, one wonders if they might have answered that in fact they were there to learn and not to do philosophy. It may be argued that the aim of academic philosophy as taught at the university is not to do philosophy but to learn it as a condition for doing it later, but the usual fact of the matter is that, in 'learning' it, students tend to form a kind of relationship to philosophy that infinitely postpones their doing it, and in some cases actually prevents it. As Rancière would put it, what they learn is that they are inferior to the philosophers whom they are studying, and dependent on them for any knowledge they acquire. They are taught in such a way that renders it difficult or impossible to see themselves as active subjects of philosophical thinking. The moment of actually doing philosophy will never arise in the context of this relationship to the discipline.

The children, on the other hand, have learned another relationship to philosophy through their experiences of thinking, and they see themselves as active participants in the enterprise. They understand themselves as doing what philosophers do, and thus they see themselves as philosophers. Many will question whether what they are doing is actually philosophy at all. I for one am not sure. How could we be sure without first staking a contestable cultural/historical claim on a given definition of philosophy? Wouldn't we need to ask the students themselves about their own conception of philosophy before we could consider that question? In any case, even if they are not doing philosophy, some meaningful learning may emerge in their acting *as if* they were doing philosophy. Moreover, these young people made it clear from the outset that they were not just 'visiting' a university—in fact their remark implies that they understood themselves as being in order to do just what one is expected to do in that sort of a place. They affirmed that they were not just second-category visitors—that they had every right to do what is supposed to be done there, a right that trumps age or social position. This represents not philosophical but political learning: they have discovered and affirmed a primary public space for thinking, and claimed the universal right to participate actively in that space and others like them. As such, these students showed that what they had learned about philosophy in school—about the specific relationship to thinking that is practised in the experiences we offered them—is in no way restricted to school. Their understanding of the enterprise is simple, clear, and direct, and they take the practice absolutely seriously—they understand it implicitly as a way of thinking that results in significant personal development of the one who practises it. This is what these students learn: in fact, they do not learn philosophy; rather they learn to build a relationship to philosophy through thinking with others. Meanwhile, what this experience with philosophy—this active relationship to thinking— may bring forth in them is something that we cannot and should not anticipate, lest we fall back into the illusion that we have 'taught them something'.

SPEAKING WITH THE HEAD

The second example that I want to offer comes from another group of students from the same school, this time in their own classroom in their worn and threadbare school in the suburbs. We were discussing the meaning and significance of doing philosophy, in a classroom that we had equipped specifically for our sessions. Like the one at the university, we have removed the hard benches, painted the walls with bright colours, and put in some lighter and softer furniture. The students and teachers from this school call this space the 'thinking classroom' (*Sala do pensamento*). So, when we asked our students what they thought about their experience with philosophy so far—if they had learned anything from it and if so what, and what kinds of effects they found in themselves as a result this practice—they began offering ideas and examples. One of them—I shall call him Vinicius—spoke about some of the different things he could now do that he could not before. In fact, they did not sound particularly unique; but he finished his intervention with a remark that commanded our attention. He said, 'Before philosophy I spoke with my mouth; since I have been doing philosophy I speak with my head.'

The image stuck us immediately as significant, but we did not pursue it in the conversation, or even attempt to develop a hermeneutical path in order to determine the exact meaning of his intervention. In fact, he may have intended to say something that we did not understand him to be saying, or vice versa; but to inscribe what children say in the grid of our own adult hermeneutical devices is perhaps not that interesting after all. Depending on our presuppositions and theoretical lenses and frameworks, a number of possible interpretations may emerge, but it might be more interesting to listen to this voice from the standpoint of our own experience, even though the resulting interpretation may not necessarily correspond at all to what Vinicius was 'actually' saying. In other words, instead of proposing and defending an interpretation of what he said, I want to draw some implications from it for my own thinking about our practice. As such, they are childlike words that will be read in a childlike way.

The first idea inspired by Vinicius's words is that whatever he understands by 'the mouth' and 'the head', the former expresses a kind of being which is in a relation of part to whole with the latter. The mouth is a part of the head, and there are lots of other parts in a head besides the mouth. This signifies to me that if, before his philosophical experience, he spoke only with his mouth, and since then speaks with his whole head, he has more options for speaking now than he had before.

Secondly, we do in fact speak with our mouths, but we do not literally or specifically speak with our heads, even though our mouths are located in our heads. In effect, we can say that we speak with our heads only in an indirect or metaphorical way. This capacity for indirect or metaphorical speech suggests that through the experience of philosophy he learned to explore another dimension of language than the one he was accustomed to. Before his experience with philosophy, 'speaking' belonged to one semantic register, and 'head' to another. After philosophy, he could calmly put these two registers together, in his thinking and in his speech. He learned that he could use the words not only to say what they are 'supposed' to say (and therefore to think only what 'ought' to be thought) but in a second order way. He learned to think and speak in a broader dimension than the one we are used to in everyday language.

Thirdly, the expansive image—that is, from part to whole—employed by Vinicius is interesting, not only because it expresses an enlargement and complexification of his capacity for speaking and thinking, but it also signals a movement from an ordinary and naturalised relationship to what it is supposed to be thought and spoken, to an extraordinary and unnatural form of relationship. In effect, it is not a natural thing to say—we are not supposed to be speaking with our heads, but with our mouths. His image represents a kind of desacralisation of the function of both head and mouth; it is in fact illogical to move the speaking function from the mouth to the head. As such, Vinicius expresses a kind of salutary indiscipline in his thinking through philosophy; through our thinking experiences he learned to deconstruct the framework that disciplined the way he thought and spoke about his own thinking and speaking. What seemed unnatural before philosophy now was seen as a conquest.

These are just a few examples of a more extended practice. My own strong impression is that, through the philosophical experiences of thinking we have offered, these groups of young people have begun to attach much more value, care and attention to what they say and think than before they began seeing themselves as doing what philosophers do. And they share this process with their other teachers, who also take part in this enlargement of the possibilities of speaking and thinking. Coincidently, they find more sense and meaning in the experience of school itself.

IN CONCLUSION

The primary aim of this paper has been to explore how the relationships between philosophy and childhood could be thought and practised from a perspective other than the traditional Western one, which I have traced to Plato. In this sense, I have tried to offer conceptual elements towards a reterritorialisation of the relationship between childhood and philosophy, to put it in Deleuzian terms. These elements include some diverse philosophical approaches to childhood and to the practice of philosophical thinking, as well as some concrete examples from my own practice. It has not been my intention to build a set of claims about the relations I am exploring, nor to found an educational model—which, although it may have been a tactical necessity in order to introduce philosophy into childhood education a few decades ago, is no longer that productive. And in order to maintain a fluid and emergent relation between theory and practice, I have called on a rather extended number of authors and categories, whose ideas act to deconstruct both traditional views of childhood and implicitly, of childhood education.

My colleagues and I have never been very sure of how to justify the name 'philosophy' in this enterprise, undertaken in a social and pedagogical zone that, in many ways, could not be further from the familiar terrain of philosophy as understood in the academy. Nor is the difficulty here an issue of class: it would probably be easier to bring philosophy as academically understood to the more privileged zones of the upper middle class private school, but probably even harder to bring it as an experience of transformative thinking. An institutionalised context pushing so obdurately in other directions makes us question not only how to do philosophy in such a setting, but whether it is possible at all in the way we understand philosophy. It seems most probable that the 'childhood of education'—that new beginning so relentlessly invoked by the new understanding of the relationship between the child and time that I have sketched above—implicitly entails the 'childhood of school'. In its present form, the school is actually hostile to the form of childhood that we seek to foster and care for. It must find itself in a new relationship to childhood before philosophy, as an experience of transformative thinking, can really be practised in it. But the schools we find are the ones we have, and the lack of meaning that we observe there cries out to us, and compels us to enter them. We do so *as if* it were possible to establish a new educational relationship to childhood there, and work fully expecting an emergence that cannot be predicted, but that fills us with the energy to continue thinking a new location for the practice of philosophy in the education of childhood. Through what we call philosophy, children of all ages are open to an ageless childhood in their thinking experience and in their lives. The energies generated by the encounter between childhood and philosophy are unpredictable, and oblige us to pay close attention to what might emerge from it, all the while expecting the unexpectable (as Heraclitus says in his fragment 18) and unlearning the learned, on the assumption that another world is not only possible, but is in fact already present.

NOTES

1. All translations in this paper are the author's unless otherwise specified.
2. For the following, see Deleuze, 1990, chap. 5: Politique: 16. 'Contrôle et devenir'.
3. For the following, cf. Deleuze and Guattari, 1980, 10. 1730—'Devenir-intense, devenir.-animal, devenir-imperceptible', pp. 285 ff.
4. All references in this section from Chapter 5, 'Survivant. Arendt', are quoted from the Spanish translation (Lyotard, 1997).
5. This specific project began in 2007. For a detailed description of a one year experience with adults in these settings, see Kohan and Wozniak, 2010.
6. See for example, 'Entretien avec Michel Foucault' (by D. Tromabadori) in Foucault, 1994, pp. 41–95.
7. The word 'spiritual' is full of metaphysical and theological connotations, but the other expressions discussed—and ultimately rejected—by Hadot seem to present other problems. He considers the term 'thinking' or 'intellectual' exercises, but affirms that both terms seem to leave aside a fundamental dimension of 'spiritual exercises': imagination and sensibility. Other expressions he considers are 'ethical' and 'psychological' exercises, but both are too limiting in that they do not denote the transformation of the world view and of the personality of the person involved in this practice.
8. For the complete list, see Hadot, 1993, p. 25 ff.
9. The issue is certainly more complex in the three conversations he describes in *Apology* 21b–23d, but this simplification seems enough for the present argument.
10. In English: 'Does Philosophy fit in Caxias?! *A Public School Gambles on Thinking*'. The original Portuguese, 'Em Caxias a Filosofia En-caixa?!', plays with the word 'Caxias' which is a name of a city close to Rio de Janeiro, but also signifies 'fit'. Online at: www.filoeduc.org/caxias (Portuguese).
11. Most of these students don't even consider the possibility of entering a university in the future. No one has done that in their families, and completing elementary school is considered a great achievement.

REFERENCES

de Barros, M. (1999) *Exercícios de ser criança* (Rio de Janeiro, Salamandra).
de Barros, M. (2000) *O livro das ignorâças* (São Paulo, Record).
Deleuze, G. (1968) *Différence et répétition* (Paris, PUF).
Deleuze, G. (1990) *Pourparlers* (Paris, Les Éditions de Minuit).
Deleuze, G. and Guattari, F. (1980) *Mille Plateaux. Capitalisme et schizophrénie* (Paris, Les Éditions de Minuit).
Deleuze, G. and Guattari, F. (1991) *Qu'est-ce que la philosophie?* (Paris, Les éditions du Minuit).
Foucault, M. (1984) *Histoire de la sexualité* (Paris, Gallimard, vol. II: L'usage des plaisirs).
Foucault, M. (1994) *Dits et Écrits* (Paris, Gallimard. vol. IV).
Foucault, M. (2001) *L'herméneutique du sujet* (Paris, Gallimard-Seuil).
Hadot, P. (1993) *Exercices spirituels et philosophie antique* (Paris, Albin Michel).
Heraclitus (2001) *Heraclitus*, M. Marcovich, ed. (Sankt Augustin, Academia Verlag).
Kohan, W. and Wozniak, J. (2010) Philosophy as Spiritual Exercise in an Adult Literacy Course, *Thinking: The Journal of Philosophy for Children*, 19.4, pp. 17–23.
Liddell, H. and Scott, R. (1966) *A Greek English Lexicon* (Oxford, Clarendon Press).

Lipman, M. (1988) *Philosophy Goes to School* (Philadelphia, PA, Temple University Press).
Lipman, M. (1998) The Contributions of Philosophy to Deliberative Democracy, in: D. Evans and I. Kuçuradi (eds) *Teaching Philosophy on the Eve of the Twenty-first Century* (Ankara, International Federation of Philosophical Societies), pp. 6–29.
Lyotard, J-F. (1997) *Lecturas de infancia* (Buenos Aires, EUDEBA).
Plato (1990) *Platonis Opera*, J. Burnet, ed. (Oxford, Oxford University Press).
Rancière, J. (1987) *Le maître ignorant* (Paris, Fayard).

11

'In Charge of the Truffula Seeds': On Children's Literature, Rationality and Children's Voices in Philosophy

VIKTOR JOHANSSON

INTRODUCTION

How can professional philosophy with its sophisticated expressions and forms of reason speak for children or give children a philosophical voice? How can children have a voice in philosophy? Gareth Matthews' texts implicitly respond to these questions. His conversations with children show how philosophy can speak for children and how children speak for philosophy. This article can be read as an attempt to reconstruct Matthews' philosophy of childhood in the light of these questions. I suggest that we can acknowledge children both as rational beings who can actually contribute to philosophy by educating philosophers and as learners who sometimes can be reached by the sophisticated language of philosophers. I further claim that if philosophy turns to children's literature as a source for its investigations it is possible to embark on a search for children's voices in philosophy as an education for both philosophers and children. This is vital to any attempt to philosophise with children because it demonstrates how we, in many ordinary contexts, actually acknowledge children as rational conversational partners who contribute to our understanding of ourselves as rational beings. Or, put differently, children's literature becomes a way to explore not only our relationship with children, but also how such relationships can be a philosophical education for both children and adults. This emphasises both the role philosophical reflection can play in establishing a rational community encompassing children and adults, and how this is possible through an acknowledgement of children's rationality. Clearly, if there is

Philosophy for Children in Transition: Problems and Prospects, First Edition. Nancy Vansieleghem and David Kennedy. Chapters © 2012 The Authors. Editorial organization © 2012 Philosophy of Education Society of Great Britain. Published 2012 by Blackwell Publishing Ltd.

something to these suggestions, doing philosophy with children has, at least on the face of it, a role in establishing this community.

THE LORAX AND RESPONSIBLE CHILDREN

In Dr Seuss' *The Lorax* (1971) the Once-ler gives the last seed of the Truffula Trees to a child; a seed with which the child can re-establish the paradisiacal world once destroyed by the Once-ler's greed. The Once-ler says,

> You are in charge of the Truffula Seeds.
> And Truffula Trees are what everyone needs.
> Plant a new Truffula. Treat it with care.
> Give it clean water. And feed it fresh air.
> Grow a forest. Protect it from axes that hack.
> Then the Lorax and all his friends
> may come back.

This gesture seems to suggest that children, this child, may be responsible agents that can handle such a task. We can respond to such gestures in children's literature in at least two ways: (i) We can take this as an illustration of an empirical possibility. We may accordingly be inclined to investigate whether this is a real possibility. Do children *demonstrate* or *manifest* the ability to take such responsibilities? (ii) We can take this story as an invitation to imagine that we are can *acknowledge* children as responsible and rational agents, which means that *our* attitude to children is as vital for our conception of them as rational as their ability to demonstrate rational capabilities. This also means that the child and the Once-ler share the same fate; they both bear the responsibility and the consequences of one another's lives and actions.[1] The Once-ler's instructions to treat the seed with care, ultimately giving the seed to the child, can be seen as an acknowledgement of that shared fate, or as I shall put it: speaking for the child and letting the child speak for him.

To my mind there are several things in *The Lorax* that prompt this second kind of response. The figure of the Once-ler is clearly an adult. For instance, he opens up a successful shop, and he starts a corporation and establishes a factory with many employees. When the Once-ler first comes to the Land of the Truffula Trees, however, it is depicted as an Eden where fantastic animals play while the Once-ler enjoys nature. Inspired by his new environment and using a Truffula tree, he creates his first Thneed, the production of which eventually destroys the Truffula trees, along with the beautiful landscape, and exploits its resources. One moral of *The Lorax* is that the child has to take responsibility as a result of the irresponsibility of adults. The message seems to be that we have to trust our children, that they are our only hope. How can we even think otherwise? Who else will take responsibility for the future of humanity? But are we justified in giving children this form of responsibility? Is it a responsibility they can fulfil? In what sense can we understand children as rational responsible beings, and in what sense do we speak for children as sharing our fate?[2]

The hopes and doubts expressed in these questions are related to how we live with children as rational beings and moral agents, and to children's roles in our form of life. Our children are the future of humanity, and in some sense the future of rationality. If, as I suggest, our response to children's literature can be conceived as an acknowledgement of a shared responsibility or community of reason, then children's literature can help us to acknowledge the kinds of life we can live with children as co-representatives of our community of reason, as co-founders of our forest of Truffula Trees, our restored future world. If our response is one of acknowledgement, we need to pay attention to how children's literature can help us to be honest about the lives we live and may live with children.

RECONSIDERING GARETH MATTHEWS' PHILOSOPHY OF CHILDHOOD

In an early paper 'Philosophy and Children's Literature', before his ground-breaking work on the philosophy of childhood, Gareth Matthews surveys how philosophical thought, what he calls 'philosophical whimsy', is presented in children's literature. By referring to a few empirical examples of children raising the same philosophical questions and making the same philosophical claims he finds in children's literature, Matthews argues that 'what philosophers do (in rather disciplined and sustained ways) is much closer than usually appreciated to what at least some children rather naturally do (albeit fitfully, and without the benefit of sophisticated techniques)' (Matthews, 1976, pp. 14–15). As he proceeds in his work on philosophy of childhood and philosophy for children, Matthews extends his empirical examples of children's philosophical reasoning. This allows him to make the forceful claim, against Piagetian research on children's development, that our interactions with children really ought to be understood as interactions with rational beings or moral persons (Matthews, 1996, p. 27). Matthews justifies his claims by finding empirical evidence of children demonstrating philosophical abilities.

Although I agree with Matthews' conclusions—that children's thoughts may be closer to what philosophers do and that we ought to acknowledge children as rational beings and moral persons—I believe that his claims can be strengthened if we take a different route from our readings of children's literature. This route not only re-evaluates children's assumed or denied rationality but also reformulates how rationality is to be pictured. It involves reading children's literature not only as illustrating and presenting philosophical issues that children may think of, but as a philosophical expression of the existential problems that are latent in our relationships to children: this elucidates how we in fact live with children and how we *might* live with them. In the light of this it is possible to reconsider Matthews' conversations with children. These conversations do not have to be understood primarily as empirical evidence for children's philosophical abilities but rather as illustrations of how philosophical conversations with children can demonstrate our acknowledgement of children's voices as making claims to be involved in our community of reason. Different philosophy for children programmes may offer ways to emphasise this communality.

In this article I propose that children's literature can invite us to acknowledge children as rational responsible beings. I argue that the basis for children's capabilities to reason lies as much in our acknowledgement of them as reasonable as in their attempts to reason with us. Such an acknowledgment means to speak for children as rational beings. To speak for children as rational we are not dependent on children manifesting empirical evidence of reason. Instead, such acknowledgement is a claim to community with children and as such a claim to shared rationality. Reading children's literature philosophically can be a way to help us see more clearly our role in giving the children a voice in our communities of reason. If we are blind to our role in our rational communities with children, we are also blind to their role in those same communities. We are blind to their rationality. We 'are missing something about [ourselves], or rather something about [our] connection with these people, [our] internal relation to them' (Cavell, 1979, p. 376).

IMAGINATION, COMMUNITY AND LITERATURE: LIVING WITH ANIMALS

The imagination called for by stories is significant with regard to the acknowledgment of children's voices. Consider the reply that is given by J. M. Coetzee's character, Elisabeth Costello, when, having just spoken of Ted Hughes' poem 'The Jaguar',[3] she is asked about how far we can imagine the inner life of an animal:

> I would reply, writers teach us more than they are aware of. By bodying the jaguar, Hughes shows us that we too can embody animals—by the process called poetic invention that mingles breath and sense in a way that no one has explained and no one ever will. He shows us how to bring the living body into being within ourselves. When we read the jaguar poem, when we recollect it afterwards in tranquillity, we are for a brief while the jaguar. He ripples within us, he takes over our body, he is us (Coetzee, 1999, p. 53).

A major setback in Costello's reasoning is that it immediately invites a sceptical reply. In what sense can a reader of 'The Jaguar' actually get inside the jaguar? We may simply notice that since the jaguar's senses and expressions are so different from ours, we can ask whether it is possible to come close to anything like embodying the animal. The poem may create an illusion (if even that) of our coming closer to the jaguar experience, but can we really tell whether we have come any closer?

Nonetheless, Costello's reading of Hughes' poem can give us another kind of answer. It shows us the power and importance of human imagination. It is only in philosophising or in intellectualising Costello's response that we would raise the question of the *actual* embodiment of the animal (see Diamond, 2006, pp. 103–105). Both the example of Costello's reasoning and 'The Jaguar' are works of literature. We know that Costello's reasoning is imagined and that the sense of the jaguar rippling within us when reading Hughes' poem is imagined. We do not know anything about Costello outside of our and Coetzee's imagination and we do not know anything about the jaguar's experience besides what Hughes invites us to imagine.

The apparent illusion of understanding the jaguar is not an illusion at all. This imagining of the other is all we have to go on if we want to understand one another, whether an animal or a human. Even though some philosophers may have claimed to overcome sceptical arguments about other minds, we do not usually think of those (most of us do not know them) when we engage with others. In interacting with others we do not act on a certainty of understanding the other or of being understood by the other. Rather, this interaction is a matter of attuning ourselves to the other by acknowledging their words and actions as our words and actions—which means making a claim to a shared community. Understanding the other may thus be conceived as having a clear overview of how we live and possibly can live with that particular other—how we live with a jaguar, how we live with a child, even how we live with ourselves.

Costello shows that Hughes speaks *for* the jaguar; he gives the jaguar a voice in a human language, as Coetzee gives voice to Costello and her equally wild sensitivities. This is remarkable about poems like 'The Jaguar'. Hughes not only invites us to imagine being the jaguar, he makes this possible by using his words in such a way that we can imagine being a *jaguar*. Other words may not succeed in this. Indeed, Hughes' words, or Costello's use of them, may not do this to all of us. That does not even happen in the story about Costello: she is quite alone in her approach to animals. However, in speaking for the jaguar, in trying to put the jaguar's experience into words, Hughes also claims that we have enough in common with the jaguar to understand it, enough in common to put its experience into words. This is what 'speaking for' means here; it is a claim to a shared community (Cavell, 1979, p. 20). It is an acknowledgement of the other.

Although in reading 'The Jaguar' our imagination appears to help us acknowledge what we share with an animal and to find something in common with it, can it be said that we share what might be called a *rational community* with children? We are certainly not always inclined to think so, as shown by the helplessness of our reason in the face of children's dissonance (see Johansson, 2010). Children's literature can challenge the stability of our reason and challenge our inclination to respond to children in certain ways. Children's literature may even lead us to identify imaginatively with or to embody the central (child-)characters and to follow their ways if reasoning. Just as Costello is affected in reading Hughes' poem, so we also may be affected by reading about Costello.

Though we may recognise that some children do reason and express themselves comprehensibly, it seems much more difficult to acknowledge them as persons that we can reason with about the same issues as adults. We live as if some human beings were children; we project that aspect onto young human beings. To be sure, there is nothing wrong in seeing some human beings as children, but some of our ways of picturing children may blind us to other aspects of our lives with children. For example, as Dewey notes (1916, p. 46), our understanding of children as immature may lead us to focus on capabilities they lack rather than capabilities they have. Our (mis)understanding of children, at least for some of us, is then similar to our (mis)understanding of animals. Because they are different from us, and of course children are not as different from adults as animals, we do not always see the shared features that can establish a community of reason. We do not always recognise how we actually live with children. Although in some respect we live with children as if they were human, in other respects we may fail to acknowledge that children are a part of our communities of reason. We lack a clear view of our lives with children (Wittgenstein, 1953, §122). We attempt to teach children our ways of reasoning, but we are blind to children's ways of reasoning. Thus, it seems fair to assume that the asymmetry between the child and the adult in the ability to reason in particular contexts may give us a limited picture of children, a picture that may obscure other possible ways of living and reasoning with children. Pictures of such asymmetries, if these are the only pictures we have of childhood, feed our tendency to think of children merely as uncompleted adults or rational not-yets.

RATIONALITY AND CHILDREN'S LEGAL RIGHTS

An example of how talk of rational abilities may blind us to other aspects of our community with children, which distinguishes my position from Matthews', is to be found in his discussion of children's legal rights. Matthews raises this issue through the illustrative example of the Gregory Kingsley case, where, in a Florida State court in 1992, a child claimed a standing legal petition to terminate his biological parents' legal right to him. This finally led to a divorce between Gregory and his biological parents. Is this reasonable? Can we give children the legal right to petition on their own behalf? Matthews and I are in agreement in saying yes.

Matthews maintains this position by asking two principal questions: (i) Is the child sufficiently rational, or rational in the right way, to be able to be self-determining? (ii) Would it be in the child's own interest to restrict the child's ability to be self-determining (Matthews, 1996, p. 70)? Matthews' answer to both these questions is: 'It depends'. Some children would be sufficiently rational, and then it would not be in their interest to restrict their *ability* to be self-determining. He suggests that children become gradually more self-determining as their rational abilities mature and that Gregory demonstrated a sufficient rational ability to be self-determining in this case (p. 79).

I think Matthews' argument is misleading. It is not solely a matter of the child's rational *ability*, or his power to demonstrate that *ability*. In fact, talk about rationality solely as an ability seems confused. Rather we should acknowledge the child as a human being and a rational conversational partner. In Stanley Cavell's words, 'the basis of it seems to lie in us' (Cavell, 1979, p. 433). I understand this to draw out part of the moral aspect of Wittgenstein's saying: 'My attitude towards him is an attitude towards a soul. I am not of the *opinion* that he has a soul' (Wittgenstein, 1953, Part II §22).

But still, rational? Can we really acknowledge small children as *rational*? If Hughes can have some of us imagine that we have enough in common with a jaguar for us to imagine that we become a jaguar, can we not imagine children sharing enough with us to be a part of our rational community? It all depends on whether we speak for children and acknowledge them as having a voice of their own in our community. Of course, this is not wholly independent of children's abilities. Even though the basis of acknowledgment lies in us, we cannot share a human form of life with just anything without risking our sanity. If I insist on treating rocks as moral persons and trying to involve them in rational deliberation, it is reasonable to question my sanity, or at least my understanding of certain language-games. I find it tragic that my sanity may be similarly questioned if I do the same with children. We seem to need a clear view of our lives with children to understand the extent of our actual acknowledgment of children's voices and possible future lives with children—that is, a clear view over the multifarious different ways in which we respond to children's expressions as rational or not.

Dr Seuss' gesture can remind us how we do in fact live with children— that we do share a fate, a future world and a community—as is evident in the way that Seuss lets Once-ler teach the child protagonist how his world became desolate. This gesture also allows us to picture the possibility of a new kind of life: it allows us to picture a mythology of a paradisiacal forest of Truffula Trees where the animals' joyous games and practices are acknowledged as valuable. We imagine a possible life depicted as a return to the colourful world of childhood fantasy. This return to childhood fantasy, as a way of reasoning, can be realised if we (re)turn to children's literature.

CHILDREN'S LITERATURE AND CHILDREN'S REASONS: *WHERE IS MY SISTER?*

Remember how Costello begins her clarification of her reading of Hughes poem by saying 'writers teach us more than they are aware of'. This shows how Costello reads the poem as more than a text, as something that establishes a commonality with animals, illustrating how literature can challenge our imagination by inviting us continually to look beyond the text and towards what the text does to us when we read it. Children's literature can invoke similar challenges. As Hughes' poem suggests our common fate with animals, reading children's literature may draw our attention to particular aspects of children's reasoning. This may challenge our understanding of rationality, a challenge brought home to us by the dissonance between the established logic in adults' reasoning and the whimsical expressions of children's play and imagination. (Are children's 'whimsy' and grown-ups 'sophistication' expressions of different modes of rationality?)

In the picturebook *Var är min syster?* (Where is my Sister?), the Swedish writer and illustrator Sven Nordqvist (2007) invites us into a child's world (or two children's worlds). As in Coetzee, this is an example of a fictional character giving an account of another's reasoning. Even though the child-protagonist in this story is an animal, this book can be read as a conceptual investigation of our acknowledgment, acceptance and responses to the other as a human being.

A small animal, most likely a mouse, asks an adult elderly animal, possibly a mole, to help him look for his big sister. They take off on a journey through an extraordinary landscape in a balloon in the shape of a pear. The bulk of the story is told through a series of fanciful pictures of landscapes, with mixed perspectives, varying scales and seemingly out-of-place objects. The illustrations, which remind me of how I played in my own childhood and of how I now enjoy playing with children, seem to be of what goes on in a child's mind when playing a role-game or letting their imagination flow as they discover the world: a truck is needed to pick up a spruce cone; a knight rides a snail in a medieval joust; someone really small uses an axe to harvest carrots. The words accompanying the story told by the pictures share these characteristics. Reading the book with the pictures is not only a matter of reading the text, but also of playing with pictures and language in conversation with the child (the child we are reading with or the child in ourselves, in me). The book both depicts and enacts children's play.

In giving an account of what his big sister has told him, the younger brother says:

> If we are among the clouds
> we can fly, she says.
> Because if one won't do that one will fall,
> and if one falls one will die,
> but we cannot die
> because first we shall grow old,
> so we can fly
> if we are among the clouds.[4]

Some of the premises in this 'argument' are obviously false and its logic does not fit adults' established ways of reasoning. It appears as if the adult and the child in this story are at a moment where Wittgenstein would say that reasons come to an end (cf. Wittgenstein, 1953, §211). There is a dissonance between the adult's and the child's practice of reasoning. The fully-grown animal's incredulous answer is not very surprising.

> She reasons in her own way, your sister.
> Just don't believe everything she says.
> It is probably good to begin by practicing flying
> no more than a yard above the ground
> and have someone on the ground catch you
> if it does not turn out well (Nordqvist, 2007).

This response, by actually responding to the child's thinking, acknowledges that the child's reasoning is a way to reason even though it may not be a very reliable one—if acted upon, it might even be dangerous. The child's argument, if we can call it that, does not need to be a valid argument according to our adult standards for it to enter into the 'space of reasons,' to use Wilfred Sellars's term (1963, p. 169). Of course, grown-ups, philosophers even, also frequently reason poorly. Hence, by responding to the child's reasoning as reason, good or bad, we acknowledge the child as taking a position in our rational community. Even if we have standards for good reasoning, those standards do not necessarily have reasons themselves (Wittgenstein, 1953, §§477–85). Thus, our reasons come to an end when we realise that nothing more, nothing less, than our actually acknowledging the child's reasoning as reason initiates the child in our community of reason. This is how our community of reason is born and reborn (Cavell, 1979, p. 125).[5] Within such communities we can raise questions about good or bad reasoning, we can correct the child's reasoning and often be right to do so, and the child can question our reasoning. But it is nonsense to think of this child's reasoning, or ours, as good or bad if we do not acknowledge what the child does, and what we do, as reasoning.

Nevertheless, it is not enough to speak for the child or let the child speak for us as members of a community of reason since we have doubts about the rationality of the child's actual argument. We may find it difficult to see the point of the child's ways of reasoning even if we accept it as such. The combination of pictures and words in Nordqvist's book may help us overcome this and actually enter into the child's world, which is visible in these words and pictures. It becomes clearer as the characters continue through another landscape and the young animal tells us something about his sister that may give us a clue about where to find her. Our mouse explains:

> Then she was gone the whole day
> But she came home when it was dark.
> She said that she had seen a road
> that maybe led to Africa
> and China or Greenland
> or maybe around the whole world.
> Another time I shall go there, she said.
> It was behind a couch.
> A blue road. Or a yellow road
> behind a green chair.
> Or maybe it was a great ocean,
> I don't really remember.
> –It would be good to know
> if we shall look
> behind an ocean or a couch.

The pictures in the book are the source of these bewildering thoughts. As noted, they depict the child's description. Or, rather, the reverse: the child's words describe something we find in the pictures (the pictures tell the story and the words depict the pictures), pictures that appears to mix up scales and perspectives, fantasy and reality. This is important, if we notice that after flying through the child's landscapes, the child's world, the adult animal is now more humble in his response. He acknowledges the child's fantasy worldview and seems to realise that the quest is as much a game, or role-play, as it is an actual search for the sister. He can see a reason or a point in the child's whimsical sentences. His response thus become a way of speaking for the child—an acknowledgment that, as they both become attuned to this game, the question as to whether they should search behind a couch or an ocean is critical.

To follow the story, both in the pictures and in the words, we must be able to imagine what the child sees, to enter into the child's fantasy. Letting ourselves do this is not so much a matter of attuning the child to our practices but of attuning ourselves to the practices of the child. In this way, reading children's literature with children and entering those imaginative worlds together is making a claim for community. Reading children's literature with children is a step towards such community, but of course we may also enjoy reading children's books by ourselves and such solitary reading is also a way to explore our lives with children.

This kind of philosophy or way of philosophising seems to me particularly fruitful both for attempts to philosophise with children and for any philosophy that claims to say something about our relationships with children. Children's literature can awaken the imagination that is needed to see the whimsical thoughts of children as autonomous thought; it can awaken the imagination we need in speaking for children. This makes it possible for us not only to become attentive to children's voices, but also to awaken the imagination needed for us to grow into autonomous beings, constantly transforming our mutual attunement and reclaiming our community of reason. Philosophy for children and philosophy of childhood are thus ways of coming to clarity about the life we live with them and our shared fate in that life, as well as of achieving clarity about the life with children we want.

PHILOSOPHY AND CHILDREN'S VOICES: ESTABLISHING A COMMUNITY OF REASON

If speaking for a rational community and letting participants in that community speak for us is crucial, can philosophy have a role in this? Can philosophy speak for children? We have seen that in reading children's literature we can give voice to children, but can I give a philosophical account where I speak representatively for children without writing for them as my readers? Can philosophy speak for children? If, as Cavell suggests, philosophy can be an 'education for grown-ups' (1979, p. 125), can it also be an education for children? What does it take for philosophy to be an education for children?

I do not think these questions can be dealt with without acknowledging the separation between children and their elders. Let me explain. Cavell ends *The Claim of Reason* by saying that Shakespeare's Othello and Desdemona, lying dead on their sheets, form an emblem of the truth of scepticism. They form 'an emblem of human separation, which can be accepted, or granted or not' (Cavell, 1979, p. 496). Perhaps poetry or literature can find redemption for them, by, as Cavell suggest, making 'room for hell in a juster city' (ibid.), room for separateness. But then again, is such redemption acceptable to philosophy if philosophy still hopes to *overcome* the scepticism of other minds, that is, to overcome the fact of human separation, rather than acknowledging it? Does this mean that philosophy should become literature? Cavell ends *The Claim of Reason* with a question. 'But can philosophy become literature and still know itself' (ibid.)?

I turn Cavell's philosophy (as an education for grown-ups) to work on our relationships with children, to our lives with children and by doing so sketch out how philosophy also can be an education for children. This interest corresponds to Cavell's attention to the educative aspects of acknowledging the separateness in relationships in adult marriages. In Cavell's readings this acknowledgment fails in marriages such as Othello and Desdemona's, or Nora and Torvald's in Ibsen's *A Doll House*, and is successful in what he calls remarriage comedies (Cavell, 2005, p. 122). If reading these films and plays and noticing the education or lack of education these couples provide for each other may be a philosophy for grown-ups, then can readings of children's literature be philosophy as education for grown-ups? Can philosophy become children's literature and still know itself?

Philosophy, Cavell maintains, can be an education for grown-ups. I claim that philosophy also can be an education for children. This does not only mean a philosophical activity that involves philosophical conversations with children in schools. It also means that philosophy itself can give voice to children and educate children. I introduce this idea as a way to extend Wittgenstein and Cavell's philosophy in order to rethink why we want children to be involved in philosophical practices and why we need philosophy in schools.

Consider how Cavell calls our attention to some aspects of learning languages in the opening of Wittgenstein's *Investigations*. There, famously, by referring to St Augustine's *Confessions*, Wittgenstein introduces the idea that philosophical pictures of language may mislead us. Continuing the confessional mode of both Augustine and Wittgenstein, Cavell asks, 'But what happens if "my elders", all of them (those bigger people from whom, according to Augustine's passage, I learn to use words), will not accept what I say and do as what they say and do? Must they? Is it only natural to them? Is it their responsibility?' (Cavell, 1979, p. 28) Notice Cavell's wording and the voice he is expressing here. It is as if a child were saying this. Cavell is using a child's wording. He says '*my* elders' (which are Augustine's words) and, 'those bigger people', emphasising that there are people bigger than he is. Notice also that Cavell continues Augustine's confessional use of the first-person. Giving voice to his own childhood worries (cf. Cavell, 2010, pp. 19–21, 30–31, 100, 110), Cavell speaks representatively for children, lending his voice to express the doubts of a child being initiated into a linguistic community.

Emphasising how tragedy (scepticism) and the problem of representativeness are interlinked he continues,

I would like to say: If I am to have a native tongue, I have to accept what 'my elders' say and do as consequential; and they have to accept, even have to applaud, what I say and do. We do not know in advance what the content of our mutual acceptance is, how far we may be in agreement. I do not know in advance how deep my agreement with myself is, how far my responsibility for the language may run. But if I am to have my own voice in it, I must be speaking for others and allow others to speak for me. The alternative to speaking for myself representatively (for *someone* else's consent) is not: speaking for myself privately. The alternative is having nothing to say, being voiceless, not even mute (Cavell, 1979, p. 28).

There is a lot going on in this passage. I shall bring out a few ideas that are relevant for my purposes here. It is still the child, Stanley Cavell, who speaks. Cavell is giving voice to those who seldom have a voice in philosophy. When Cavell says, 'I would like to say', it is as if he gives voice to a child's anxiety over whether he will be able to speak comprehensibly together with his elders. However, the child Cavell realises that this uncertainty, or anxiety, about whether agreement will be reached is not only his, but also his elders'. What the child expresses, and in a way discovers, is a separateness between him and his elders.

Henrik Ibsen explores such separateness in the relation between a child and her elders in his play *The Wild Duck*. In the final act, Hedvig, a fourteen-year-old girl, shoots herself to show her love to her doubting father, Hjalmar. Hjalmar doubts whether Hedvig actually is his daughter. Hedvig overhears him saying, 'Oh, what proof could she give me? I don't dare hope to be reassured from that quarter' (Ibsen, 1884, p. 211). This drives Hedvig to take extreme measures to have her love acknowledged. Nonetheless, the cause of Hjalmar's doubts is not Hedvig herself, but an early affair that his wife, Gina, had. To Hjalmar, this confirms a separateness in his family and brings his doubts to the fore. It introduces a distance, a difference, between him and his daughter that his (dogmatic) picture of the ideal family does not allow for.

Hedvig not only struggles with having her voice heard and acknowledged by her elders, especially her father. She also has to struggle with her elders' tendency to use vague metaphors about idealistic moral ideas and to speak outside the everyday contexts of language. Her elders' confused talk makes her simple questions unanswerable. Likewise she struggles with Hjalmar's tendency not fully to mean what he says. This makes her subject to the whims of her elders, to not being able to trust them (Moi, 2006, pp. 263–64). In both cases, her elders are reluctant to take full responsibility for their words, which means that no one speaks for Hedvig. It means that no one can speak for her.

When Hjalmar discovers that his life with Hedvig does not fit his picture of their relationship, he seems unable to respond to her, unable to speak for what could have been a community between them. Why should he speak for her: they are separate, and she is other? Hedvig and Hjalmar are separate, she is other, and as long as Hjalmar (falsely) takes himself as 'the man of the house', the breadwinner and the one who decides the point of their speech, Hedvig is voiceless. Her words not so much lack meaning, but they have no room, no point, in Hjalmar's world where father and daughter are one. What is the point of speaking if we are not separate? And further, what is the point of speaking if the other is completely separated or without any ability to understand us? This is part of Cavell's struggles in speaking as a child. It is a struggle with the language of our elders. It is a language that gives us the possibility to speak in community and to express our position, it gives us a voice—but on the conditions of our elders' conventions for speech, for judging what is worth saying, which means that those conventions may also limit our room to express our position and limit our voice and our humanity.

Unlike Hjalmar (more like Hedvig) the child Cavell, like most children, accepts what this separateness demands of him if he wishes to enter the linguistic community of his elders and find his voice in that community. (This is not necessarily what he wants to do or should do. There are many reasons for children to detach themselves from their native community.) The child, in Cavell's passage, knows that, in speaking, he is also speaking representatively for his community; he speaks as if they do what he does. But he also lets his elders speak for him, speaking as if he does what they do. The education, taking place when a child learns to speak and enters a linguistic community, is consequently both for the child and the elder. Both of them strive to find their voice in the community that is becoming theirs as they acknowledge each other's words as words. Hence, acknowledging the child's reasons and words as our words is not a matter of translating their language into our language, or our reason into their reason, as if we spoke two different languages. Rather, it is to acknowledge their reasons as reason and their language as language, just as we recognise the jaguar's experience as our experience. Of course there is a limit to what we can recognise as our language or as our experience; few, if any, of the jaguar's expressions will be taken as language. But such limit is not set *a priori*. Rather it is something we will have to experience in our conversation with others.

Nonetheless, in this passage, Cavell never loses sight of the possibility of a sceptical outcome of the child's and his elder's interactions, an outcome where they do not, or cannot, acknowledge one another. Cavell says things such as '*If* I am to have a native tongue', '*if* I am to have my own voice', 'We do not know in advance' and 'I do not know in advance', indicating that he continual struggles with his uncertainty over how far (even if) he and his elders can go on together (Cavell, 2005, p. 203). Cavell invites us to read his text as he reads Wittgenstein: 'Now it is becoming clear that each of the voices and silences of the *Investigations* ... are meant as ours, so that the teacher's and the child's positions, among others, are ours, ones I may at any time find myself in' (Cavell, 1990, p. 83). Sceptical voices are not only expressed and heard by philosophers, but also in literature and in everyday life. Here we find that the sceptical voices are both heard and expressed by a child struggling to find a native tongue. In reading Cavell the teachers', the elders', and the children's voices are ours. Their struggles with scepticism are our struggles. Thus philosophising with children is not only about enhancing children's philosophical abilities: it is also about struggling together with the doubts we are faced with in philosophy, in literature and in our everyday interactions with others; it is about acknowledging that human life is inherently subject to scepticism.

In such a philosophy of childhood, the philosopher speaks representatively for the child and the child speaks representatively for the philosopher. That is how philosophy can be an education both for children and for grown-ups. In a sense, in speaking representatively for children, philosophers of education allow themselves to become children or recognise children's voices in themselves the same way that Costello uses Hughes' poem in order to think herself into the being of a jaguar (Diamond, 1991, pp. 42–48). They acknowledge the child in themselves and children's struggles with the discovery of being separate from others. The philosopher struggles with the sense that others are enigmatic and incomprehensible, that we are not understood by others (Cavell 2002, p. 263; 1990, p. 23). The education of the philosopher and the child consists in the ways that their voices form a community of reason, thought and language, and their transformations of one another's voices in participating in this community. When reading *Var är min syster?* or *The Lorax* and letting them speak for our possible rational community with children, we do not only educate ourselves. Because our reading may transform our conversations with children, which changes the conditions for children's voices in our community, this can also be an education of children even when we read children's literature without them present other than as characters in books. This is not an education of a particular child or a particular philosopher, but an acknowledgement of our shared community and of the ways that such community can transform itself in our conversations when we speak for one another. That means that philosophers of childhood, as so much children's literature (though clearly not all children's literature invites such readings), should not only speak *with* children and *about* children, but also *for* children and *as* children in order to give voice to their struggles to become part of our communities of reason.

TELLING A STORY ABOUT CHILDREN AND PHILOSOPHY: MATTHEWS AND CAVELL

I may seem unfair to Matthews' struggles to argue for children's rationality. Admittedly, I am impatient with his claims when he speaks as a philosopher trying to argue his position. My point has been rather different from his. The question of children's rationality becomes a real worry because it leaves us in a position where our arguments lose their force. If we cannot acknowledge children's expressions as reasons despite our worries about how well they reason according to our standards, then we have no common ground, our reasons come to an end, and there is no point in arguing with them. We acknowledge children as reasoning with us and in doing so we create a common ground from which we can advance conversations and sow doubts about our and others' arguments. ('She reasons her own way, your sister. Just don't believe everything she says.'). This means that the question of rationality becomes a different question from what Matthews may have had in mind. Whereas Matthews appears to claim that, since some children can reason philosophically, we should involve them in philosophical conversations, my claim is that we involve children in philosophical conversations to *establish* a community of reason, to make a claim of reason.

Nonetheless, when Matthews speaks for or lends his voice to children, a different scene is played out. Then his approach is transformed into a serious *acknowledgment* of children's thoughts. He actually demonstrates the kind of conversation with children I call for, both in his ways of writing, in speaking for children in his books, and in the actual conversations with children that motivate his writing. My worry is that what his philosophical style tells us is not fully compatible with his claims as a philosopher.

In *Dialogues with Children,* Matthews tells us a multi-layered *story* of his philosophical conversations with the children at a Scottish music school. Though this story evidently is based on his actual study of these children, Matthews does not present his findings as conventional empirical research (e.g. as a developmental psychologist might do). Rather he chooses a narrative structure with which he can engage his readers in a more literary manner. The tone of his prose, although interposed with some 'adult' philosophical terminology, is suggestive of the conversations he has with children, as if his readers were also children. Thus, Matthews invites us to acknowledge children's reasoning, or, so to speak, their philosophical language-games. However, this is only audible to us as long as we allow ourselves to take both Matthews and the children's accounts seriously, despite their lacking 'the benefit of sophisticated techniques'. This means *acknowledging* the account as a philosophical account, is an invitation to enter into discussion with children and with Matthews as a child, as well as an invitation to speaking for a shared community with them.

On a further note, Matthews' worry is not merely that the complexity and even geniality of children's philosophical thoughts are not acknowledged. He is also worried about the lack of philosophical thought in adults' lives in general, which may cause adults and psychologists (and perhaps even teachers) to fail to acknowledge philosophical aspects in children's thinking (Matthews, 1992, pp. 116–19). When we encounter the philosophical thoughts of children, we do not always recognise them as such, not only because of their at times unsophisticated expression but also because of our unfamiliarity with philosophy. In Matthews' words: 'What we as adults don't do, when we talk to children, is discuss matters we ourselves find difficult or problematic' (pp. 1–2). It seems as if we—at least in Western cultures, in our established ways of adulthood—avoid philosophical examination of our lives.

Cavell puts a similar idea somewhat differently. Referring to Wittgenstein's discussion of children who respond to their teachers' instruction in a non-conventional, dissonant way, Cavell writes (now as if he were the teacher or the adult):

> When my reasons come to an end and I am thrown back upon myself, upon my nature as it has so far shown itself, I can, supposing I cannot shift the ground of the discussion, either put the pupil out of my sight—as though his intellectual reactions are disgusting to me—or I can use the occasion to go over the ground I had hitherto thought foregone. If the topic is that of continuing a series, it may be learning enough to find that I *just do*; to rest upon myself as my foundation. But if the child, little or big, asks me: Why do we eat animals? or Why are some people poor and others rich? or What is God? or Why do I have to go to school? or Do you love black people as much as white people? or Who owns the land? or Why is there anything at all? or How did God get here?, I may find my answers thin, I may feel run out of reasons without being willing to say 'This is what I do' (what I say, what I sense, what I know), and honor that (Cavell, 1979, pp. 124–25).

Here the child's questions and resistance become existential. Matthews helps us to acknowledge the reality of children asking these questions, which means recognising children's questions as having philosophical depth and importance. Nevertheless, most of us do not have straight answers to these questions. Some of us might even believe that no one has an answer to these questions, and yet we are not satisfied. Such dissatisfaction may lead to a disgust, not only for the child's questioning of our way of life and thought, but for philosophy as such. I am inclined to think of this as an anxiety over the groundlessness of our practices. The authority of adulthood's established ways is in question if we take the child's philosophical questions seriously.

There seems to be at least two ways out of this reluctance to children's philosophical questionings. (i) One way would be to continue our resistance to philosophy. We can hold that the philosophical thoughts of children are nonsensical, irrelevant and essentially confused. Thus, we may claim that children should be educated out of their philosophical confusion to leave philosophy as it is and help children (and ourselves) to do other things than ask these seemingly confused questions. (ii) The second route, which I embrace, would be to acknowledge philosophical worries, whether in children or adults, as a part of the human condition. We may, as Cavell and Matthews emphasise, feel lost in the face of children's philosophical questions. Nonetheless, this loss puts us in a position where we can find and found our communities and ourselves again, where we can re-establish our communities and ourselves. This means that we engage in conversation with children not to establish set answers to their questions (building new moral and metaphysical systems), but to found a way, as Cavell puts it, 'on the way, *by* the way' (Cavell, 1981, p. 137). To borrow and freely to adapt phrasing of Naoko Saito in respect of Cavell: Philosophical conversations with children involve the task of founding a community (see Saito, 2005, p. 134).[6] Then, indeed, children do speak for philosophy.

Thus, we can read Matthews' attempts to promote philosophy with children as an acknowledging of a shared fate with children, as if our acknowledgment of children's philosophical questions established that they shared our deepest human concerns. When children raise questions about knowledge, scepticism, reality, ontology, beauty, morality, the meaning of life and so on, and we, despite their, to our adult minds, unsophisticated expression, acknowledge those questions as pertinent to us in our human condition, we enter into a conversation that reshapes or revolutionises the very foundations of our communities. In such conversations we speak for a transformed community where children are invited to found our ways of speaking, thinking and living. To philosophise with children is to say, 'You are in charge of the Truffula seed', or 'you and I are responsible for our future community of speech and reason'. I believe this is something philosophy for children programmes, depending on their design (one may certainly question if a 'programme' is the right way to go about it), could do, but also that this something we can do in many, perhaps more ordinary conversations with children, if we take their questions and assertions seriously.

I have suggested that philosophy related to childhood can be a speaking for children and an education of children by the reforming of our shared fate and community as much as a speaking for adults and educating them. Read and written in this way, children's literature will become a call for acknowledging the rationality of both children and grown-ups and serve as philosophical education of both. Children's literature can open our ears to children's philosophical thoughts and invite us to philosophise with children. Being engaged in philosophy for children is being engaged in our community of reason.

Perhaps one can summarise this text as an attempt to show how an acknowledgment of children as rational beings is an acknowledgement of children as human beings that we educate and are educated by. As human beings, they are both responsible for and subject to our community of reason and our shared future. If the questions we recognise as philosophical (questions of knowledge, or morality, or justice, or being or meaning) are essential to how we live and shape our communities, then philosophy for children programmes can be a way to acknowledge that children are both participants in and responsible for our lives and communities.[7]

NOTES

1. Cf. Cora Diamond's reading of Dickens' *A Christmas Carol* (Diamond, 1991, pp. 29–51).
2. Admittedly, *The Lorax* is a text much about environmental issues. The reading that I suggest of the text as being about our moral lives with children is not separable from its environmentalism. Rather the environmental issue strengthens my attempt to show that we share a fate with our children, that we share a responsibility for a future world and that our actions and expressions form our shared future.
3. The second half of the poem is what seems to illustrate Costello's point. It reads,

> But who runs like the rest past these arrives
> At a cage where the crowd stands, stares, mesmerized,
> As a child at a dream, at a jaguar hurrying enraged
> Through prison darkness after the drills of his eyes
> On a short fierce fuse. Not in boredom—
> The eye satisfied to be blind in fire,
> By the bang of blood in the brain deaf the ear—
> He spins from the bars, but there's no cage to him
> More than to the visionary his cell:
> His stride is wildernesses of freedom:
> The world rolls under the long thrust of his heel.
> Over the cage floor the horizons come. (Hughes, 1972, p. 3)

4. This and the following excerpts from *Var är min syster?* are my own translations.
5. This paragraph is partly a response to some worries raised by in conversation with Michael Peters.
6. The original reads: 'Philosophical writing, then, involves the task of "founding a nation"' (Saito, 2005, p. 134).
7. Most of this article was written during a stay at Department of Education Policy, Organization, Leadership, University of Illinois, funded by the Fulbright Commission. I have benefited from the comments of Nicholas C. Burbules, Michael A. Peters, Pradeep A. Dhillon, Klas Roth, Martin Gustafsson and Adrian Thomasson, Paul Standish and the editors of this issue. Early drafts of the paper have been presented at PESA in Honolulu 2009 and at ECER in Helsinki 2010. A special thanks to Stijn Mus who is responsible of giving a rather rough draft of the paper to Nancy Vansieleghem. I thank Michael Kress for proofreading the text. All remaining faults are of course my own.

REFERENCES

Cavell, S. (1979) *The Claim of Reason* (Oxford, Oxford University Press).
Cavell, S. (1981) *Senses of Walden* (Chicago, IL, Chicago University Press).
Cavell, S. (1990) *Conditions, Handsome and Unhandsome: The Constitution of Emersonian Perfectionism* (Chicago, IL, University of Chicago Press).
Cavell, S. (2002) *Must we mean what we say?*, 2nd edn. (Cambridge, Cambridge University Press).
Cavell, S. (2005) *Philosophy the Day after Tomorrow* (Cambridge MA, Belknap Press of Harvard University Press).
Cavell, S. (2010) *Little Did I Know: Excerpts from Memory* (Stanford, CA, Stanford University Press).

Coetzee, J. M. (1999) *The Lives of Animals* (Princeton, NJ, Princeton University Press).

Dewey, J. (1916) *Democracy and Education*, in: *The Middle Works of John Dewey, 1899–1924*, Vol. 9 J. A. Boydston ed. (Carbondale, IL, Southern Illinois University Press).

Diamond, C. (1991) The Importance of Being Human, in: D. Cockburn (ed.) *Human Beings* (Cambridge, Cambridge University Press).

Diamond, C. (2006) The Difficulty of Reality and the Difficulty of Philosophy, in: A. Crary and S. Shie (eds) *Reading Cavell* (London, Routledge).

Hughes, T. (1972) *The Jaguar, Selected Poems* (New York, Harper and Row).

Ibsen, H. (1884) *The Wild Duck*, in: *Ibsen: Four Major Plays, Vol. 1*, R. Fjelde, trans.; J. Templeton, ed. (New York, Signet Classics).

Johansson, V. (2010) The Philosophy of Dissonant Children: Stanley Cavell's Wittgensteinian Philosophical Therapies as an Educational Foundation, *Educational Theory*, 60.4, pp. 469–486.

Matthews, G. (1976) Philosophy and Children's Literature, *Metaphilosophy*, 7.1, pp. 7–16.

Matthews, G. (1992) *Dialogues With Children* (Cambridge MA, Harvard University Press).

Matthews, G. (1996) *The Philosophy of Childhood* (Cambridge MA, Harvard University Press).

Moi, T. (2006) *Henrik Ibsen and the Birth of Modernism: Art, Theater, Philosophy* (Oxford, Oxford University Press).

Nordqvist, S. (2007) *Var är min syster?* (Stockholm, Opal).

Saito, N. (2005) *The Gleam of Light: Moral Perfectionism and Education in Dewey and Emerson* (New York, Fordham University Press).

Sellars, W. (1963) *Science, Perception and Reality* (New York, Humanities Press).

Wittgenstein, L. (1953) *Philosophical Investigations*, 4th edn. (Oxford, Blackwell Publishing).

12

Brilliance of a Fire: Innocence, Experience and the Theory of Childhood

ROBERT A. DAVIS

> There are childhood reveries which surge forth with the brilliance of a fire
> (Gaston Bachelard, 1971, p. 100)

MYTHOLOGIES OF INNOCENCE

Across a broad range of discourses, from critical theory to the literature of professional education, the concept of childhood innocence is the most regularly reviled of a constellation of ideas associated with the supposedly orthodox Western construction of childhood.[1] Amidst the general revision made in the last twenty years to the theory of childhood originally associated with the work of Philippe Ariès, the hostility towards the principle of childhood innocence, given definitive expression by Ariès (1962, pp. 100–119), has not only survived the process of revision but actually intensified, invigorated by the poststructuralist challenge to the key signifiers of essentialised or unitary identity.[2] Of all of the pioneering interpretations first proposed by Ariès, the critique of 'innocence' as a universal and defining property of childhood seems at first glance the most obviously valid and unassailable. Advances in the social sciences, deeper engagements with the (often frightful) lives of historically- and culturally-situated children and, above all, the expanding ethnographic record of varied, multiple childhoods across many societies and epochs all seem to point irresistibly to the factitious character of the concept of childhood innocence and its questionable basis in a contingent and historically-specific set of circumstances with little or no salience for the experience of children in the modern globalised world (Lancy, 2008).

Philosophy for Children in Transition: Problems and Prospects, First Edition. Nancy Vansieleghem and David Kennedy. Chapters © 2012 The Authors. Editorial organization © 2012 Philosophy of Education Society of Great Britain. Published 2012 by Blackwell Publishing Ltd.

The alleged redundancy of the idea of innocence is, however, only part of the opposition it continues to excite. In the rigorous application of the hermeneutic of suspicion to a cluster of inherited perceptions of childhood, innocence is censured not simply as a fraud, but also as a pernicious abstraction, damagingly implicated in the exclusion of children from the morally complex realm of the social where such absolutes can have little meaning or explanatory significance. Hence, Marina Warner criticises what she memorably terms the 'manichaean diptych' of angel and devil in which the received imagery of childhood innocence traps children, burdening them with an ideal of perfection so unsustainable that each inevitable lapse from it in the everyday lives and behaviours of young people is invariably condemned as deviant (Warner, 1994, pp. 33–48). Owain Jones attacks the promulgation of the myth of childhood innocence for its collusion with a set of cultural assumptions that differentiate children according to markers of class, environment and race. Rural, white, prosperous children have a special access to the legacy of innocence denied their poor, urban and often ethnically mixed counterparts (Jones, 2002). It is through work of this kind that the antipathy towards childhood innocence becomes embedded in the values of professional education, in areas such as the preparation of childcare practitioners.[3]

Perhaps the most antagonistic response to the traditions of childhood innocence comes currently from the movements in critical theory heir to the Foucauldian project of denaturalising the genealogies of human sexuality. Ariès' discussion of childhood innocence, with its celebrated attention to the intimate training of the infant Louis XIII and the sexual mores of the *ancien régime* French court, anticipated something of this line of analysis. Exposing the ideological processes by which normative constructions of sex and gender are authorised and regulated has since become one of the principal targets of the postmodern interrogation of the canons of Enlightenment rationality. Childhood innocence is, in this critique, a definitive and pejorative context for the reproduction of the univocal narratives of sexual destiny through which dominant patterns of gender and desire are first created and then policed. The attack on the disciplinary function of childhood innocence that arises out of these objections has taken two main forms in recent times. James Kincaid and his followers have cast a withering veil of scepticism over the literature of innocence from the 19th and 20th centuries, locating within its alleged displacements and evasions the hypocritical concealment of predatory paedophilic longings and the stimulus to child-molestation (Kincaid, 1992, 1998; McCreery, 2004). More radically still, and with an importantly contrasting goal, the primacy accorded sexual self-fashioning in certain strains of postmodern thought, such as Queer Theory, prompts the denunciation of childhood innocence as one of the cornerstones of the heteronormative life-schedule, supporting the patriarchal structures of compulsory heterosexuality and fixed gender determination.[4] Innocence is no longer simply an irrelevant historical curiosity in these readings, it is a central reference point in a wider mythology of childhood that helps uphold an unjust moral order in which both adults and children are subject to the oppressive politics of purity. Eroticised objects of an alienated adult gaze, children confined within the economy of innocence are denied full sexual and ethical agency, whilst at the same time functioning symbolically to validate a dialectic of vulnerability and corruption that constrains adult sexual autonomy. As Lesnik-Oberstein and Thomson observe,

> The child has thus a strange identity, one that is not at one with itself, even in the act of figuring the very thing that is at one with itself . . . In this way, it incorporates into itself the dialectic it is called upon to forestall. So it is in its absolute singularity that it is read as the most stable, the most fixed, the unquestioned and unquestionable—universally. In short, it is without question (Lesnik-Oberstein and Thomson, 2002, pp. 35–46).

Contemporary scholarly opposition to the concept of the innocence of childhood serves several distinct polemical purposes. They each share, however, the broadly Arièsian understanding of the origin of the myth of innocence and trace the ideological pedigree of the concept almost without exception to the same historical conjuncture. This is vital to an understanding of the widespread indictment of innocence in the literature of childhood studies, its unanimity perhaps jarring ironically with a disciplinary ethic that elsewhere proclaims the virtues of alterity and the eschewal of closed explanatory systems. Higonnet sums up an academic consensus that has solidified in the literature into an overarching orthodoxy:

> Historians date the modern, western concept of an ideally innocent childhood to somewhere around the seventeenth century. Until then, children had been understood as faulty small adults, in need of correction and discipline, especially Christian children who were thought to be born in sin (Higonnet, 1998, p. 8).

Interestingly, the imprecise reference to the 'seventeenth century' starting-point, which is vaguely indebted to Ariès' chronology, is rarely followed through in these statements of a supposedly self-evident historical truth. The conventional historiography of innocence almost always leaps from gesturing tokenistically to a presumed but barely acknowledged 17th-century bench-mark on to Rousseau or some other foundational moment of the Romantic movement. For it is, of course, with Romanticism that the trouble with innocence really begins (Haudrup, 2000, pp. 39–59). The zealous rejection of one myth—the conceit of childhood innocence—is matched by the convenient embrace of another: the myth of origins, which strives to assign the emergence of innocence to a specific and decisive turning point in early modern European culture's perception of the child.

The allusion to a vaguely realised pre-Romantic backdrop to the rise of innocence has a potential to open up lines of enquiry into the area that few commentators have pursued.[5] Probing the late Renaissance interest in the transcendentalism of childhood not only converges with new post-Ariès assessments of the emergence of the modern institutions of childhood (Somerville, 1992; Classen, 2005; Cunningham, 2006), it also holds forth the prospect of reconnecting critical awareness with a wider and more ancient historical grammar of innocence embracing the cultural work of a range of discursive genres, including theology, philosophy, mysticism and poetics. This task, it can be seen, furthers the genealogical endeavour by problematising an accepted critical dogma and excavating the hidden history of the elusive idea of innocence in order more effectively to comprehend its sources and evaluate its continuing influence. The general resistance to such a move within the broad critique of innocence may reflect the impact of prevailing disciplinary specialisations. It might also point, however, to an implicit recognition that the current academic consensus on the concept performs a pivotal—even necessary—function in the wider critical appraisal of childhood in contemporary culture and society (Masschelein, 2003; Ryan, 2008).

HISTORIES OF INNOCENCE

Insistence on a High Romantic turning point in the fortunes of childhood innocence rests upon a view of preceding values that oversimplifies the legacy of the deep past while subduing those elements within it that complicate the contrived contrast of perceptions before and after the decisive Romantic intervention. In a more nuanced historiography of innocence, the Romantic account of childhood can be seen to participate in a rich and variegated movement of feeling with roots running far back into the religious, philosophical and aesthetic traditions of Western culture. Acknowledging this truth does not erase the memory—or the inheritance—of the pessimistic moral and theological systems, derived chiefly from the Augustinian fall-redemption paradigm and its Calvinst variants, in which childhood was also systematically configured in the late medieval and early modern periods (Somerville, 1982; Stables, 2008, pp. 51–56). It is precisely from the logic of such antitheses that a more generous account of the lineage of childhood innocence is seeking to escape. It may nevertheless be significant that much contemporary theorising about childhood echoes the fatalistic, querulous tone of some of the bleakest of the early modern Christian commentators. That a pre-Romantic Christian emphasis upon the depravity of childhood existed, interdependent with a widespread punitive regime of adult control and surveillance of children in church, home and school, is not in dispute (Thomas, 1990; Orme, 2006, pp. 128–163). It requires to be set alongside, however, another tradition of thought with equally profound investments in Judaeo-Christian scripture and doctrine—including largely forgotten but influential movements of speculative Christian mysticism in which the image of the child played a commanding role.

Contrary to the findings of Ariès, there existed in the Middle Ages a large corpus of Christian writings devoted to descriptions of the innocence of childhood and the uniqueness of children's experience. The 12th-century mystic Hildegard of Bingen compared the goodness of children to the brightness of the angels (1986, p. 299). Dante could write that '. . . In little children only mayst thou seek/True innocence and faith . . . '; (1962, p. 229). Latin lexicographers wrongly traced the etymology of *puer*, a boy, and *puella*, a girl, to *puritas*, meaning 'pure'; and one divine could write 'Children are as pure as heaven' (Shahar, 1990, pp. 17–20; Schultz, 1995; Orme, 2001, pp. 188–189). The formulation most readily associated with Rousseau, that 'There is no original perversity in the human heart. There is not a single vice about which one cannot say how and whence it entered . . .' (1979, p. 56), has powerful affinities with elements of the English Puritan and Rhineland inner light movements of the centuries that preceded Rousseau and by the Continental variants of which he was clearly influenced. It is the dissenting tracts and Puritan psychobiography of 17th-century writers, such as the Digger Gerrard Winstanley, which, in the English tradition especially, form the crucible in which the modern conception of childhood innocence finds its most defiant assertion: '. . . a childe that is new borne, or till he grows up to some few yeares . . . is innocent, harmeless . . . And this is *Adam*, or mankinde in his Innocency' (Sabine, 1941, pp. 494–495). The image of the child as representative of a prelapsarian perfection and unity of being is a perennial metaphor in the literature of religious mysticism, alchemy and the esoteric tradition.

Recent scholarship into the prehistory of Romanticism has shown that the teachings of the Protestant inner light sects made an immense contribution to the development of psychological interiority in European thought and writing (Berlin, 1993; Beiser, 2003), including the preservation and consolidation of the tradition of childhood innocence in a period of religious confrontation and cultural crisis. In the European context especially, belief in the fundamental innocence of childhood—understood, it ought to be emphasised, as a *type* of the radical innocence of general humanity—can be interpreted as a form of resistance to the dominant cultural hegemony of the contending fall-redemption theologies of Protestant Predestinarians and Counter-Reformation Jansenists. To espouse an alternative, subterranean tradition, conveyed from antiquity through Christian Neoplatonism and its multiple philosophical progeny, became the signature of a particular style of European spiritual dissenter, cutting across confessional divides (Marcus, 1978). Jeremy Taylor typifies, in the turbulent English setting of the 1640s and 50s, the Anglo-Catholic protest against the Calvinist emphasis on the polluted origins of the unregenerate human infant, mired in the concupiscence of Original Sin. For thinkers like Taylor, the innovative Puritan attention to childhood and domesticity was an undoubted stimulus for renewed psychological interest in, and moral solicitude towards, the young. It also, however, repeatedly pathologised children and reinforced a repellent ontology of generational separateness based upon its characteristically despondent disciplines of introspection:

> But it is hard upon such mean accounts to reckon all children to be born enemies of God ... full of sin and vile corruption when the Holy Scriptures propound children as imitable for their pretty innocence and sweetness, and declare them rather heirs of heaven than hell. ... These are better words than are usually given them; and signify, that they are beloved of God, not hated, designed for heaven and born to it ... not born for hell: that was 'prepared for the devil and his angels' not for innocent babes. This does not call them naturally wicked, but rather naturally innocent, and is a better account than is commonly given them by imputation of Adam's sin (Taylor, 1655, pp. 164–165).

Thirty years previously, John Earle, the Bishop of Salisbury, in his hugely popular collection of 'characters', *Microcosmographie* of 1628, extended the *theological* defence of the innate innocence of childhood by interpreting it as a recapitulation of the originary innocence of the Garden of Eden: 'A *Child* is a Man in small letter, yet the best Copie of ... *Adam* before he tasted of *Eve*, or the Apple ... His father hath writ him as his owne little story, wherein he reades those dayes that he cannot remember; and sighes to see what innocence he hath out-liu'd ...' (Earle, 1628, p. 185). The references by Winstanley and Earle to parallels between the innocence of childhood and the prelapsarian condition of the first human beings is a poorly understood element in the symbolic pattern of innocence in Christian thought. In the divided England of the middle of the 17th century, the theme was taken up by a generation of Anglican clergymen-poets, at odds with the prevailing theological and political temper of their time and place, yet of vital importance in the transmission of key features of a suppressed Christian tradition, included in which were a set of core beliefs about the spiritual cache surrounding the image of the child (Martin, 1938). To the evangelical imagination, the translation of this vein of thought to the plane of inner, psychological experience made the child described by those writers into an emblem of privileged sensitivity and freshness of sensation—the ultimate icon of wholeness, integration and the transformation of the imperfection of the world into the possibilities of new life:

> Certainly Adam in Paradise had not more sweet and curious apprehensions of the world than I when I was a child ... All appeared new, and

strange at first, inexpressibly rare, and delightful and beautiful. My knowledge was divine ... I seemed as one brought into the estate of innocence ... Boys and girls tumbling in the street, and playing were moving jewels ... (Traherne, 1990, p. 226).

This is Thomas Traherne writing in 1668, almost a century and a half before Blake and Wordworth. Traherne declares that, as a child, 'I felt a vigour in my sense/That was all spirit ... I nothing in the world did know/ But 'twas divine' (p. 5). Many currents of thought are clearly evident in utterances of this kind, but the consistency and the coherence of the underlying complex of ideas are irreducible, and form an indispensable foundation for much subsequent understanding of the quickened awareness, and the spiritual and moral sensibility, of the child. Viewed—when considered at all—as a local aberration, Traherne in fact typifies a powerful, if deliberately marginalised, vector in English piety of the period.

An interesting locus of the wider movement of feeling from which this inclination emerges can be seen in the writings of Traherne's older contemporaries, the twin brothers Thomas and Henry Vaughan. The general tenor of Thomas Vaughan's abstruse, alchemical speculations shares the attitudes of those late Renaissance mystics for whom the child is a central representation of both continuity and renewal: 'This *Consideration* of my self when I was a Child, hath made me since examine Children ... A Child I suppose, *in puris Naturalibus*, before education alters and ferments him ... Notwithstanding, I should think, by what I have read, that the naturall disposition of Children ... is one of those things, about which the *Antient Philosophers* have busied themselves even to some curiosity' (Vaughan, 1984, p. 521). Thomas Vaughan here shows the influence of a number of Continental thinkers, principally Weigel, Gorlitz, and the great German mystic Jacob Boehme, whose works were much translated into English in the second half of the 17th century. Boehme's principal concern is to defend early childhood as the naturalistic expression of an essential unity of being upon which the sovereignty of the mature, integrated self depends. It is a view with affinities to Platonism, but distinguished by a belief—which foreshadows Wordsworth—in the uniqueness of the psychological chemistry through which infants, especially, construct a pre-rational picture of the world. This is a condition, Boehme insists (mischievously inverting a familiar educational metaphor), from which adults, in proximity to infants, can continue to be enriched: 'Little Children are our Schoolmasters ... they bring their sport from their Mothers wombe, which is a Remnant of Paradise' (1647, p. 130). By 'sport', Boehme means 'play', and his delight in children's instinctive and spontaneous inclination to play represents one of the first reflections upon the link between innocence and play in the veneration of childhood. In another typical inversion of what had by then become a clichéd simile in popular devotional writing, the Philosopher in Boehme's *Aurora* of 1656 poses the question 'To Whom now shall I liken the Angels?' He provides his own answer: 'I will liken them to *little* children, which walk in the fields in *May*, among the *flowers*, and pluck them, and make curious Garlands, and Poseys, carrying them in their hands rejoicing' (Boehme, 1656, p. 321).

Thomas Vaughan's brother, the poet-priest Henry Vaughan, advances a still more personalised and visionary rendering of these beliefs, dwelling upon the redemptive possibilities of capturing the child's '... age of mysteries! which he/Must live twice that would God's face see,' and 'by mere playing go to Heaven.' For Henry Vaughan, 'the white designs that children drive' ('Child-hood': 1983, p. 288) include an innate perception of the pristine integrity of the created order, with the sanctity of which the child has profound spiritual affinities:

> Happy those early days when I
> Shined in my angel-infancy
> Before I understood this place
> Appointed for my second race,
> Or taught my soull to fancy aught
> But a white celestial thought ... ('The Retreat', Vaughan, 1983, p. 172).

At the heart of this view of the child lies the evolving modern belief in the continuity of the self though time, and it is from this point that increasing emphasis is placed upon the connection between healthy early childhood experience and the moral and psycho-spiritual well-being of the adult individual. These ideas are of course central to the educational philosophies of late Renaissance thinkers such as Locke and Comenius (Singer 2005). Ever since the affinities between Henry Vaughan and Wordsworth were first identified by Bishop Trench in 1868—focused mainly upon the striking similarities between Vaughan's poem 'The Retreat' and Wordsworth's 'Intimations Ode'—the preoccupation with innocence in the writings of Vaughan and his contemporaries has been interpreted proleptically and recruited to a teleology that privileges rather than analyzes the seeming originality of the Romantic transformation of perceptions of childhood.[6] Yet there is a compelling justification, given the climate of enquiry in which Vaughan's outlook was formed, to look backwards in time rather than forwards, to probe more deeply into the historical genealogy of this version of innocence, grappling with the still earlier sources upon which Vaughan and his contemporaries quite expressly drew.

Traherne, the Vaughan brothers, and the broader range of Anglican writers such as Herrick and Herbert who participated in the anti-Calvinist defence of childhood, belonged to a wider coalition in latitudinarian

Protestant thought in the Europe of the later Reformation. They looked to a recovery of the wisdom of the early Church Fathers and of pre-Nicene patristics as a means of combating the morbidity of extreme Calvinism whilst avoiding the errors of Rome (Walker, 1964, p. 11). This was a quest that incurred the wrath of Calvin and his followers, who accused their opponents of Pelagianism and Arianism and of denying the gravity of Original Sin. In their revolt against what they saw as the fatalism of the Calvinist doctrines of depravity and atonement, the Anglican school, centred on the Cambridge Platonists, drew deliberately upon the writings of the 2nd-century Church Fathers Irenaeus of Lyons (c125–202) and Origen (c185–254) as a means of refuting propositions they had come to regard as the consequences of a perverse Calvinist interpretation of Augustine. The 17th-century passion for the writings of Irenaeus, in particular, fed directly into the work of the Cambridge Platonists and through them exercised an immense influence on Traherne and the Vaughan brothers (Grant, 1971). One of the main sites of contention in this struggle, signalled implicitly in the repeated invocations of the figure of Adam in the literature cited above, was the early chapters of the Book of Genesis and, especially, the disputed interpretation of the character of the prelapsarian condition enjoyed by Adam and Eve. It seems clear that in his reflections upon of the Pauline account of the Fall and the symbolism of the relationship between God and the primal humans, Irenaeus of Lyons had come to consider Adam and Eve to be, at least metaphorically, *children*:

> Adam and Eve ... 'were naked and were not ashamed,' for there was in them an innocent and infantile mind, and they thought or understood nothing whatsoever of those things that are wickedly born in the soul through lust and shameful desires. For at that time they preserved their nature intact, since that which was breathed into the handiwork was the breath of life; and while the breath remains in its order and strength, it is without comprehension or understanding of what is evil.[7]

At the heart of Irenaeus' soteriology is the story of God's paternal care for the infants in the Garden. The complication of the ontological freedom accorded the first humans is that they are by necessity placed by their Creator in a condition of endless becoming—even, self-fashioning—which leaves their 'discretion still underdeveloped' and their free wills prey to 'the deceiver'. For Adam 'was a child and had need to grow so as to come to his full perfection' (Irenaeus, 1952, pp. 12, 14). The key biblical doctrine underpinning Irenaeus' unflinchingly orthodox yet ultimately optimistic view of the Fall is the Genesis statement that humanity is made, first and foremost, in the *image* of God. As Marshall and Parvis have proposed, the distinctive character of this emphasis on the concept of the *imago dei* resides in its materiality: matter and flesh are good and whole. The corporeal embodiment of the individual infant signifies the integrity of 'something bodily and physical in which all human beings share.' It is, they argue, 'not lost at the Fall but rather remains as a locus of God's saving power in the world . . . It is inclusive, it sees things from the side of the most vulnerable, and it points ahead' (Marshall and Parvis, 2004, p. 324). The innocence of childhood is, for Irenaeus and the Renaissance poetic theologies shaped by his rediscovery, not static, but dynamic and developmental. It is an image of absolute dependence and absolute potential. In the prosecution of these arguments, Irenaeus typifies an important yet often overlooked strain in early Christian theodicy, with roots in the highly pro-juvenile language of the New Testament. Here the fundamental dignity of the person of the child is shown to derive not from the exercise of reason or moral capability (about the validity of each, in a child, there might legitimately be doubt), but from the mere fact of being: the possession of a body, and a body viewed as a reiteration of the innocence and vulnerability of the divine child laid in the manger. The essentially incarnational quality of patristic thinking on these questions, taken up in the writings of Clement of Alexandria (c150–215), Tertullian (c160–220) and Cyprian (c208–258), defied the norms of pagan antiquity in proposing the innocence of childhood as a blueprint and inspiration for the Christian life. This innocence is, moreover, not simply nostalgia for the apparent absence of sin in the prologue to lived, rational experience. It is a set of positive values attached to the state of childhood, centred upon children's physical presence, their spontaneity, their predispositions, their appetites, their capacity for play and their relationship with their parents—of which Clement, in particular, has a markedly optimistic view (Bakke, 2006, pp. 58–72). Commenting on the implications of this neglected cluster of New Testament and patristic convictions, the theologian Hans Urs von Balthasar has noted that through it,

> . . . the ways of the child, long since sealed off for the adult, open up an original dimension in which everything unfolds within the bounds of the right, the true, the good, in a zone of hidden containment which cannot be derogated as 'pre-ethical' or 'unconscious,' as if the spirit of the child had not yet awakened, or was still at the animal level—something it never was, not even in the mother's womb. That zone or dimension in which the child lives, on the contrary, reveals itself as a sphere of original wholeness and health (von Balthasar, 1991, pp. 11–12).

Von Balthasar's bold additional claim that 'everywhere outside of Christianity the child is automatically sacrificed' (von Balthasar, 1968, p. 257), underlines (with a grim and unwitting irony, perhaps, given the recent record of some of the ministers of his Church) the contrast between the early Christian valorisation of the child and the often destructive classical asymmetry of adult and child out of which the calamitous practices of infanticide and pederasty were sanctioned in the ancient world. The Christian opposition to such social practices was a frequent source of controversy in the Roman Empire and laid an important foundation for the development of the Christian understanding of childhood generally and the innocence of childhood in particular (Gundry-Volf, 2001).

INNOCENCE RECLAIMED

The reclamation of these enduring ideas in certain areas of Reformation theology—largely in response to the internecine crisis of Calvinism—can be shown to be a far more significant aspect of the history of innocence than is commonly acknowledged. As appreciation increases of the extent to which core Romantic principles germinated in the milieu of dissenting Protestant spiritualities, represented by key transitional figures such as Hamann and Swedenborg, so the persistence of the subversive legacy of innocence assumes a subtly altered place in the intellectual ancestry of Romanticism (Balfour, 2002). Indeed, John Mee has gone so far as to claim that English High Romanticism is at its core a mutation of the Reformation virtue of 'enthusiasm', with everything this entails for the social control of the disruptive spiritual and libidinous energies of childhood (Mee, 2003). Recognising the indebtedness of writers such as Blake and Wordsworth to the legacy of dissenting thought refurbishes understanding of their strategic application of the concept of innocence to the prophetic project of redeeming childhood from the dominant functional, performative and disciplinary discourses of early industrial society. In keeping with the prevailing critical scepticism towards innocence, the direction of contemporary Romantic theory is strongly inclined against this claim, dwelling instead upon the centrality of innocence to a wider, sinister cultural programme of containment and self-regulation in which Romantic notions of an ideal childhood are discursively located (Plotz, 2001, pp. 56–60). Even seemingly progressive social endeavours—most especially modern, child-centred education— allied to the Romantic vision of childhood as a state inherently innocent, free and sometimes even ecstatically captivated by the wonder of a prodigal world, survive little of the withering accusatory glare of post-Romantic ideological suspicion. Every cultural undertaking involving the idealised image of the child is, in this critical scrutiny, always from its inception fatally haunted by the contradictions of the Romantic inheritance, prey to its displacements and suppressions of everything in actual childhood that is not compliant with the normative overarching ideal (Bunyard, 2010).

Powerful though this critique can often be, and prudent though it is to treat the transcendental claims of Romantic argument with caution, wholesale repudiation of the Romantic defence of childhood involves a denial of the sophistication with which Romantic art confronts the paradoxes and crises of childhood innocence in a perilous and volatile world. As Roni Natov has shown, William Blake's famous affirmation of the condition of innocence exuberantly celebrates the fundamental *plasticity* of early childhood, its capacity to respond to experiences of conflict and stress just as readily as it embraces those vouchsafing attachment and fulfilment (Natov, 2003, pp. 9–21). The dialectic of Innocence and Experience is acted out in both the psyche of the child and in the disfigured cultural order of which he or she is a part. As well as ratifying the child's vital access to an atavistic unity of being, Blake's *Songs of Innocence and of Experience* repeatedly confront the child's primal fear of abandonment and represent it poetically and visually as an anxiety overcome only after great struggle. The Chimney Sweeper, the Little Girl Lost, the Little Boy Lost—all the various child-protagonists of Blake's songs—endure the impact of a ruthless adult society in which childhood is tyrannised by overlapping forces of economic, racial and religious subordination. The innocence embodied in these compelling personalities is elevated to a form of *resistance* by its moral intelligence and its access to resources of the imagination that reproach the brutality and hypocrisy of the zone in which childhood finds itself repeatedly confined:

> They clothed me in the clothes of death,
> And taught me to sing the notes of woe.
>
> And because I am happy, & dance & sing,
> They think they have done me no injury:
> And are gone to praise God & his Priest and King
> Who make up a heaven of our misery. ('The Chimney Sweeper', Blake,
> 1988, p. 22)

The endurance and transformative power Blake associates with innocence is forged out of its engagement with, and not its flight from, the oppressive delusions of experience and its diminished version of human purpose. Radical innocence overcomes these limitations not by recourse to an unsatisfactory transcendentalism, but by the assertion of authentic and humanising ideals consistent with the propensities and appetites of childhood itself. Freedom of movement, familial belonging, natural compassion, desire (including, daringly, sexual desire), resilience, and continuity with the ecology of other living things represent, in Blake's poetry of childhood, properties that are *constitutive* of innocence, affording eventual access to a higher synthesis in which the 'contrary states' of Innocence and Experience are transformed. The child, for Blake, is a source of human feeling that opposes limits, particularly those limits associated with the patriarchal power of the despotic father God and his secular successors in the rationalist systems of production and authority governing the institutions of early industrial society. The innocent child is not an escape from these systems, nor is she even simply a victim. Rather, she is—as she was for Blake's dissenting forebears—a dangerous memory, both individual and collective, of a different way of thinking about human destiny.

The Romantic enunciation of innocence is not exhausted by Blakean dialectics. It has many subtle inflections, covering the spectrum from the vatic exaltation of childhood to a conciliatory ceremonial naturalism healing the division between adult and child within highly specified hierarchies of social relation. The children who populate Wordsworth's poems, such as 'We Are Seven' or 'Anecdote for Fathers', once again refuse an easy or complacent staging of this reconciliation of the generations, emphasising instead the evasive and refractory quality of the adult-child encounter and its ironically contrasting styles of reasoning:

> Oh dearest, dearest Boy! My heart
> For better lore could seldom yearn
> Could I but teach the hundredth part
> Of what from thee I learn. ('Anecdote for Fathers', Wordsworth, 1992, pp. 132–134).

Wordsworth has been rightly praised for 'giving voice' to children, if also, more recently, admonished for his frequent neglect of the real children in his care. Plotz is surely wrong, however, in her suggestion that the concept of childhood innocence barely interested him (2001, pp. 55–58). Facile, sentimental definitions of innocence certainly bored Wordsworth, as they did Blake. Nevertheless, Wordsworth's efforts to extend conversational voice to marginal and isolated figures were clearly founded upon the recognition he wished to confer on the 'state of greater simplicity' defended in the Preface to the *Lyrical Ballads* and in his time conventionally dismissed by high art (Wordsworth, 1992, p. 60; Marcus, 1985). Indeed, it is the dialogic quality of Wordsworth's poetry of engagement that allows him in narrative poems such a 'The Idiot Boy' and 'Michael' to adjudicate between different versions of innocence across a range of personalities and landscapes within the poems, including those of mature adult protagonists emotionally bonded with children and alive to the uniqueness of their response to experience. The outcome of such an encounter with innocence is, for the adult, most certainly gain and not loss. Indeed, it may be by virtue of a parallel synergy of hopes and interests across the generations that, as Barbara Garlitz has so ably demonstrated, Wordsworth's most ecstatic articulation of the innocent sublimity of childhood, the 'Immortality Ode', assumed almost scriptural levels of cultural authority in egalitarian educational circles in 19th-century Britain (Garlitz, 1966; Halpin, 2008). Surfacing in diary entries, letters, essays, sermons, manifestos and political speeches, the rhetoric of the 'Immortality Ode' was powerfully and deliberately harnessed to radical demands for the extension of mass education and early claims for the recognition of children's rights. Two important correctives to the standard critique of the language of innocence emerge from this. First, the frequently suspect transcendentalism of the concept of innocence is seen to possess an unexpectedly progressive political traction. Second, the 'democratisation' of innocence in its passage from elite to popular culture, and in its potent enrichment of the discourses of educational access, underscores a vital if often obscured principle at the heart of the Wordsworthian defence of the innocence of childhood *tout court*—that is, that innocence is an *entitlement* of childhood as well as a *privilege* of it (Dunne, 2008).

INNOCENCE, EXPERIENCE, COMPETENCE

The organic, abiding view of childhood innocence as a mobilising virtue in the creation and revival of a more general adult vitality contests many of the critical orthodoxies of contemporary critical theory, education and psychology (Saward, 1999). It is certainly highly significant that the perceived Romantic recovery of the radical innocence of childhood in the period from approximately 1750–1830 paralleled the rise of industrial-bureaucratic state and its emblematic institutions of disciplinary regulation and standardisation. Foremost among these lay the gradual extension of mass elementary schooling to the general population, characterised by its patterns of classroom aggregation and simultaneous instruction modelled on the early factory system (Hamilton, 1989, pp. 97–120). Orthodox histories of popular education, anchored in a dominant humanistic narrative of enlightened educational progress, inclined until comparatively recently to identify this movement, even in its obvious myriad imperfections, with the steady realisation of the ideals of key Enlightenment activists such as Comenius, Locke and Helvétius and their advocacy of popular schooling as remedy for the ignorance, oppression and sectarianism of previous eras. This version of the history of education is not by itself false, but it is incomplete, especially in its understanding of the cultural and ideological influences through which mass education was resourced and implemented from the early industrial period onwards.

   Even if Foucauldian and post-Foucauldian critiques of the role of popular schooling in the covert reproduction of docile subjectivities is in the final analysis to be challenged for its fatalism, the seemingly benign practices of interactive learning and teaching in the institutions of progressive education in the late Enlightenment period have nevertheless been implicated in the governance of children's minds and bodies in forms of lasting and subtle significance to modern societies. The advent of mass education—including, indeed, those versions openly declared to be emancipatory and inclusive—has been firmly embedded in the expansion of the complex legal, political, economic and cultural apparatus of the modern state and its increasingly searching demands on, and promises to, its 'citizens'. This explains why in both Europe (Gill, 2010, pp. 229–255) and the United States (Brewer, 2005, pp. 129–150) arguments raged in the late-18th and early-19th centuries over the proper supervision of mass education and its relationship to political participation and state power. Even the champions of a radically 'democratised' concept of public education, such as Noah Webster or Mary Wollstonecraft, explicitly defended the role of the school in the nurture of a thoroughgoing social and political literacy which would 'claim' children for reason and republican virtue, if necessary by wresting them away from all other rival or regressive loyalties, including those of family and sect. Contemporary manifestations of education for citizenship, and the confident, applied rationality of P4C, may believe they have overcome or even abolished this tension, but the spectre of 'regulated childhoods' remains palpable in the ways in which discursive boundaries are set and emotional and investments moderated across these activities.

Of course the educational zone that stood historically in many respects outside this structure of increasing surveillance and regulation proved to be the site most hospitable to the discourse of Romantic innocence and its attendant pedagogical values. Both in theory and practice, infant or kindergarten education in Europe and America developed through its leading early 19th-century exponents such as Pestalozzi and Froebel a defining philosophy of learning destined to form the core of progressive, child-centred education as the industrial era unfolded (Davis, 2010). It is in fact difficult to overstate the extent to which the ethics of infant education through most of the 19th century reproduced the Romantic rhetoric of childhood innocence as both a general theory of childhood and a convincing rationale for early learning. Indeed, it is only the subsequent steady encroachment of more obviously performative constructions of effective nursery education that has obscured this history, colluding in the annexation of the pre-5 environment by the competence-driven objectives of the primary or elementary classroom. Any suggestion that the rich, Romantic language of childhood innocence represents only a decadent, even disquieting, imposition on the lives of real children is rebutted in the recognition of the combative force it has assumed (and in some sense retains) in the defence of early childhood from the encroachments of instrumentalised conceptions of education—even those beguilingly tricked out in the garments of empowerment and participation. Against these pressures and inducements, the traditions of innocence understood in their full complexity propose a startlingly fresh vision of the child—a child who is endowed, Adam Phillips suggests,

... with an astonishing capacity for pleasure and, indeed, the pleasures of interest; with an unwilled relish of sensuous experience which often unsettles the adults who like to call it affection. This child who can be deranged by hope and anticipation—by an ice-cream—seems to have a passionate love of life, a curiosity about life, that for some reason isn't always easy to sustain ... Because it is easy to sentimentalize and to idealize, the visionary qualities of the child, this part of the legacy of romanticism—which is in Blake and Wordsworth and Coleridge most explicitly—has been abrogated by psychoanalysis (Phillips, 1998, pp. 21–22).

Phillips' wry yet penetrating commentary artfully positions psycho-analysis rather than philosophy as the unsuspecting heir to this aspect of Romanticism, at least with respect to its place in the histories of innocence. Psychoanalysis inherits, perhaps without wishing to, the imagery of childhood laid down in the palimpsest of pagan, Christian and Romantic speculation with which this essay has been concerned. But this is an imagery that surely cannot be contained within the therapeutic parameters of the psychoanalytic project, even at its most compensatory. Always, the tradition of which innocence is such a potent expression pushes against these constraints, its inner dynamic urging a return that is also a renovation; its impulse utopian rather than arcadian in the future educational possibilities towards which it points.

NOTES

1. The range of literature in which this view is expressed is too vast to record exhaustively. In the sociology of childhood see, most recently, Shanahan, 2007; Wyness, 2006, pp. 11–26; Meyer, 2007; Jones, 2009, pp. 108–117. See also James *et al.*, 1998, pp. 12–20. In the literature of child protection, an important statement is Kitzinger, 1990. In Cultural Studies, see Jenkins, 1998. In the visual arts the key text remains Higonnet, 1998; see also Langmuir, 2006, pp. 33–67. In literary studies, see Zornado, 2001, pp. 101–135. In the philosophy of education, Baker, 2001, pp. 300–323. The view persists in historical studies as well: see Gillis, 2002 and Levander, 2009.
2. Important rebuttals of Ariès may be found in Wilson, 1980 and Pollock, 1984, pp. 1–28. See also Heywood, 2010.
3. The claim of early-years education researcher, Reesa Sorin (2003), that 'Coming from an early childhood teaching background ... it is often difficult to shift from the view of the child as innocent ... Early childhood pedagogy has for many years been based on the image of the child as innocent and in need of adult direction' is typical here. See also Kehily and Montgomery, 2003, pp. 221–266. An attempt at formulating a viable understanding of 'proper pleasure' in early years settings in particular is advanced by Jones (2003).
4. See the highly controversial book by Levine, 2002; the collection of Bruhm and Hurley, 2004; and Pugh, 2011. See also Robinson, 2008.
5. A notable yet tantalising exception is Richardson, 1999. Richardson alludes to the revival by Wordsworth and some of his contemporaries of 'obscure seventeenth-century Anglican writers such as Vaughan and Earle' (p. 25).
6. See Zimmer, 2002, pp. 30–65 and McMaster, 1935.
7. Irenaeus of Lyons, *Epideixis*, 14. Cited and translated by Steenberg, 2004. See also Harrison, 1992.

REFERENCES

Ariès, P. [1962] (1971) *Centuries of Childhood: A Social History of Family Life*, R. Baldick, trans. (London, Jonathan Cape).
Bachelard, G. (1971) *The Poetics of Reverie: Childhood, Language and the Cosmos*, D. Russell, trans. (Boston, MA, Beacon Press).
Baker, B. (2001) *In Perpetual Motion: Theories of Power, Educational History and the Child* (New York, Peter Lang).
Bakke, O. M. (2006) *When Children Became People: The Birth of Childhood in Early Christianity*, B. McNeil, trans. (Minneapolis, MN, Fortress Press).
Balfour, I. (2002) *The Rhetoric of Romantic Prophecy* (Stanford, CA, Stanford University Press).
von Balthasar, H. U. (1968) *Man in History: A Theological Study*, W. Glen-Doepel, trans. (London, Sheed and Ward).
von Balthasar, H. U. (1991) *Unless You Become Like This Child*, E. Leiva-Merikakis, trans. (San Francisco, CA, Ignatius Press).
Beiser, F. C. (2003) *The Romantic Imperative: The Concept of Early German Romanticism* (Cambridge, MA, Belknap Press of Harvard University Press).
Berlin, I. (1993) *The Magus of the North: J.G. Hamann and the Origins of Modern Irrationalism* (London, John Murray).
Blake, W. (1988) *The Complete Poetry and Prose of William Blake*, rev. edn., D. V. Erdman ed. (New York, Doubleday).
Boehme, J. (1647) *XL. Questions Concerning the Soule. Propounded by Dr. Balthasar Walter. And answered by Jacob Behmen*, J. Sparrow, trans. (London, Matthew Simmons).
Boehme, J. [1656] (1997) *Aurora*, W. Law, trans. (Whitefish, MT, Kessenger Publishing).
Brewer, H. (2005) *By Birth or Consent: Children, Law and the Anglo-American Revolution in Authority* (Chapel Hill, NC, University of North Carolina Press).
Bruhm, S. and Hurley, N. eds (2004) *Curiouser: On the Queerness of Children* (Minneapolis, MN, University of Minnesota Press).
Bunyard, D. (2010) Subjectivity Unbound: Escaping the Mortal Engines, in: M. O'Loughlin (ed.) *Imagining Children Otherwise: Theoretical and Critical Perspectives On Childhood Subjectivity* (New York, Peter Lang), pp. 157–179.
Classen, A. ed. (2005) *Childhood in the Middle Ages and the Renaissance: The Results of a Paradigm Shift in the History of Mentality* (Berlin, de Gruyter).
Cunningham, H. (2006) *The Invention of Childhood* (London, BBC Publications).
Dante, Alighieri (1962) *The Divine Comedy: Paradise*, D. L. Sayers and B. Reynolds, trans. (Harmondsworth, Penguin).
Davis, R. (2010) Government Intervention in Child-Rearing: Governing Infancy, *Educational Theory*, 60.3, pp. 285–298.
Dunne, J. (2008) Education and Childhood, *Yearbook of the National Society for the Study of Education*, 107.1, pp. 258–273.
Earle, J. [1628] (1899) *Microcosmographie* (London, J.M. Dent).
Garlitz, B. (1966) The Immortality Ode: Its Cultural Progeny, *Studies in English Literature, 1500–1900*, 6.4, pp. 639–649.
Gill, N. (2010) *Educational Philosophy in the French Enlightenment: From Nature to Second Nature* (Farnham, Ashgate).
Gillis, J. R. (2002) Birth of the Virtual Child: Origins of Our Contradictory Images of Children, in: J. Dunne and J. Kelly (eds) *Childhood and its Discontents: The Seamus Heaney Lectures* (Dublin, The Liffey Press), pp. 31–51.
Grant, P. (1971) Original Sin and the Fall of Man in Thomas Traherne, *ELH*, 38.1 (1971), pp. 40–61.
Gundry-Volf, J. M. (2001) The Least and the Greatest: Children in the New Testament, in: M. J. Bunge (ed.) *The Child in Christian Thought* (Grand Rapids, MI, Eerdman's Publishing), pp. 33–36.
Halpin, D. (2008) In Praise of Wasting Time in Education: Some Lessons from the Romantics, *Forum*, 50.3, pp. 377–382.

Hamilton, D. (1989) *Towards a Theory of Schooling* (London, The Falmer Press).
Harrison, C. (1992) Childhood in Early Christian Writers, *Augustinianum*, 32.1, pp. 61–76.
Haudrup, P. (2000) Childhood and the Cultural Constitution of Vulnerable Bodies, in: A. Prout (ed.) *The Body, Childhood and Society* (London, Palgrave, 2000), pp. 39–59.
Heywood, C. (2010) *Centuries of Childhood:* An Anniversary—and an Epitaph?, *The Journal of the History of Childhood and Youth*, 3.3, pp. 341–365.
Higonnet, A. (1998) *Pictures of Innocence: The History and Crisis of Ideal Childhood* (London, Thames and Hudson).
Hildegard of Bingen (1986) *Scivias*, B. Hozeski, trans. (Rochester, NY, Bear and Co).
Irenaeus of Lyons (1952) *Proof of the Apostolic Preaching*, J. P. Smith, trans. (Westminster, MA, Newman Press).
James, A., Jenks, C. and Prout, A. (1998) *Theorizing Childhood* (London, Polity Press).
Jenkins, H. (1998) Introduction: Childhood Innocence and Other Myths, in: H. Jenkins (ed.) *The Children's Culture Reader* (New York, New York University Press), pp. 1–41.
Jones, A. (2003) The Monster in the Room: Safety, Pleasure and Early Childhood Education, *Contemporary Issues in Early Childhood*, 4.3, pp. 235–250.
Jones, O. (2002) Naturally Not! Childhood, the Urban and Romanticism, *Research in Human Ecology*, 9.2, pp. 17–30.
Jones, P. (2009) *Rethinking Childhood: Attitudes in Contemporary Society* (London, Continuum).
Kehily, M. A. and Montgomery, H. (2003) Innocence and Experience, in: M. Woodhead and H. Montgomery (eds) *Understanding Childhood: An Interdisciplinary Approach* (London, John Wiley and Sons), pp. 221–266.
Kincaid, J. (1992) *Child-Loving: The Erotic Child and Victorian Culture* (New York, Routledge).
Kincaid, J. (1998) *Erotic Innocence: The Culture of Child Molesting* (Durham, NC, Duke University Press).
Kitzinger, J. (1990) Who Are You Kidding? Children, Power, and the Struggle Against Sexual Abuse, in: A. James and A. Prout (eds) *Constructing and Reconstructing Childhood* (London, The Falmer Press, 1990), pp. 158–166.
Lancy, D. F. (2008) *The Anthropology of Childhood: Cherubs, Chattel, Changelings* (Cambridge, Cambridge University Press).
Langmuir, E. (2006) *Imagining Childhood* (London, Yale University Press).
Lesnik-Oberstein, K. and Thomson, S. (2002) What is Queer Theory Doing With the Child?, *Parallax*, 8.1, pp. 35–46.
Levander, C. F. (2009) Innocence, Childhood, in: R. A. Shweder (ed.) *The Child: An Encyclopedic Companion* (Chicago, IL, University of Chicago Press), pp. 501–503.
Levine, J. (2002) *Harmful to Minors* (Minneapolis, MN, University of Minnesota Press).
Marcus, L. M. (1978) *Childhood and Cultural Despair: A Theme and Variations in Seventeenth-Century Literature* (Pittsburgh, PA, University of Pittsburgh Press).
Marcus, S. (1985) Some Representations of Childhood in Wordsworth's Poetry, in: J. H. Smith and W. Kerrigan (eds) *Opening Texts: Psychoanalysis and the Culture of the Child* (Baltimore, MD, Johns Hopkins University Press).
Marshall, K. and Parvis, P. (2004) *Honouring Children: The Human Rights of the Child in Christian Perspective* (Edinburgh, St Andrew Press).
Martin, L. C. (1938) Henry Vaughan and the Theme of Infancy, in: J. Dover Wilson (ed.) *Seventeenth Century Studies Presented to Sir Herbert Grierson* (Oxford, Oxford University Press), pp. 243–255.
Masschelein, J. (2003) The Discourse of the Learning Society and the Loss of Childhood, *Journal of Philosophy of Education*, 35.1, pp. 1–20.
McCreery, P. (2004) Innocent Pleasures? Children and Sexual Politics, *GLQ: A Journal of Gay and Lesbian Studies*, 10.4, pp. 617–630.
McMaster, H. N. (1935) Vaughan and Wordsworth, *Review of English Studies*, 11.43, pp. 313–325.
Mee, J. (2003) *Romanticism, Enthusiasm and Regulation: Poetics and the Policing of Culture in the Romantic Period* (Oxford, Oxford University Press).

Meyer, A. (2007) The Moral Rhetoric of Childhood, *Childhood*, 14.1, pp. 85–104.

Natov, R. (2003) *The Poetics of Childhood* (London, Routledge).

Orme, N. (2001) *Medieval Children* (New Haven, CT, Yale University Press).

Orme, N. (2006) *Medieval Schools* (New Haven, CT, Yale University Press).

Phillips, A. (1998) *The Beast in the Nursery* (London, Faber and Faber).

Plotz, J. (2001) *Romanticism and the Vocation of Childhood* (London, Palgrave).

Pollock, L. (1984) *Forgotten Children: Parent-Child Relations From 1500–1900* (Cambridge, Cambridge University Press).

Pugh, T. (2011) *Innocence, Heterosexuality and the Queerness of Children's Literature* (Abingdon, Routledge).

Richardson, A. (1999) Romanticism and the End of Childhood, in *Literature and the Child: Romantic Continuations, Postmodern Contestations*, J. H. McGavran, ed. (Iowa City, IA, University of Iowa Press), pp. 23–44.

Robinson, K. H. (2008) In the Name of 'Childhood Innocence': A Discursive Exploration of the Moral Panic Associated with Childhood and Sexuality, *Cultural Studies Review*, 14.2, pp. 113–129.

Rousseau, J-J. (1979) *Emile*, A. Bloom, ed. and trans. (New York, Basic Books).

Ryan, P. J. (2008) How New Is the 'New' Social Study of Childhood? The Myth of a Paradigm Shift, *Journal of Interdisciplinary History*, XXXVIII.4, pp. 553–576.

Sabine, G. H. ed. (1941) *The Works of Gerrard Winstanley* (Ithaca, NY, Cornell University Press).

Saward, J. (1999) *The Way of the Lamb: The Spirit of Childhood and the End of the Age* (Edinburgh, T. & T. Clark).

Schultz, J. A. (1995) *The Knowledge of Childhood in the German Middle Ages, 1000–1350* (Philadelphia, PA, University of Pennsylvania Press).

Shahar, S. (1990) *Childhood in the Middle Ages* (London, Routledge).

Shanahan, S. (2007) Lost and Found: The Sociological Ambivalence Toward Childhood, *Annual Review of Sociology*, 33, pp. 407–428.

Singer, E. (2005) The Liberation of the Child: A Recurrent Theme in the History of Education in Western Societies, *Early Child Development and Care*, 175.6, pp. 611–620.

Somerville, C. J. (1982) *The Rise and Fall of Childhood* (London, Sage).

Somerville, C. J. (1992) *The Discovery of Childhood in Puritan England* (Athens, GA, University of Georgia Press).

Sorin, R. (2003) Research with Children: A Rich Glimpse into the World of Childhood, *Australian Journal of Early Childhood*, 28.1, pp. 32–33.

Stables, A. (2008) *Childhood and the Philosophy of Education: An Anti-Aristotelian Perspective* (London, Continuum).

Steenberg, M. C. (2004) Children in Paradise: Adam and Eve as 'Infants' in Irenaeus of Lyons, *Journal of Early Christian Studies*, 12.4, pp. 1–22.

Taylor, J. (1655) *Unum Necessarium; Or, The Doctrine and Practice of Repentance* (London, James Flesher).

Thomas, K. (1990) Children in Early Modern England, in: G. Avery and J. Briggs (eds) *Children and their Books: A Celebration of the Work of Iona and Peter Opie* (Oxford, Oxford University Press), pp. 45–77.

Traherne, T. (1990) *Selected Poems and Prose*, A. Bradford ed. (Harmondsworth, Penguin).

Vaughan, H. (1983) *The Complete Poems*, A. Rudrum ed. (Harmondsworth, Penguin).

Vaughan, T. (1984) *The Works of Thomas Vaughan*, A. Rudrum ed. (Oxford, Clarendon Press).

Walker, D. P. (1964) *The Decline of Hell: Seventeenth Century Discussions of Eternal Torment* (London, Routledge and Keagan Paul).

Warner, W. (1994) Little Angels, Little Devils: Keeping Childhood Innocent, in *Managing Monsters: Six Myths of Our Time: the Reith Lectures 1994* (London, Vantage), pp. 33–48.

Wilson, A. (1980) The Infancy of the History of Childhood: An Appraisal of Philippe Aries, *History and Theory*, 19, pp. 132–153.

Wordsworth, W. (1992) *Lyrical Ballads*, M. Mason ed. (London, Longman).

Wyness, M. (2006) *Childhood and Society: An Introduction to the Sociology of Childhood* (London, Palgrave Macmillan).

Zimmer, R. B. (2002) *Clairvoyant Wordsworth: A Case Study in Heresy and Critical Prejudice* (London, Writers Club Press).

Zornado, J. (2001) *Inventing the Child: Culture, Ideology and the Story of Childhood* (New York, Garland Publishing).

Index